C
Fi

F

F

E

Ja
ar
b
3
l

w
A
t
p
o
t
is

Applied User Data Collection and Analysis Using JavaScript and PHP

14
15
16
17
18
19
20
21
22
23
24
25
26
27
28
29
30
31
32
33 }
34 ?

S.
er

4.
Ir
in

E
F
u
e

Applied User Data Collection and Analysis Using JavaScript and PHP

Kyle Goslin
Markus Hofmann

CRC Press
Taylor & Francis Group
Boca Raton London New York

CRC Press is an imprint of the
Taylor & Francis Group, an **informa** business

A CHAPMAN & HALL BOOK

First edition published 2021
by CRC Press
6000 Broken Sound Parkway NW, Suite 300, Boca Raton, FL 33487-2742

and by CRC Press
2 Park Square, Milton Park, Abingdon, Oxon, OX14 4RN

CRC Press is an imprint of Taylor & Francis Group, LLC

ISBN: 978-0-367-75682-6 (hbk)
ISBN: 978-0-367-75680-2 (pbk)
ISBN: 978-1-003-16354-1 (ebk)

Typeset in Computer Modern font
by KnowledgeWorks Global Ltd.

For Amanda and Noah.
For when distraction was needed, and for when it was not. — Kyle

In memory of Johann Trautwein, who, as an early adopter of computing, not only paved my path to the world of informatics but also instilled many other values I cherish. A true gentleman - missed but never forgotten by all who knew him. — Markus

Contents

Preface

The driving force behind any web application is the users of the application and the developers creating the application. During development, however, the interests and needs of the user can often fall behind, in favor of what the developer *thinks* they need. This development style often leads to complicated user interfaces, poor design choices, and content overload.

To mitigate against this, the daily interaction a user can have with an application and their overall opinion should be considered paramount during development. This book aims to provide the tools and knowledge required for the collection and analysis of data, irrespective of the format or source.

This book places a dividing line between the types of data that can be collected from users. *Active data* is defined as data that is collected by providing the user with the means to enter their opinion, and sentiment, toward a feature or topic. These solutions can often be seen on websites in the form of rating systems, feedback boxes, and user surveys. In contrast to this, *passive data* is defined as the data that is collected in the background without any direct user interactions. This data takes the form of browser fingerprinting, IP addresses, geolocation data, time spent on pages, and the location of the mouse during interactions with an application.

With the advent of cloud storage solutions, more data is being retained than before. Sales data, transaction logs, and user surveys all become sources for data analysis. Data can come from a number of different sources, some of which may have existed before an application has been developed. Emphasis is placed on collecting this data and placing it in a usable format for analysis.

After this data has been collected, the analysis process can begin. For each different data type—e.g., numeric or text—statistics and visualizations can be generated. This book provides the foundations for creating meaningful insights and visualizations from the data that are relevant to both business and developer needs.

As with any new technologies, a common issue with any new solution is integrating it into an existing system or implementation. To aid development, each of the examples in this book has been developed in isolation to allow for easy integration. An emphasis is placed on the diversity of technologies to provide a well-rounded understanding of what is available.

The complete development life-cycle is described in this book, outlining how data can be collected, analyzed, and reported to the key stakeholders in a project.

Authors

Kyle Goslin
TU Dublin
Dublin, Ireland

Markus Hofmann
TU Dublin
Dublin, Ireland

Acknowledgments

I would like to thank Amanda for her continued support allowing me to hide away in my office to write and review no matter the weather inside or outside the house. Your opinions and sentiment mean more to me than any other. I would also like to thank my parents, Ted and Claire, for their unwavering support of all things academic. The pursuit of knowledge and taking risks were always encouraged, as the reward was always better once failure had, many times, been achieved. I would also like to thank my brother, Darragh, for being the ears of patience when frustration or writer's block dawned.

I would also like to thank Daniel McSweeney, head of the Department of Informatics at TU Dublin Blanchardstown campus, for his support and encouragement. Ideas were always met with guidance and reflection. I cannot forget my co-workers in Peter Alexander, Tara Cambell, Jane Hanratty, and all others in office A57 for their ongoing support and encouragement. The experience is always better when shared. I would also like to thank Philip Kavanagh for his technical review of this book.

This book was the combination of many ideas and concepts derived from teaching at TU Dublin, Blanchardstown campus. I would like to thank my students, who are the lifeblood of academia.

— Kyle Goslin

List of Figures

List of Tables

CHAPTER 1

Introduction

1.1 INTRODUCTION

Understanding a user's needs and requirements is one of the main driving forces for any business. Collected data provides insights into how users feel about a given feature or topic and how they work on a day to day basis. This data can be gathered directly from users by providing simple questions and allowing the user to select an option from a predefined list, or to enter their own text-based responses.

Although asking a user for their opinion is possible, other methods can be used to gather data. Data can be collected indirectly through a web application by monitoring the interactions and behaviors a user has with it. The collected data can be processed to generate meaningful statistics and visualizations, providing both overviews and a deep-dive analysis of user interests and needs.

Each different data type, such as numerical data and text data, comes with methods of identifying importance and relevance. Both quantitative and qualitative analysis approaches can be used to extract these insights. In this book, we explore the different methods available for data collection, extraction, and analysis. This book aims to describe the many different approaches that can be taken with the aim to capture as much data as possible for analysis.

To provide a complete solution, the process of developing and deploying the developed solutions on a cloud-based server is explored with additional features such as report generation and delivery. An emphasis in this book is placed on the diversity of technologies exposing you to many different alternatives for data collection and analysis, providing you with the tools needed to develop a well-rounded solution.

1.2 WHO THIS BOOK IS AIMED AT

This book is aimed at web application developers who have some knowledge with the basics of JavaScript and PHP. This book builds on this basic knowledge and provides complete working examples that can easily be deployed into existing web applications.

This book is not directed toward people who do not have these skills, however, the knowledge about gathering data and generating insights are still valuable to gain an understanding of what tools and approaches are available if you do have developers to implement these solutions.

1.3 TECHNOLOGIES USED

In this book, a clear line between the technologies used throughout the chapters can be seen. On the client-side, e.g., in the web browser of the user, HTML and JavaScript will be used. On the server-side, PHP version 7.4[1] running on an Apache version 2.4 web server[2] is used to do the bulk of the processing of the data, e.g., storing the information in a database and calculating statistics.

JavaScript is used as it provides the ability to manipulate and present data to the user without the need to redirect the user to multiple different pages. Using the collected data, visualizations will be created using JavaScript and HTML/CSS libraries. As JavaScript is a browser-based programming language implemented by individual web browser vendors, each of the browsers can have slight variations as to how it is interpreted. To side-step the problem of cross-browser compatibility issues, we will utilize JavaScript libraries wherever possible. The main JavaScript library that is used in this book is jQuery version 3.5.[3]

jQuery offers all the features that plain JavaScript has to offer, but all of the cross-browser issues have been thoroughly tested. Any new user to JavaScript often searches for code and finds browser-specific JavaScript code, considering this the correct solution. But code that may work correctly in one browser may not work on a different browser. Much to the developer's frustration, even a different version of the same browser may also cause issues when the sample code is run. For this reason, we will use libraries extensively to fast track the development process.

To aid the visualization process, JavaScript-based libraries such as

---

[1] https://www.php.net
[2] https://www.apache.org
[3] https://www.jquery.com

D3.js, Charts.js, and *Google Charts* are explored as they offer high-quality interactive visualizations. A focus is placed on the diversity of the libraries used in this book to provide a learning experience with different code bases.

As all data collected needs to be retrieved for analysis, different data sources will be explored. Examples of this include utilizing comma-separated value (CSV) files, simple text files, JSON files, and database tables. In this book, the core database we will be using is the MySQL 8 community edition[4] database as it is free, widely used, and integrates with PHP.

Although many different web browsers exist, Google Chrome[5] version 80 was used during the development of the examples in this book.

1.4 VARIATIONS OF DATA

In this section, we will begin the process of breaking down the two approaches that can be taken to gather data from users. The first approach is *active data collection*, whereby the user is directly polled to provide answers or judgments. The second approach is *passive data collection*, whereby all of the data is gathered in the background without the need for user intervention. Examples of this include gathering data by listening to the browser environment. As a user navigates a web application, data can be recorded and saved for future retrieval.

Data can come in both structured and unstructured formats. An example of structured data is a database table that contains the user level of interest graded by the user between one and ten. The only possible variations of this data are the numbers between the ranges provided to the user. An additional component of this structured data is the processing speed, as little to no processing is required since the data is already in the desired format. To gain insights from this data, simple metrics such as the total, sum, and average can be used.

Structured data is in contrast to unstructured data that may be held in any number of different storage locations such as a text file, CSV file, or a database table. This form of data inherently has no structure to it. This adds complexity to processing the data as it is not just a simple calculation or predefined column in a table. To extract meaning from this

---

[4]https://dev.mysql.com/downloads/mysql
[5]https://www.google.com/chrome

data, additional processing such as identifying relevance and importance must be performed.

After processing, additional steps can be performed to identify the relationships between individual pieces of data. Examples of this include the use of charts to visualize these relationships. As the quantity of data grows during the interactions with an application, methods of filtering the data to provide focus on the crucial trends can be performed.

1.4.1 Active Data

Active data is any data that has been directly provided by a user. This data can be collected by asking a user their opinion about a topic to a brief "yes" or "no" answer to a question. Often users do not have the time to give a wealth of information outlining how they feel about a particular page or subject. This often leads developers to consider the best time or approach to take to pose questions to the user.

The disadvantage of active data is that there is a cost associated with interacting with users. At the end of any process, many users simply do not want to leave any form of data and consider the process an annoyance. Example of active data include:

- Number of times a user has shared or "liked" a particular page on a website through a social media interface.

- Leaving a rating for a product on a website.

- Answering the questions in a survey.

- Setting custom options on a website.

1.4.2 Passive Data

Passive data is data collected in the background of an application without any user intervention. Although the user is navigating through content and selecting different articles of interest, at no time is the user ever formally requested to provide input about what they are currently viewing or their opinions. Passive data collection approaches include:

- Length of time a user remains on a section of web application or viewing a page.

- Statistics about popular pages that a user is viewing.

- Amount of time a user has spent inside of a particular collection of pages that are all directly related to each other.

- Demographic of a user.

- Click times when users are interacting with an application.

- Log files generated by an application.

- Geographic location/IP address of a user.

- Application usage patterns.

1.5 WHAT YOU NEED

As the focus of this book is the development of web applications, a complete server stack is required. The three main technologies that are used throughout this book include an Apache web server with the PHP module and a MySQL database. For new developers, consider using a pre-packaged solution such as XAMPP[6] that is a preconfigured solution for web developers offering all of these services without the need for any effort installing and configuring each of the individual components. XAMPP is currently available for Microsoft Windows, Apple Mac, and Linux distributions.

Alternatives to XAMPP include tools such as MAMP[7], EasyPHP[8], and AMPPS.[9]

To aid the development process, JavaScript libraries are used throughout this book. Instead of downloading the JavaScript files required for each different example, and to ensure the latest available codebase is used, Content Delivery Networks (CDN) are used where possible. These can be seen in the opening lines of each example.

As most PHP libraries are available pre-packaged, we will use the command line application *composer*. This is a dependency management tool for PHP. Composer can be downloaded from *https://getcomposer.org/download*. During the installation process of composer, it will ask to point to the location of the *php.exe* file. If you are using a local web server, this is typically installed inside of the *php/* folder that is detected automatically. Once composer has been installed,

---

[6]https://www.apachefriends.org
[7]https://www.mamp.info/en
[8]https://www.easyphp.org
[9]https://www.ampps.com

open a command prompt and navigate to the root folder of your project. After this, issue the *composer init* command to begin the creation process of the *composer.json* file.

Composer is different from other tools as it does not work on a per-system basis, it is focused on a per-project basis. Each individual project will have a collection of libraries specified that are defined inside of the *composer.json* file. This is a human-readable file that contains a list of different requirements for a given PHP project in JSON format.

An example of this is a composer file that defines a reference to the *PHPinsight* package along with the version number of the package. Additional PHP packages to add to a project can be found at *https://packagist.org*. Below is a sample of the JSON in a *composer.json* file.

```
{
    "require" : {
            "jwhennessey/phpinsight": ">=2.0.9"
    }
}
```

After the *composer.json* has been added to the project folder, composer can be used to manage additional packages. By opening up a command prompt and navigating into the root of the project where *composer.json* is located, the *install* command can be issued to composer. By doing this, the contents of the JSON file are parsed, and all specified dependencies are downloaded and installed into the project.

```
composer install
```

In cases where we want to add a new dependency to the project we can use the *require* command:

```
composer require jwhennessey/phpinsight
```

This process greatly improves the manual installation process of different packages that make up a project.

1.6   DEVELOPMENT ENVIRONMENT

Through the course of this book, a heavy focus is placed on the client-side programming language JavaScript. When working with JavaScript, a very small issue with one section of code can quickly bump into other sections, causing a cascade of errors. To help during the debugging process of JavaScript, the *console.log()* function should be used frequently. This function can be called from any location inside of a web page as long as it is placed inside a JavaScript *script* tag. Sample Code 1 shows a simple example of a web page with a call to this function.

```
1   <!DOCTYPE html>
2   <html>
3       <head>
4           <meta charset="utf-8">
5           <title>Hello World</title>
6       </head>
7       <body>
8           <p>Hello World!</p>
9
10          <script>
11              console.log("Hello world!");
12          </script>
13      </body>
14  </html>
```

SAMPLE CODE 1: Sample HTML document with embedded JavaScript.

To access this console log in Google Chrome, the *Ctrl+Shift+I* keys can be pressed together to view the developer tools, as shown in Figure 1.1.

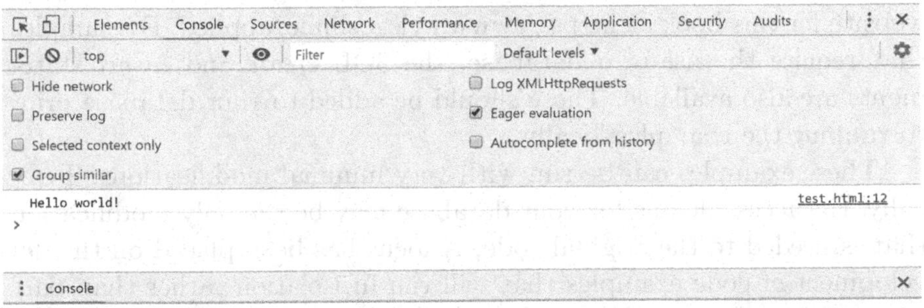

FIGURE 1.1: Viewing the developer console in Google Chrome.

This console provides information about the errors that are encountered in JavaScript code and also information about which line the error has occurred on. Individual JavaScript variables, objects and strings can be passed to the *console.log()* function. To aid the debugging process, calls can be made to the function to print before and after a piece of JavaScript code has run. This allows us to easily see if the code has run as expected.

As working with a local web server is designed to mimic the behavior of a commercial server for development purposes, sometimes unwanted features are implemented. One example of this is the browser-based website caching that is performed when a local web page is opened. As changes are being made to an application during the course of development, the browser will often not render the latest version of the code, opting to return a cached version. To prevent this, the developer tools allow us to disable this caching feature.

By entering into the *Network* tab in Google Chrome developer tools, the option to *disable cache* can be ticked during development, as shown in Figure 1.2.

FIGURE 1.2: Disabling the cache in the developer console.

1.7 CODE EXAMPLES

This book contains a number of JavaScript/HTML and PHP code examples that can be run on your local Apache/PHP/MySQL server. To aid development, complete examples can be downloaded from the official website for this book at https://www.kylegoslin.ie/applied. For samples that require the use of a database, the SQL *create* and *insert* statements are also available. These should be added to your database prior to running the examples locally.

These examples can be run with very minimal modifications. Typically, the access details for your database may be the only modification that is needed to the original code. A focus has been placed on the development of code examples that will run in isolation rather than part of a larger framework. This provides the opportunity for these examples to be placed into an existing application.

Although security is a significant component of web application development, it is not the focus of this book. For this reason, if any examples are used in a live environment, additional care should be taken to implement correct security mechanisms.

1.8 BOOK OUTLINE

In this section, a brief outline of the structure of this book is presented.

Chapter 1: *Introduction*, provided an outline of the core types of data that can be gathered for analysis and the tools required to get started. Chapter 2: *Active data collection* explores the various approaches that can be used to collect data from a user directly, such as rating stars, binary feedback, and custom response forms. The foundation of JavaScript tools that are used through this book is explored.

Chapter 3:*Passive Data Collection*, provides an outline of the passive data collection processes. Common data sources such as cookies, server-side sessions, and files are explored as possible data sources. The interactions that a user has with an application are explored, detailing how data can be gathered using additional JavaScript tools and third-party resources. As social media is a common source of data, the process of gathering data from a social media website is explored using authenticated API calls.

Once data has been gathered, a method of viewing the results can be implemented. In Chapter 4: *Custom Dashboards*, the process of creating a custom visualization dashboard with login and registration pages is described. To aid the visualization of data, the process of adding simple bar charts in both single and multi-column form are described. This provides a data analyst with the means to dynamically add visualizations based on data from any source dynamically.

In addition to numeric data, text forms the basis of many data sources. In Chapter 5: *Working with Text*, the processing of text is described. The identification of stop words is first described along with the process of identifying red-flag terms that help identify terms of interest. To gain a deeper insight into the context of text, n-grams are described. To further aid this, the process of sentence completion, word stemming, and synonym detection is described to provide the data analyst with a method of identifying other relevant text of interest. To add a numeric component to text, a focus is placed on term weighting approaches. Finally, when working with text-based feedback records, an approach for sentiment analysis is described.

For gathered data, visualizations can easily be applied. In Chapter 6: *Text Visualization*, the process of generating visualizations is described. Word clouds are described to view the frequency of individual terms. The relationships between data are outlined using a tree-based graph format. To identify the relationships between custom terms of interest on any given day, a linked graph is described. As data is often collected at different times, a time-series analysis approach is described for positive and negative feedback records.

Chapter 7: *Time-based Feedback Analysis* outlines the time-based component of data and how it can be used for the segmentation of data. As time is an ongoing entity, an approach based on time segment analysis and visualization is described, allowing for individual time windows to be viewed. The area of real-time feedback analysis is described for situations where the data collection process is actively happening. To view larger data sets in a single visualization, the process of creating positive and negative feedback calendars for a given year is described. To view large data sets on a smaller scale, the process of viewing custom color-coded feedback heat map is described.

For any type of data, statistics can be derived. In Chapter 8: *Feedback Statistics and Overviews*, the basics of statistics is described with complete examples. As working on large data sets is often time-consuming, the process of working with representative samples is described. The process of calculating the percentage difference is then described as most of the statistics generated can be represented as a percentage.

Finally, Chapter 9: *Hosting, Reporting, and Distributing*, the process of PDF report generation based on PHP is described. As many of the tasks that are performed on data are performed on a daily basis, the process of task scheduling is described for both local and external services. To provide the key stakeholders with the generated reports, the process of integrating a cloud-based e-mail service is described. Finally, once a complete application has been developed, the process of hosting a PHP/JavaScript application on the Amazon Lightsail is described.

1.9 SUMMARY

This chapter introduced the tools and environment needed for running the examples in this book. The concept of passive and active data was described, outlining that data does not directly need to be harvested from a user. Indirect methods, such as logging interactions with an application and identifying relevant data sources, e.g., existing files and social media streams, can be used to gather data for analysis. In Chapter 2, the process of collecting data through active methods is described to begin the cycle of data collection for analysis and visualization.

Active Data Collection

2.1 INTRODUCTION

In this chapter, we will describe the process of collecting data from users directly. This is done through the use of simple binary choices, text-based content, and star ratings. The data is categorized as *active data*, as the user is required to participate in the data collection process. However, gathering data directly from users can be difficult, as users are often unwilling to put time into the process. We attempt to make the process of gathering data as simple and unobtrusive as possible for the user.

2.2 BINARY DATA COLLECTION

Many modern web applications provide the user with a simple data collection mechanism in the form of a binary choice. Typically, this is the result of answering a question. A simple *Yes* or *No* input field can quickly gather a user's opinion with minimal effort. These mechanisms purposely limit the number of options and interactions a user can have. The submission process for this data can also be automatic to prevent the user from selecting a choice and then unintentionally forgetting to press the submit button.

To aid the process of future analysis, each page in this sample application is considered an individual article. Each article has a unique *ID* to differentiate articles from one another.

Example 1: Binary data collection

This example consists of three core files and one library:

1. create.sql — This file is used to create the *yesno* database table.

2. binary.html — The main HTML/JavaScript binary data collection interface.

3. ajax.php — Used to receive data and store it in a MySQL database.

4. jQuery — Used to perform a JavaScript *POST* to the ajax.php page.

Example code: create.sql

Before creating the user interface, a new MySQL database table is first required to be titled *yesno*, as shown in Sample Code 2. The table consists of four different attributes, where two of these are automatically generated when a new record is inserted. The first of these is the *ID* column that is auto-incremented and a primary key. Every time a new record is created in the database, the *ID* will increment by 1. This is useful for uniquely identifying the record in the future. The second column is titled *mytime*. Every time a new record is created, the current time stamp on the server will be logged with the record. The third and fourth columns are the two that will vary depending on what article is being viewed by the user, and the choice selected.

As the *articleid* is numeric, the data type for this will be set to *int*. The *result* column, however, contains the string *Yes* or *No*. To hold this, the *result* column data type is set to *varchar*.

```
1   CREATE TABLE `yesno` (
2       `id` INT NOT NULL AUTO_INCREMENT,
3       `mytime` TIMESTAMP NOT NULL DEFAULT CURRENT_TIMESTAMP ,
4       `articleid` INT,
5       `result` VARCHAR (10),
6       PRIMARY KEY ( `id`)
7   );
```

SAMPLE CODE 2: create.sql — *yesno* database table SQL.

Example code: binary.html

In Sample Code 3, on line 1, a reference to the jQuery[1] Content Delivery Network (CDN) is first added. Two radio buttons are added along with a simple *div* tag to make the form uniquely identifiable on lines 4 and 6.

---

[1]https://code.jquery.com

JavaScript will be responsible for listening to the changes that have been made to the form, and also for passing the data off to the web server to be saved in a database table. In the example code, both of the radio buttons have the same *name* attribute. This is done as both are part of the same group, preventing both from being selected at the same time.

On line 10, a jQuery *click()* listener is added. This listens to clicks that are made on the radio buttons. When identifying the radio buttons, the *input:radio* value is passed to the jQuery selector specifying that we are interested in the radio buttons that have the *name* attribute defined as *answer*. When either of the radio buttons is clicked, the JavaScript inside of the click function will trigger. Inside this function on line 11, we can use the keyword *this*, which represents the radio button that has just been clicked. Using this, we can call the *val()* function that will return the value from the radio button that has been selected.

After this on line 12, a custom JavaScript function titled *saveAnswer()* is called. When called, the current value the user has selected will be passed to this function. The *saveAnswer()* function on line 15 takes a single parameter in the form of the value the user selected. Inside this function, a jQuery *POST* is added on line 16 to send the *answer* variable to a server-side page titled *ajax.php* to save the data to the database table. Inside the jQuery *POST* the first parameter that is passed is *ajax.php*. This is a reference to the page that will handle the database interactions. A custom *type* parameter is added so we can reuse the same *ajax.php* page for multiple different purposes by uniquely identifying the different types of requests we are sending to the page.

The *type* variable is set to *yesno*. Next, we will pass the *articleid* that is used to identify the page where the data has come from. The *articleid* is set to *1221*. The final parameter that is passed is titled *result*. The value for this variable comes from the user selection that was passed to the *saveAnswer()* function titled *answer*. On line 18, a *done()* function is added. This function is called when all of the processing has been completed, and the data has been sent to the database. A simple *alert()* function is added on line 19 to tell the user *Thank you!* after they have submitted the data.

```
1   <script src="https://code.jquery.com/jquery-3.5.1.min.js"
2     crossorigin="anonymous">
3   </script>
4   <div id="binaryfeedback">
5       Are you happy with this service?
6       <input type="radio" name="answer" value="Yes"> Yes
7       <input type="radio" name="answer" value="No"> No
8   </div>
9   <script>
10  $( "input:radio[name=answer]" ).click(function() {
11      var val = $(this).val();
12      saveAnswer(val);
13  });
14
15  function saveAnswer(answer){
16      $.post( "ajax.php", { type: "yesno", articleid: "1221",
17      result: answer })
18      .done(function( data ) {
19          alert('Thank you!'+data);
20      });
21  }
22  </script>
```

SAMPLE CODE 3: binary.html — Yes/No options being presented to the user.

Example code: ajax.php

In Sample Code 4, a new PHP page is created titled *ajax.php*. This additional page is never directly opened by the user; it is called dynamically through the jQuery *POST* function. When this page is called every time the data will be saved to a database table using a PHP Data Object (PDO). On line 2, the *POST* variable is referenced to extract the value that was passed across from the JavaScript request. On line 3, a simple *if statement* is used to check what value the *type* variable contained. If the type was set to *yesno*, a call is made to the *yesNoLog()* PHP function on line 4. After the *if statement*, the function definition for the *yesNoLog()* function is added on line 6.

In the body of the PHP function on lines 7 and 8, two variables are created to catch the values that have been sent across from the jQuery *POST* request. It is important to ensure that the variable names inside the *POST* match to the variables that were sent across using the JavaScript *POST* earlier. In this example the *articleid* and the *result* are extracted from the *POST*. Once the variables have been gathered, a connection to the database can be made. The database interactions is performed inside of a *try-catch* statement that begins on line 9. The *host, dbname, user,* and *pass* variables are defined on lines 10 to 13.

These variables reflect the MySQL database that is being used. On line 14, a new PHP PDO is created. On line 16, a simple SQL *INSERT* statement is created. Two question marks are inserted at the end of the statement. These are unnamed placeholders that hold the place for the variables that will be appended.

The two variables that we caught from the *POST* are passed to the SQL statement using the *bindParam()* function on lines 19 and 20. This is a safe method of passing variables to a database without causing any security issues as sanitization is performed on the variables. As the *articleid* is an integer, the type of parameter being added is set to PARAM_INT. The type of *result* being added is set as a PARAM_STR. The final step in this process is to run the SQL statement. On line 21, the *execute()* function is called. A *catch* is added on line 22 to complete the *try-catch* block. If any errors are presented when connecting to the database or running the code, the *catch* block will run, and the *getMessage()* function will be called to retrieve the error message.

```php
1   <?php
2   $type = $_POST['type'];
3   if($type == 'yesno'){
4       yesNoLog();
5   }
6   function yesNoLog(){
7       $articleid = $_POST['articleid'];
8       $result = $_POST['result'];
9       try {
10          $host = 'localhost';
11          $dbname = 'bookexamples';
12          $user = 'sampleuser';
13          $pass = '3C9038A509BE6145AAD6827B4568AD918BC3DAC0';
14          $DBH = new PDO("mysql:host=$host;dbname=$dbname",
15              $user, $pass);
16          $sql = "INSERT INTO `yesno` (`articleid`, `result`) VALUES
17              (?, ?);";
18          $sth = $DBH->prepare($sql);
19          $sth->bindParam(1, $articleid, PDO::PARAM_INT);
20          $sth->bindParam(2, $result, PDO::PARAM_STR);
21          $sth->execute();
22      } catch(PDOException $e) {echo $e->getMessage();}
23  }
```

SAMPLE CODE 4: ajax.php — PHP logging binary choice to the *yesno* database table.

Output

Figure 2.1, shows the output of these radio buttons with a small question such as *Are you happy with this service?*

Are you happy with this? ● Yes ● No

FIGURE 2.1: Yes and No binary options.

In Figure 2.2 the alert box that is shown to the user after the data has been recorded in the database table is shown.

FIGURE 2.2: Alert box showing the selected radio button value.

2.3 TEXT-BASED DATA COLLECTION

A further adaptation to a basic binary data collection process can be added to include an additional text field that only appears if a user selects the *No* option. Although text requires additional processing to quantify and gather insights from, it nonetheless is useful as a number of derivative statistics can be drawn from this data.

Example 2: Providing an option to gather text

This example consists of three core files and one library:

1. create.sql — This file is used to create the *whyanswerlog* database table. This table has an additional column to store text.

2. binary.html — The main HTML/JavaScript binary data collection interface with an additional text field.

3. ajax.php — Used to receive data and store it in a MySQL database table.

4. jQuery — Used to add a click handler and to perform a JavaScript *POST* to the ajax.php page.

Example code: create.sql

To store text, an additional database table is required. In Sample Code 5, the *result* column is set to 500 characters to allow for the text-based answer.

```
1  CREATE TABLE `whyanswerlog` (
2      `id` INT NOT NULL AUTO_INCREMENT,
3      `mytime` TIMESTAMP NOT NULL DEFAULT CURRENT_TIMESTAMP ,
4      `articleid` INT,
5      `result` VARCHAR (500),
6      PRIMARY KEY ( `id`)
7  );
```

SAMPLE CODE 5: *whyanswer* log database table SQL.

Example code: binary.html
In Sample Code 6, on line 5, a *div* tag is added to hold the text area for the user to elaborate on why they chose *No*. On line 11, a simple submit button is added to trigger the saving process. The submit button has an *onclick* set to call the *saveWhyAnswer()* JavaScript function.

On line 14, a *click()* handler for the radio button is added. On line 19, a simple *if statement* that will check to see if the user clicked *No* is added. If they did, we will call the *findOutWhy()* function that will trigger the input field for user input to open on line 20. On line 31, a function titled *findOutWhy()* is added. Inside this on line 32, the jQuery *show()* function is called on the jQuery selector that references the *explainwhy* div tag.

When the user clicks the submit button, a call is made to the *save-WhyAnswer()* function as shown on line 34. In this function on line 35, the text entered by the user is gathered using the *getElementById()* function that takes a reference to the *whyanswer* text area. On line 36, the *POST* function is called that is similar to the previous example. On line

39 a simple *alert()* statement is used to present the user with the text *thank you for your comments!.*

On line 42, when the page is finished loading, a shorthand version of the *document ready* function is used. This ensures that the page is loaded, and all the different elements on the page are ready. Once the page has fully loaded, jQuery is used to hide the *div* that we have just created using the *hide()* function on line 43 until the user selects the *No* option.

```
1   <script src="https://code.jquery.com/jquery-3.5.1.min.js"
2    crossorigin="anonymous"></script>
3   <input type="radio" name="answer" value="Yes"> Yes <br>
4   <input type="radio" name="answer" value="No"> No<br>
5   <div id="explainwhy">
6       Sorry to hear you were not happy,<br>
7       Would you like to say why?<br>
8       <textarea id="whyanswer" rows="5" cols="50">
9       </textarea>
10  <br>
11  <button onclick="saveWhyAnswer()">Submit</button>
12  </div>
13  <script>
14  $( "input:radio[name=answer]" ).click(function() {
15
16      var val = $(this).val();
17      saveAnswer(val)
18
19      if(val == 'No'){
20          findOutWhy();
21      }
22  });
23
24  function saveAnswer(answer){
25      $.post( "ajax.php", { type: "yesno", articleid: "1221",
26       result: answer })
27      .done(function( data ) {
28          alert('Thank you!');
29      });
30  }
31  function findOutWhy(){
32      $("#explainwhy").show();
33  }
34  function saveWhyAnswer(){
35      var answer = document.getElementById('whyanswer').value;
```

```
36    $.post( "ajax.php", { type: "whyanswer", articleid: "1221",
37      result: answer })
38      .done(function( data ) {
39          alert('Thank you for your comments!');
40      });
41  }
42  $(function() {
43      $("#explainwhy").hide();
44  });
45
46  </script>
```

SAMPLE CODE 6: binary.html — HTML form with additional *div* tag allowing the user to enter comments.

Example code: ajax.php

Instead of using the *ajax.php* page for one purpose, it was set up in the previous example to use the *type* variable that allows us to perform multiple different functions with the same page. In Sample Code 7, we will add an *else if* statement on line 6 that will be used to redirect the flow of execution to the *whyAnswer()* function if the *type* variable is set to *whyanswer*. In the *whyAnswer()* function on lines 28 and 29, the two variables *articleid* and *result* are first extracted from the *POST* variable.

A connection to the database is created on line 39 inside the *try-catch* statement. A simple *INSERT* statement is used on line 37 to put the record in the database table. The values for both columns are represented with question marks that are later replaced by values when a call is made to the *bindParam()* function on lines 40 and 41. As the result contains text, the data type in the second *bindParam()* call is set to *PARAM_STR*.

```
1   <?php
2   $type = $_POST['type'];
3   if($type == 'yesno'){
4       yesNoLog();
5   }
6   else if($type == 'whyanswer'){
7       whyAnswer();
8   }
9   function yesNoLog(){
10      $articleid = $_POST['articleid'];
11      $result = $_POST['result'];
```

```
12      try {
13          $host = 'localhost';
14          $dbname = 'bookexamples';
15          $user = 'sampleuser';
16          $pass = '3C9038A509BE6145AAD6827B4568AD918BC3DAC0';
17          $DBH = new PDO("mysql:host=$host;dbname=$dbname", $user,
18           $pass);
19          $sql = "INSERT INTO `yesnolog` (`articleid`, `result`)
20           VALUES (?, ?);";
21          $sth = $DBH->prepare($sql);
22          $sth->bindParam(1, $articleid, PDO::PARAM_INT);
23          $sth->bindParam(2, $result, PDO::PARAM_STR);
24          $sth->execute();
25      } catch(PDOException $e) {echo $e;}
26  }
27  function whyAnswer(){
28      $articleid = $_POST['articleid'];
29      $result = $_POST['result'];
30      try {
31          $host = 'localhost';
32          $dbname = 'bookexamples';
33          $user = 'sampleuser';
34          $pass = '3C9038A509BE6145AAD6827B4568AD918BC3DAC0';
35          $DBH = new PDO("mysql:host=$host;dbname=$dbname", $user,
36           $pass);
37          $sql = "INSERT INTO `whyanswerlog` (`articleid`, `result`)
38           VALUES (?, ?);";
39          $sth = $DBH->prepare($sql);
40          $sth->bindParam(1, $articleid, PDO::PARAM_INT);
41          $sth->bindParam(2, $result, PDO::PARAM_STR);
42          $sth->execute();
43      } catch(PDOException $e) {echo $e;}
44  }
45  ?>
```

SAMPLE CODE 7: ajax.php — Additional PHP function to insert text a user has entered into a database table.

Output

Figure 2.3 shows the result of selecting *No* on the Yes/No radio buttons. A question is prompted to the user along with a text area where they can describe their issue.

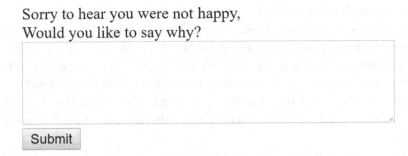

Sorry to hear you were not happy,
Would you like to say why?

Submit

FIGURE 2.3: No option expanding allowing the user to expand their response in text format.

2.4 STAR RATINGS

The star rating allows us to gather opinions on a defined scale from a user with the least amount of user interaction. Star ratings allow the user to rate typically on a range between one and five. This method proves to be very unobtrusive, as the user does not need to click an additional submit button to send the result to the server.

The rating system comes in two main varieties, one that allow the user to provide responses in the form of a star rating, while the other show previous user ratings. The process of gathering statistics and presenting them to the user in star form will be discussed at the end of this chapter. As star ratings are commonplace on websites such as Amazon and eBay, many vendors offer free and open-source star rating solutions. Each of these implementations come with a varying degree of abilities and handlers to respond to the input entered by the user. The overall look and feel of the rating approach are the main factors in deciding which implementation to use. In this example, we will be looking at the RateYo![2] star rating package.

Example 3: Star rating

This example consists of one file and two libraries:

1. rating.html — This provides the star rating interface to the user.

2. jQuery — This library is used to access the jQuery selector.

3. RateYo! — Used to provide a star rating interface.

---

[2]https://rateyo.fundoocode.ninja

Example code: rating.html

In Sample Code 8, three references are included. The first of these is the reference to jQuery on line 1, the second is the reference to the CSS file on line 3, and the last is a reference to the RateYo JavaScript file on line 6. After the files have been included, a *div* tag is included on line 9 that will be converted into the star rating system. The *ID* of the *div* tag is set to *rateYo*. On line 11, a shorthand for the *document ready* function is added.

The jQuery selector is used to select the *rateYo div* tag on line 12. On this *div* the *rateYo()* function is called. Inside of this, the *onSet* on line 13 takes a reference to the function that is called when a star is clicked. In this example, a simple alert statement is added on line 14 to indicate to the user the rating they selected. The rating made by the user is available through the *rating* variable.

```
1   <script src="https://code.jquery.com/jquery-3.1.0.min.js"
2         crossorigin="anonymous"></script>
3   <link rel="stylesheet"
4         href="https://cdnjs.cloudflare.com/ajax/libs/rateYo/2.2.0/
5         jquery.rateyo.min.css">
6   <script src="https://cdnjs.cloudflare.com/ajax/libs/rateYo/2.2.0/
7         jquery.rateyo.min.js">
8   </script>
9   <div id="rateYo"></div>
10  <script>
11  $(function () {
12      $("#rateYo").rateYo({
13      onSet: function (rating, rateYoInstance) {
14          alert("Rating is set to: " + rating);
15      }
16      });
17  });
18  </script>
```

SAMPLE CODE 8: rating.html — Star rating interface.

Output

Figure 2.4 shows an example of what the star rating looks like when loaded.

FIGURE 2.4: Star-rating example.

Example 4: Saving a star rating

After a user has clicked on a star, the only thing that is changing is the star on the page. No data is being stored in a database table that can be retrieved later.

This example consists of three files and two libraries:

1. create.sql — Used to create the *starratinglog* database table.

2. rating.html — This provides the rating stars to the user that can be selected.

3. ajax.php — This page receives the rating and stores it in a database table.

4. jQuery — Added to perform a JavaScript *POST* to the *ajax.php* page.

5. RateYo! — Used to provide a star rating interface.

Example code: create.sql

To store the data, a new database table is required, as shown in Sample Code 9. This table contains an *ID* field that is unique and auto-incremented. This is followed by the *mytime* that holds the time stamp when the record was created. The *articleid* column is used to hold a reference to the article being viewed by the user. The result entered by the user is placed inside the *result* column. As the user cannot select half stars, the data type for this is set to *int*.

```
1  CREATE TABLE starratinglog(
2      `id` INT NOT NULL AUTO_INCREMENT,
3      `mytime` TIMESTAMP NOT NULL DEFAULT CURRENT_TIMESTAMP ,
4      `articleid` INT,
5      `result` int,
6      PRIMARY KEY ( `id`)
7  );
```

SAMPLE CODE 9: Sample *starratinglog* table SQL.

Example code: rating.html

In Sample Code 10 on line 14 the *saveRating()* function is called that takes in a single parameter titled *rating* that contains the rating the user selected. On line 18, the function is defined. In this function, on line 19 a call to the jQuery *POST* function is performed. The *type* of request being performed is titled *starrating*. The *articleid* being viewed is set to *1221* and the *userrating* is set to *rating* that is dynamically set when a star is selected. On line 22, an *alert()* call is added to present the user with the text *Thank you for your rating!* when a rating is selected.

```
1   <script src="https://code.jquery.com/jquery-3.5.1.min.js"
2          crossorigin="anonymous"></script>
3   <link rel="stylesheet"
4         href="https://cdnjs.cloudflare.com/ajax/libs/rateYo/2.2.0/
5         jquery.rateyo.min.css">
6   <script src="https://cdnjs.cloudflare.com/ajax/libs/rateYo/2.2.0/
7         jquery.rateyo.min.js">
8   </script>
9   <div id="rateYo"></div>
10  <script>
11  $(function () {
12      $("#rateYo").rateYo({
13      onSet: function (rating, rateYoInstance) {
14          saveRating(rating);
15      }
16      });
17  });
18  function saveRating(rating){
19      $.post( "ajax.php", { type: "starrating", articleid: "1221",
20       userrating: rating })
21      .done(function( data ) {
22          alert('Thank you for your rating!');
23      });
24  }
25  </script>
```

SAMPLE CODE 10: rating.html — Star rating with *saveRating()* function.

Example code: ajax.php

A second page titled *ajax.php* is added that is responsible for processing the request. In Sample Code 11, on line 2, the *type* variable is first gathered from the *POST*. A check is performed on line 3 to see if the *type* of request that was sent is equal to a *starrating*. If it is, then a call is made to the PHP function *starRatingLog()* on line 4. Inside of the *starRatingLog()* function on line 7 and 8, the *articleid* and the *userrating* are extracted from the PHP *POST* and placed inside local variables.

On line 14, a connection is made to the database to insert the record into the *starratinglog* database table. As the first two columns of this table are auto-generated, only the *articleid* and the *result* are required for the *insert* statement. Inside the statement on line 16, two question marks hold the position where the values will be placed. The *bindParam()* function is used on lines 19 and 20 to place the value into the statement before it is executed.

```php
1   <?php
2   $type = $_POST['type'];
3   if($type == 'starrating'){
4       starRatingLog();
5   }
6   function starRatingLog(){
7       $articleid = $_POST['articleid'];
8       $result = $_POST['userrating'];
9       try {
10          $host = 'localhost';
11          $dbname = 'bookexamples';
12          $user = 'sampleuser';
13          $pass = '3C9038A509BE6145AAD6827B4568AD918BC3DAC0';
14          $DBH = new PDO("mysql:host=$host;dbname=$dbname", $user,
15           $pass);
16          $sql = "INSERT INTO `starratinglog` (`articleid`, `result`)
17           VALUES (?, ?);";
18          $sth = $DBH->prepare($sql);
19          $sth->bindParam(1, $articleid, PDO::PARAM_INT);
20          $sth->bindParam(2, $result, PDO::PARAM_INT);
21          $sth->execute();
22      } catch(PDOException $e) {echo $e;}
23  }
24  ?>
```

SAMPLE CODE 11: ajax.php — Saving a star rating to the *starratinglog* database table.

Example 5: Retrieving star ratings

As the star rating can be used to gather opinions from a user, the opposite to this is to display the average star rating. This is done by gathering the ratings that have previously been saved by users. Although the database table will hold lots of data from different star ratings across a website, we must ensure that we get only the ratings for the current article under consideration.

This example consists of two files and one library:

1. star.php — This provides the rating stars to the user that can be selected and also shows a preset rating.

2. ajax.php — This page receives a new rating and stores it in a database table.

3. jQuery — This is used to perform a JavaScript *GET* request.

When the rating process was first set-up, we provided a unique *ID* for each of the different star rating implementations on the website. In this example, the *articleid* is the variable that held all the information about a single instance of the star rating.

To begin, we will look at the SQL query that will be used to retrieve the average. In this example, we will use the SQL function titled *avg()* that will return the average across all of the records for the given *articleid*. To the right-hand side of this SQL query, an additional *WHERE* clause is added to narrow down the collection of records to only return the average rating of the article we are currently interested in.

```
SELECT AVG(result) FROM starratinglog WHERE articleid ='1221';
```

Example code: star.php

In Sample Code 12 on line 13, jQuery is used to perform a *GET* request to the *ajax.php* page. The *type* of request being sent is set to *getrating*. To ensure the results for a single star rating are returned, the *articleid* variable is passed that contains the *ID* of the article we are interested in. On line 14, when the jQuery function has returned a call is made to the *done()* function that returns a variable titled *data* that contains the average star rating that will be retrieved from the *ajax.php* page. On line 16, this data variable is set to be the value of the *rating* variable that dictates the number of stars that will be highlighted.

```
1   <script src="https://code.jquery.com/jquery-3.5.1.min.js"
2          crossorigin="anonymous">
3   </script>
4   <link rel="stylesheet"
5         href="https://cdnjs.cloudflare.com/ajax/libs/rateYo/2.2.0/
6         jquery.rateyo.min.css">
7   <script src="https://cdnjs.cloudflare.com/ajax/libs/rateYo/2.2.0/
8          jquery.rateyo.min.js">
9   </script>
10  <link rel="stylesheet" href="jquery.rateyo.css"/>
11  <div id="rateYo"></div>
12  <script>
13  $.get( "ajax.php", { type: "getrating", articleid: 1221})
14     .done(function( data ) {
15     $("#rateYo").rateYo({
16         rating:data,
17         onSet: function (rating, rateYoInstance) {
18     }
19     });
20  });
21  </script>
```

SAMPLE CODE 12: star.php — Using a *GET* request to retrieve the average star rating.

Example code: ajax.php
Sample Code 13 shows the *ajax.php* page. On line 2 the *type* variable is first received from the PHP *GET* request. On line 3, an *if statement* is used to check if the *type* is equal to *getrating*. If it is, then a call is made to the *getRating()* function on line 4.

On line 6, the *getRating()* function is defined. Inside this function on line 13, a connection to the database is created. On line 15, the SQL to retrieve the average rating is added. The article *ID* is left as a question mark. The *bindParam()* is used to pass in the *articleid* that was passed via the jQuery *GET* request to this page on line 18. After this query has run, on line 21, a single result will be returned. This result is placed in the *res* variable at position 0 of the returned array. The PHP *round()*

function is used to remove any trailing decimal numbers and return only an integer.

```php
<?php
$type = $_GET['type'];
if($type == 'getrating'){
    getRating();
}
function getRating(){
    $articleid = $_GET['articleid'];
    try {
        $host = 'localhost';
        $dbname = 'bookexamples';
        $user = 'sampleuser';
        $pass = '3C9038A509BE6145AAD6827B4568AD918BC3DAC0';
        $DBH = new PDO("mysql:host=$host;dbname=$dbname", $user,
         $pass);
        $sql = "SELECT AVG(result) FROM starratinglog WHERE
         articleid=?";
        $sth = $DBH->prepare($sql);
        $sth->bindParam(1, $articleid, PDO::PARAM_INT);
        $sth->execute();
        $res = $sth->fetch();
        echo round($res[0]);
    } catch(PDOException $e) {echo $e;}
}
?>
```

SAMPLE CODE 13: ajax.php — Retrieving the average star rating and printing it as a page.

Output

Figure 2.5 shows an example with a preset rating. Although a number of records exist in the database table, the average star rating achieved was 3.

FIGURE 2.5: Star rating with preset rating.

2.5 CUSTOM RESPONSE FORM

In this section, we will review the process of creating a complete response form. This form can be used to prompt users to enter longer pieces of data in different formats. Although it is possible to present the options to the user, it does not guarantee that the user will fill them all out. Custom validation is added to the form that prompts the user to enter values for each field before the form can be submitted.

To aid the layout of the form, Bootstrap is used. Bootstrap provides a default look and feel for the form. In addition to this, the Bootstrap modal will be used to present a message to the user once the form has been submitted.

Example 6: Custom response form with JavaScript validation

This example consists of three files and two libraries:

1. create.sql — This file is used to create the *servicerating* database table.

2. form.html — This contains the main HTML and JavaScript to create the form along with references to jQuery and Bootstrap.

3. saveForm.php — Receives data from the form and saves it to the database table using PHP PDOs.

4. Bootstrap — This is used to style the custom form and to add the ability to create modals.

5. jQuery – This is used to perform a JavaScript *POST* to the *ajax.php* page.

Example code: create.sql
To allow this data to be stored in the database, a new table is created titled *servicerating*. This contains an attribute for each of the form fields entered by the user. The *varchar* data type is used for text-based data and the *int* data type is used for numeric data. To uniquely identify each individual record, an *ID* column is added that is *auto-incremented* and set as a *primary key*.

```
1   CREATE TABLE `servicerating` (
2       `id` INT NOT NULL AUTO_INCREMENT,
3       `email` VARCHAR(100),
4       `fullName` VARCHAR(100),
5       `serviceRating` INT,
6       `foodRating` INT,
7       `atmosRating` INT,
8       `comments` VARCHAR(500),
9       PRIMARY KEY (`id`)
10  );
```

SAMPLE CODE 14: *servicerating* database table SQL.

Example code: form.html

Sample Code 15 outlines the HTML for a complete feedback collection form. On line 1, a reference to jQuery is first added. On line 4, the CSS for Bootstrap is included, followed by additional JavaScript required by Bootstrap on line 8. On line 12, a *div* tag is created that is used for a placeholder for error messages that will be generated if any of the form fields are left blank. On line 14, a form tag is added with the *class* attribute set to *w-25* that tells the browser to use 25% of the available space to display the components. *p-2* is used to set the padding for the form.

Inside of the *form* tag, the individual form elements can be added. It is important during this process to provide unique IDs to individual form elements. To aid the user during the process of filling out the form, individual *label* tags are added on line 16. The *for* attribute allows us to specify which form element the label is for. *aria-describedby* is used to specify a piece of text that will be displayed below the form elements.

To provide the user with a range of options to choose from, an HTML *select* is added on line 35 to 42. The user has the options between one and five. The default value for the *select* element is the first option in the list. In this example, the first option is left blank. This is useful as during the validation process, if no value was selected, an error can be thrown. This also prevents the form from being submitted with a default value.

```
1   <script
2     src="https://code.jquery.com/jquery-3.5.1.min.js"
3     crossorigin="anonymous"></script>
4   <link rel="stylesheet"
5         href="https://maxcdn.bootstrapcdn.com/bootstrap/4.0.0/css/
6         bootstrap.min.css"
7     crossorigin="anonymous">
8   <script
9     src="https://maxcdn.bootstrapcdn.com/bootstrap/4.0.0/js/
10    bootstrap.min.js" crossorigin="anonymous"></script>
11
12  <div id="error_message">
13  </div>
14  <form class="w-25 p-2">
15  <div class="form-group">
16      <label for="emailAddress">E-mail address</label>
17      <input type="text" class="form-control" id="emailAddress"
18        aria-describedby="emailHelp"
19        placeholder="Enter email">
20      <small id="emailHelp"
21        class="form-text text-muted">We'll never share your email
22        with anyone else.
23      </small>
24  </div>
25  <div class="form-group">
26      <label for="fullName">Full name</label>
27      <input type="text" class="form-control" id="fullName"
28        aria-describedby="nameHelp" placeholder="Enter full name">
29      <small id="nameHelp"
30        class="form-text text-muted">Please enter your full name.
31      </small>
32  </div>
33  <div class="form-group">
34      <label for="serviceRating">How would you rate our service?</label>
35      <select class="form-control" id="serviceRating">
36        <option></option>
37        <option value="1">1</option>
38        <option value="2">2</option>
39        <option value="3">3</option>
40        <option value="4">4</option>
41        <option value="5">5</option>
42      </select>
43  </div>
44  <div class="form-group">
45      <label for="foodRating">How would you rate our food?
```

```
46      </label>
47      <select class="form-control" id="foodRating">
48          <option></option>
49          <option value="1">1</option>
50          <option value="2">2</option>
51          <option value="3">3</option>
52          <option value="4">4</option>
53          <option value="5">5</option>
54      </select>
55  </div>
```

SAMPLE CODE 15: form.html — Complete Bootstrap feedback form part 1.

In Sample Code 16, on line 74, a submit button is added to the form. To make the form more interactive, when the form is submitted, a Bootstrap modal will be opened. On line 77, the modal begins with the *ID* set to *success*. The *role* of the *div* tag is set to *dialog*. This will be used later during the form submission to open this modal. A single close button is added to the modal allowing the user to dismiss the message on line 91.

```
56      <div class="form-group">
57      <label for="atmosRating">How was the atmosphere in the
58          restaurant?</label>
59      <select class="form-control" id="atmosRating">
60          <option></option>
61          <option value="1">1</option>
62          <option value="2">2</option>
63          <option value="3">3</option>
64          <option value="4">4</option>
65          <option value="5">5</option>
66      </select>
67  </div>
68  <div class="form-group">
69      <label for="comments">Please tell us about your experience
70          </label>
71      <textarea class="form-control" id="comments" rows="3">
72          </textarea>
73  </div>
74  <button type="submit" id="submit" class="btn btn-primary">Submit
75      </button>
76  </form>
77  <div class="modal" id="success" tabindex="-1" role="dialog">
```

```
78    <div class="modal-dialog" role="document">
79      <div class="modal-content">
80        <div class="modal-header">
81          <h5 class="modal-title">Success!</h5>
82          <button type="button" class="close" data-dismiss=
83            "modal" aria-label="Close">
84          <span aria-hidden="true">&times;</span>
85          </button>
86        </div>
87        <div class="modal-body">
88          <p>Thank you for the feedback.</p>
89        </div>
90        <div class="modal-footer">
91          <button type="button" class="btn btn-secondary"
92                        data-dismiss="modal">Close</button>
93        </div>
94      </div>
95    </div>
96  </div>
```

SAMPLE CODE 16: form.html — Complete Bootstrap feedback form part 2.

Older web forms utilised the *form* tag by appending an *action* and *method* attributes. As we are working in pure JavaScript, we will use jQuery to handle the form submission process. In Sample Code 17 on line 3, when the submit button is clicked the *preventDefault()* function is called. This function is used to suppress the default nature of the *form* tag that is to redirect to a different page. After this, a new variable titled *error* is added to store the error messages for the form, if any are present on line 4.

On lines 6—29, The jQuery selector is used to select each individual form element. The *val()* function is used to extract the value from the element. A simple *if statement* can be used to check if the value in the form field is left blank. If it is left blank, an error message is appended to the *error* variable using the += syntax.

On line 31, after the error checking has been completed, an *if statement* can be used to check if the *error* variable contains error messages or not. If an error message is present, the *html()* function is used to add the error messages gathered in the *error* variable into the *error_message div*. If the form is valid, a jQuery *POST* is performed to save the input to the database on line 33.

The *post()* function takes key-value pairs where the first variable e.g., *email*, is passed and the value is set to the value of the variable *email*. The name given to this variable has a direct link to the variable name that will be caught on the *saveForm.php* page. When the form *POST* is performed, the *done()* will be triggered on line 37. Inside of this function, the jQuery selector is used to select the *success* modal on line 39. The *modal()* function is called to make it visible to the user.

If the form is not valid, on line 43, the *error_message div* tag is selected using the jQuery selector. The HTML of the *div* tag is set to be the content of the *error* variable.

```
1   <script>
2   $( "#submit" ).click(function(event) {
3       event.preventDefault();
4       var error = '';
5
6       var email = $("#emailAddress").val();
7       if(email == ""){
8         error += 'Please enter your e-mail address<br>';
9       }
10      var fullName = $("#fullName").val();
11      if(fullName == ""){
12        error += 'Please enter your full name<br>';
13      }
14      var serviceRating = $("#serviceRating").val();
15      if(serviceRating == ""){
16        error += 'Please rate the service<br>';
17      }
18      var foodRating = $("#foodRating").val();
19      if(foodRating == ""){
20        error += 'Please rate the food<br>';
21      }
22      var atmosRating = $("#atmosRating").val();
23      if(atmosRating == ""){
24        error += 'Please rate the atmosphere<br>';
25      }
26      var comments = $("#comments").val();
27      if(atmosRating == ""){
28        error += 'Please add a comment<br>';
29      }
30
31      if(error === ""){
32          // if the form if valid
33          $.post( "saveForm.php", { type: "register", email:email,
```

```
34            fullName:fullName, serviceRating:serviceRating,
35            foodRating:foodRating, atmosRating:atmosRating,
36            comments:comments })
37        .done(function( data ) {
38            alert(data); // for debugging
39            $("#success").modal();
40        });
41    } else {
42    // if the form is not valid
43    $( "#error_message" ).html(error);
44    }
45  });
46  </script>
```

SAMPLE CODE 17: form.html — Custom JavaScript form validation part 3

Example code: saveForm.php

Sample Code 18 outlines the PHP to save the form data to a database table. This page is titled *saveForm.php*. On line 2, the *type* variable is first extracted from the *POST* variable. If the *POST* contains the term *register* then a call is made to the *registerNewUser()* function on line 4. Inside of this function, each of the variables that were *POST* using the JavaScript *POST* is extracted from the PHP *POST* and placed into local variables on lines 7–12.

Once each of the variables has been gathered a *try-catch* is added starting on line 13. Inside of this, a call to the database is made on line 18. The PHP variable *sql* on line 21 contains the raw SQL to be inserted into the *servicerating* table. This contains a reference to each individual column in the database followed by six question marks that are used as placeholders for the variables that will be bound using the *bindParam()* function on lines 26—31.

After the SQL has been prepared and the variables have been appended, a call to the *execute()* function can be performed to insert the record into the database on line 32.

```
1  <?php
2  $type = $_POST['type'];
3  if($type == 'register'){
4      registerNewUser();
5  }
6  function registerNewUser(){
```

```
7    $email =          $_POST['email'];
8    $fullName =       $_POST['fullName'];
9    $serviceRating = $_POST['serviceRating'];
10   $foodRating =     $_POST['foodRating'];
11   $atmosRating =    $_POST['atmosRating'];
12   $comments =       $_POST['comments'];
13   try {
14       $host = 'localhost';
15       $dbname = 'bookexamples';
16       $user = 'sampleuser';
17       $pass = '3C9038A509BE6145AAD6827B4568AD918BC3DAC0';
18       $DBH = new PDO("mysql:host=$host;dbname=$dbname",
19           $user, $pass);
20
21       $sql = "INSERT INTO `servicerating` (`email`, `fullName`,
22                           `serviceRating`, `foodRating`,
23                           `atmosRating`, `comments`)
24                           VALUES (?,?,?,?,?,?);";
25       $sth = $DBH->prepare($sql);
26       $sth->bindParam(1, $email, PDO::PARAM_STR);
27       $sth->bindParam(2, $fullName, PDO::PARAM_STR);
28       $sth->bindParam(3, $serviceRating, PDO::PARAM_INT);
29       $sth->bindParam(4, $foodRating, PDO::PARAM_INT);
30       $sth->bindParam(5, $atmosRating, PDO::PARAM_INT);
31       $sth->bindParam(6, $comments, PDO::PARAM_STR);
32       $sth->execute();
33   } catch(PDOException $e) {echo $e;}
34 }
```

SAMPLE CODE 18: saveForm.php — PHP used to save the form data to a database table.

Output
In Figure 2.6, the completed form layout can be seen. Figure 2.7 outlines the modal that is shown to the user after the form has been submitted.

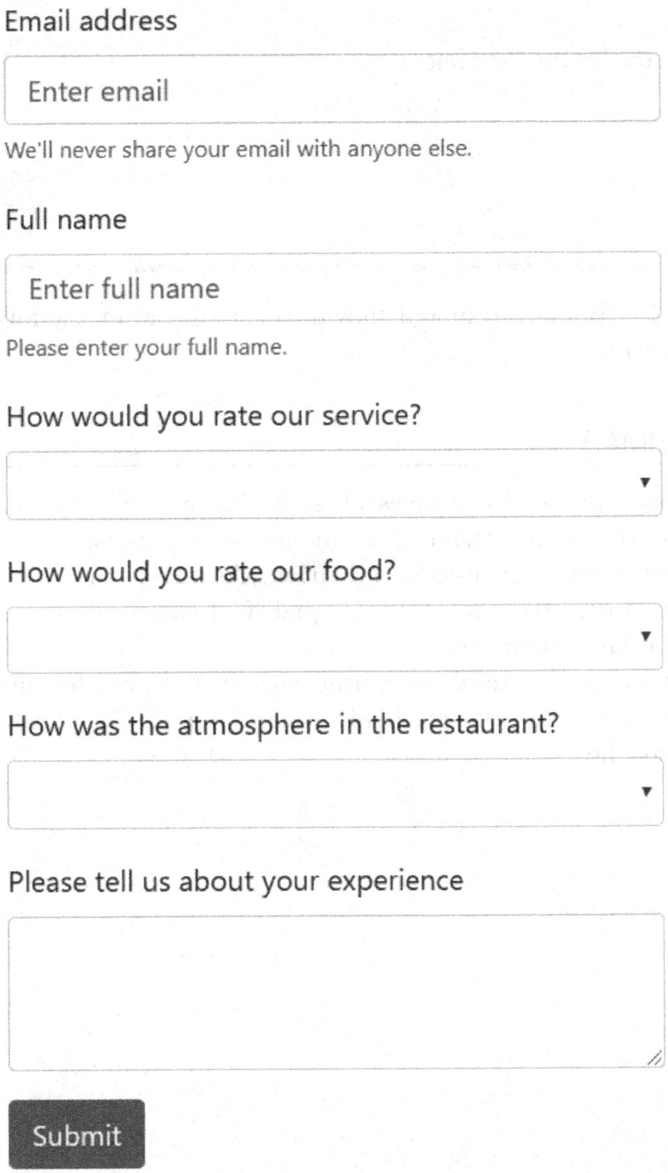

Email address

> Enter email

We'll never share your email with anyone else.

Full name

> Enter full name

Please enter your full name.

How would you rate our service?

How would you rate our food?

How was the atmosphere in the restaurant?

Please tell us about your experience

Submit

FIGURE 2.6: Completed response form.

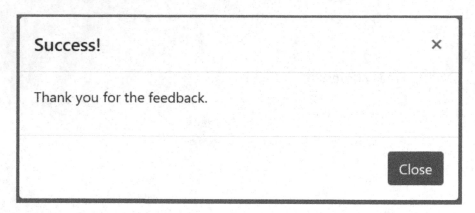

FIGURE 2.7: Bootstrap modal shown to the user after the form has been submitted.

2.6 SUMMARY

This chapter provided examples of gathering active data from a user directly by prompting them using binary selections, star ratings, and custom forms with client-side validation. Although the data received from the user directly can be of high quality, it can be a difficult process to gather in larger quantities.

To gather more data about a user without the need for direct interactions, passive collections mechanisms can be used. Chapter 3, outlines these approaches.

Passive Data Collection

Passive data is the data that is gathered in the background without any need to interact with a user. This is useful as a wide range of insights can be gathered from the user, such as: where they are from, their interests, and what environment they are currently using to access an application.

In this chapter, we explore the process of identifying different data sources and data formats. The process of extracting meaningful insights from the user is explored using both custom solutions and third-party tools.

3.1 INTRODUCTION

Although it is possible to store all the interactions a user has with a web application, not all may be useful for analysis. To reduce the duplication that can occur, a simple approach is to store data only as a result of a predefined action. Actions that can be a trigger to store data may include:

- viewing a particular product numerous times;

- viewing products that are in a similar category;

- purchasing a particular product.

When assessing what data to store, consideration should be made as to how concrete the connection is between the user and a given product or categorization. An example of this is a user who is searching through a collection of books and then decides to buy a toy. As buying a book would be considered a concrete connection, e.g., they performed the action that we want, a greater emphasis should be put on this connection.

In contrast to this, the user may be browsing books that are all of a similar topic. An analysis based on this information could prove fruitful for future sales if possible candidate books of the same topic are presented to the user. How these decisions are inferred is explored in later chapters.

Irrespective of the source of data, one common component that most data has is a temporal element, e.g., when the data was recorded. The length of time that the data is stored for can be considered relevant to the analysis process that is being performed.

3.2 COOKIES AND SESSIONS

In the early days of web development, *cookies* were used as a de facto method of storing small pieces of information in a user's web browser. As the web grew, this method of using cookies to store information was quickly outdated in favor of using server-side sessions that can hold larger amounts of data. Although sessions are commonplace in web application development, cookies have not been replaced. An example of this can be seen when a new server-side session is created in PHP. During this process, a cookie is stored in the user's web browser to identify the session they are currently associated with. A typical server-side session may only last 30 to 60 minutes, but a cookie stored in the user's web browser can persist much longer.

The reliability of cookies can be questioned, however, as users who are focused on privacy will often prevent an application from leaving cookies in their web browser. When a user deletes their browser internet history, this often includes the cookies left by websites. The association between a user and a particular collection of data on the server is now broken.

Example 1: Client-side cookies — simple set and get

Cookies are a simple method of storing data in a user's web browser. This data is stored on the client-side with no overhead to the server. To aid the process of interacting with cookies, the *js-cookie*[1] library is used. To include this functionality, a Content Delivery Network (CDN) is used

---

[1]https://github.com/js-cookie/js-cookie

to deliver a current version of the JavaScript file. The *Cookies* class can be used to set and retrieve information from cookies.

Example code: cookies.html

In Sample Code 1, on line 4, the *set()* function takes in two parameters. The first one is titled *name*, which is the key we use to access the value. This is followed by a second parameter titled *John* that represents the value. After the cookie has been created, the *get()* function on line 5 can be used to retrieve the value for a given cookie name. This value is placed into a local variable titled *name*. On line 6, the *name* variable is printed to the browser's developer console.

```
1  <script src="https://cdn.jsdelivr.net/npm/js-cookie@2/src/
2      js.cookie.min.js"></script>
3  <script>
4      Cookies.set('name', 'john');
5      var name = Cookies.get('name');
6      console.log(name);
7  </script>
```

SAMPLE CODE 1: cookies.html — Set and get for a single cookie value.

Output

To access the developer console in Google Chrome, the *Ctrl+Shift+J* keys can be pressed together. The output in Figure 3.1 shows a single variable retrieved from a cookie being printed to the console.

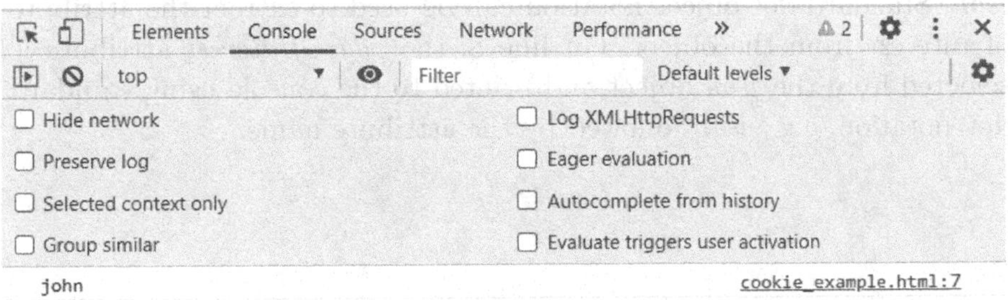

FIGURE 3.1: Value being retrieved from a cookie.

A modification can be made to the *set()* function to include the number of days after which the cookie will expire. In this example, the cookie will last for seven days.

```
Cookies.set('name', 'value', { expires: 7 });
```

The *set()* function can also be passed the domain where the cookie will be visible.

```
Cookies.set('name', 'value', { domain: 'site.com' });
```

To delete this cookie, the cookie *name* and *domain* are required. This approach prevents the process of accidentally deleting the incorrect cookie.

```
Cookies.remove('name', { domain: 'site.com' });
```

Example 2: Client-side cookies — JSON content

Although it is possible to create different cookies for each different piece of information that needs to be stored, the Cookies library provides the ability to store JSON content. This is particularly useful when more than one variable needs to be stored.

Example code: cookies_json.html
In Sample Code 2, online 6, a JSON object titled *info* is created that contains a single variable titled *pageOfInterest* with the value set to *homeware*.

Once the JSON content has been set in the cookie, on line 7, the *getJSON()* function is called to return the JSON object by name. The result from calling the *getJSON()* is stored inside of a local variable title *json*. Standard dot object notation can be used to extract the attribute of interest from the object. On line 8, the *pageOfInterest* attribute is selected from the *json* object and printed to the console using standard dot notation, e.g., *json* followed by the attribute name.

```
1  <script src="https://cdn.jsdelivr.net/npm/js-cookie@2/src/
2        js.cookie.min.js">
3  </script>
4
5  <script>
6      Cookies.set('info', { pageOfInterest: 'homeware' });
7      var json = Cookies.getJSON('info');
8      console.log(json.pageOfInterest);
9  </script>
```

SAMPLE CODE 2: cookies_json.html — Set and get JSON content.

Output

Figure 3.2 shows JSON content being retrieved and printed to the developer console.

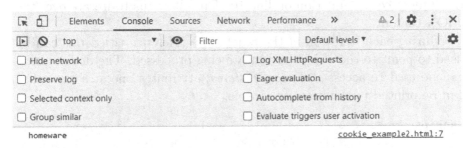

FIGURE 3.2: Set and get JSON value.

Example 3: Client-side cookies — Iterating over JSON

The previous example stored one single attribute in a JSON string. In the example JSON below, it contains two *pageOfInterest* attributes that store a reference to the type of content the user has been viewing.

```
1  [{
2              "pageOfInterest": "homeware"
3          },
4          {
5              "pageOfInterest": "cooking"
6          }
7  ]
```

Example code: iterate.html

This example contains one file and two libraries:

1. iterate.html — This file sets JSON content and then iterates over it.

2. Cookies library — This is used to interact with the cookies.

3. jQuery — Used to iterate over the JSON content.

In Sample Code 3, on line 1, the cookie library is included. On line 3, to process this JSON, the JavaScript jQuery[2] library is included in the form of a CDN reference. On line 7 the Cookies *set()* function is used to store the JSON content. After the JSON has been stored, on line 9, it can be retrieved using the *getJSON()* function that takes a single value identifying the name of the cookie to retrieve. This JSON is passed to the jQuery *each()* function on line 10. This allows us to iterate over the JSON content.

During each iteration of the function, a reference titled *this* can be used to point to the object currently being processed. The dot notation can be used to access the *pageOfInterest* attributes one at a time that can be printed to the browser console.

```
1  <script src="https://cdn.jsdelivr.net/npm/js-cookie@2/src/
2       js.cookie.min.js"></script>
3  <script src="https://code.jquery.com/jquery-3.5.1.min.js">
4       </script>
5  <script>
6  // Storing and retrieving JSON
7  Cookies.set('info', [{"pageOfInterest": "homeware"},
8       {"pageOfInterest": "cooking"}]);
9  var json = Cookies.getJSON('info');
10 jQuery.each(json, function() {
11   console.log(this.pageOfInterest);
12 });
13 </script>
```

SAMPLE CODE 3: iterate.html — Set and get JSON content that is iterated over.

---

[2]https://jquery.com

Output

Figure 3.3 shows values retrieved from JSON being iterated over and being printed to the browser console.

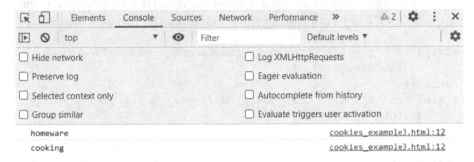

FIGURE 3.3: Iterating over JSON values.

Example 4: Client-side cookies — custom appending function

After the JSON has been read in from the cookie it is converted to JavaScript objects. At any stage in the application, if we want to update this JSON with additional JavaScript data, we can use the *push()* function and append to the JSON.

This example contains one file and two libraries:

1. appending.html — This file sets JSON content using a custom function.

2. Cookies library — This is used to interact with the cookies.

3. jQuery – Used to iterate over the JSON content.

Example code: appending.html

In Sample Code 4, the JSON is set in the *info* variable on line 8 and then read from the cookie with the the same name on line 10. The *json* variable can be used as a storage place for future additions.

On line 12, a function titled *addItem()* is added. The *push()* function on line 13 is added to the function allowing new objects to be appended to the JSON through calls to the function. This approach helps modularise the push process, allowing additional security checks to be performed on the data before it is stored if required. To append data to the JSON, a call is made to the *addItem()* function on line 16 that is passed a single string to store. In this example, the word *baking* is appended.

On line 18, the jQuery *each()* function is used to iterate over the complete JSON objects printing three values to the browser console.

```
1  <script src="https://cdn.jsdelivr.net/npm/js-cookie@2/src/
2       js.cookie.min.js">
3  </script>
4  <script src="https://code.jquery.com/jquery-3.5.1.min.js">
5     </script>
6  <script>
7  // Storing and retrieving JSON
8  Cookies.set('info', [{"pageOfInterest": "homeware"},
9  {"pageOfInterest": "cooking"}]);
10 var json = Cookies.getJSON('info');
11 // Using a function to add to JSON
12 function addItem(item){
13     json.push({"pageOfInterest": item});
14 }
15 // call the function
16 addItem("baking");
17 // view all
18 jQuery.each(json, function() {
19   console.log(this.pageOfInterest);
20 });
21 </script>
```

SAMPLE CODE 4: iterate.html — Custom function to add JSON content to existing JSON object.

Output

Figure 3.4 shows the output after the custom *addItem()* function has been called.

When working with JavaScript, all modifications that are made to a variable will be lost when the page refreshes or if the user navigates to a different page. For this reason, a regular saving process should be implemented to not only add to the object in the browser but also to a cookie for persistence.

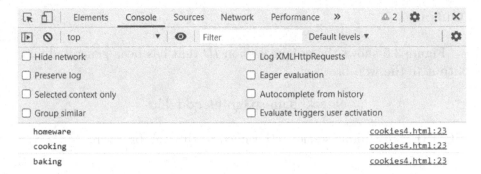

FIGURE 3.4: JSON added using custom JavaScript function.

Example 5: Server-side sessions — storing variables

As a successor to storing information in a user's web browser, server-side PHP sessions can be used. This session consists of two elements, a small cookie that is left in the user's web browser containing the *ID* number of the PHP session being used and the data stored on the server corresponding to that *ID*. At the beginning of each web page a simple call to the *session_start()* function is made. If a session exists, it will be resumed, or if no session exists, a new session will be started. After a session is created, we can simply store data in the session by creating new session variables.

Example code: session.php

In Sample Code 5, the title of the variable stored in the session is *samplevariable* as shown on line 3. The value attached to this variable is set as *Sample Value*. The unique session *ID* is retrieved on line 4 and placed in a local variable. This variable is printed to the browser on line 5.

```php
1  <?php
2  session_start();
3  $_SESSION['samplevariable'] = 'Sample Value';
4  $id = session_id();
5  echo $id;
6  ?>
```

SAMPLE CODE 5: session.php — Single string variable being set in a PHP session.

Output

Figure 3.5 shows the unique session *ID* that has been generated and output to the web browser.

9geckbbatmsb3gnlf9oqdd7l5o

FIGURE 3.5: Unique session *ID* echoed to the web browser.

Example 6: Server-side sessions — storing arrays

Sessions can also be used to hold larger quantities of data. An example of this is a simple array that contains three values. The values that are stored in the array do not need to be the same data type.

Example code: session_arrays.php

In Sample Code 6 an array titled *myArray* is created on line 3 that contains three values. On line 4, the data is placed in a session variable titled *contactinfo* by setting the session variable to the *myArray* reference. On line 5, the *contactinfo* variable is retrieved from the session. As this reference contains an array, the position number for the element of interest must be supplied when retrieving the value. The first element in the *contactinfo* session array is stored at position [0].

```php
1  <?php
2  session_start();
3  $myArray = array("John Smith", 18, "8222555");
4  $_SESSION['contactinfo'] = $myArray;
5  echo $_SESSION['contactinfo'][0];
6  ?>
```

SAMPLE CODE 6: session_arrays.php — Array being set in a PHP session.

Output

In Figure 3.6 below, the name *John Smith* will be printed in the web browser as position [0] of the array was accessed.

John Smith

FIGURE 3.6: Text output to the browser from an array stored in the session.

All of the data that is stored in a PHP session will only exist for a period of time defined by the server administrator, e.g., 30, 60, 90 minutes, etc. For this reason, if we wish to make this data persistent for a longer period of time, a database or static files must be used. Sessions are commonly used to store information about a user that has logged in to a system. When the user logs out of the system, the corresponding session will be destroyed. This can be done by making a call to the *session_destroy()* function as shown in Sample Code 7 on line 6.

```php
1  <?php
2  session_start();
3  $myArray = array("John Smith", 18, "8222555");
4  $_SESSION['contactinfo'] = $myArray;
5  echo $_SESSION['contactinfo'][0];
6  session_destory();
7  ?>
```

SAMPLE CODE 7: session_destroy.php — Destorying a PHP session after use.

3.3   READING FROM FILES

Each of the data gathering solutions we previously described centered around online applications. There are often many cases when data has been collected using an alternative tool that is not integrated into an existing application. An example of this is data that may have been manually collected using a text file, spreadsheet, or application that allows the data to be exported in a common format such as the Comma Separated Value (CSV) file. In the following section, we will explore each of these different formats and describe how data can be extracted for utilization.

Example 7: Uploading files to a web server

This example uses one library:

1. jQuery File Upload plug-in — This library is used to provide a modern look and feel to the file upload process.

When uploading files to a web server, two components are needed. The first component is the user interface uploading facility, and the second is the server-side code to receive and place the file in the desired location on the server. The process of uploading files to a web server can be done using very minimal HTML and a small amount of server-side PHP code. This process, however, does not offer the user any additional information with respect to the status of the upload or a look and feel to the uploader that would be expected in modern web applications.

In this example, we will use one of the many HTML/JavaScript file uploading libraries along with server-side PHP code. The jQuery File Upload plug-in[3] is used in this example. After downloading the source zip file from the website and extracting the contents, the folder structure shown in Figure 3.7 can be seen.

A file titled *index.html* can be seen in the root of this folder that is shown in Figure 3.8. This provides a minimal example of the capabilities of the upload tool.

Although additional functionality is shown, modifications can be made to this demo to remove elements that are not needed for this example. As the *index.html* page is responsible for the process of providing the user with the file upload experience, all additional processing is performed on the server-side using PHP. Inside of the */server/php* folder a file titled *UploadHandeler.php* can be found. This file contains all of the configurations for the file uploading process, allowing us to specify where files will be stored and restrictions that are placed on the file uploading process. As this file is large, for brevity, it is not included here in complete form.

Example code: UploadHandeler.php
The complete code described in this example can be seen in the sample code. In the *UploadHandeler.php* file, on line 104, a reference can be seen to the original file formats that are allowed during the upload process. These are originally set to allow image formats to be uploaded.

---

[3]https://blueimp.github.io/jQuery-File-Upload

cors

css

img

js

server

test

wdio

docker-compose.yml

index

LICENSE

package.json

package-lock.json

README.md

SECURITY.md

VULNERABILITIES.md

FIGURE 3.7: Folder structure of the jQuery File Upload plug-in.

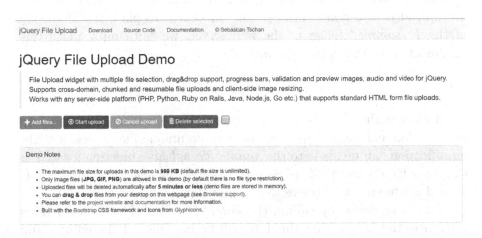

FIGURE 3.8: Default layout of the jQuery File Upload plug-in.

```
'accept_file_types' => '/\.(gif|jpe?g|png)$/i',
```

As we are working with text files and CSV files, we will replace these with the desired file extensions.

```
'accept_file_types' => '/\.(txt|csv)$/i',
```

When a file is uploaded to the server successfully, it is placed inside of the */server/php/files* folder. For security reasons, inside of this folder a *.htaccess* file is used to prevent users from executing the files in the web browser, e.g., when a user uploads a PHP file, they will not be able to run the PHP file on the server-side. By manually entering in the name of the file, e.g., *server/php/test.csv* in a web browser, the file will not be retrieved.

In this file, we can see the path to where the files are uploaded by default. This is pointing to the *SCRIPT_FILENAME* that is used to reference the current file upload directory, followed by the *files* folder. The *upload_url* references the URL to the file.

```
'upload_dir' => dirname($this->get_server_var('SCRIPT_
FILENAME')).'/files/',
'upload_url' => $this->get_full_url().'/files/',
```

For an extra level of security, it is recommended to place the files are uploaded to a non-web accessible directory. To place the file inside of the *E:/sample/* folder of the web server, we can simply make this modification to the *upload_dir* variable.

```
'upload_dir' => 'E:/sample/',
```

If the file already exists on the server, the file will automatically be given a different name. However, to provide unique file names, a slight modification can be made to the *handle_file_upload()* function located in the same file on line 1143. In Sample Code 8, the MD5 hash function is passed a reference to retrieve the current date.

This is retrieved by calling the *date()* function. The *Y-m-d H:i:s:u* references the format that the date will be in. This is followed by a full stop and a reference to the *extension* variable. This extension variable retrieves original file extension using the PHP *pathinfo()* function.

```
$extension = pathinfo($name , PATHINFO_EXTENSION);
$file->name= md5(date('Y-m-d H:i:s:u')) . '.'.$extension;
```

SAMPLE CODE 8: Modifying the UploadHandler.php file to provide unique names based on the MD5 algorithm.

When uploading files to a web server, folder permissions can often cause issues. The folder where the files are uploaded to, e.g., */files/* needs to have permissions allowing PHP to write to the folder. When working in a shared hosting environment, a review of the permissions may be required if errors relating to permissions can be seen. Adding folder permissions such as *777* is always considered bad practice. The least amount of permissions should be set on the folder to allow the file to be uploaded, but not left wide open for abuse by malicious users.

Example 8: CSV files from Google Forms

CSV files are commonly used as they allow data to be stored in a simple format, e.g., one line in the file will correspond to an individual record, and each different column in the file corresponds to a different piece of data for that record. A comma is used to separate the columns. CSV files are stored in plain text and do not require any special libraries or tools to read the content. As a result of this, they have become a widely used format for data storage.

An example of this is seen in online data collection tools such as Google Forms[4] and SurveyMonkey[5]. Both of these tools offer the ability to download all the collected data as a simple CSV file. In Figure 3.9 a simple Google Form is shown that contains one field allowing a user to enter in their e-mail address and another field that allows the user to select the option *Yes* or *No*. Although this is a simple example, this can easily be scaled to incorporate additional custom fields.

Under the *Responses* tab in Google Forms, three dots are shown in the top right hand corner as shown in Figure 3.10 which provide a list of actions that can be performed on the form data.

In Figure 3.11, the *Download responses* option is selected to export the data that has been collected using the current form. In this example, one single response was added to the form. The file that is exported from this interface is not a simple CSV file, but a compressed Zip file that

---

[4]https://www.google.com/forms/about
[5]https://www.surveymonkey.com

QUESTIONS   RESPONSES

Sample Form

Form description

Email address *

Valid email address

This form is collecting email addresses. Change settings

Are you happy with the service? *

○ Yes

○ No

FIGURE 3.9: Google Form sample.

FIGURE 3.10: Google Form export options.

contains the CSV file. This adds an additional level of processing during the extraction of data as the file must first be unzipped.

Output

Figure 3.12 shows an example of a CSV file that was generated using Google Forms to collect data. This file contains two individual records. The very first line in this file is the names of the columns. In this case, the names of the columns are the text for each individual question in the form. Below this are two individual rows of data. Each column in the file is separated using a comma, leading to the file format being called a comma-separated value. To aid the user during analysis, the first column of the row contains a unique date/time stamp followed by the individual pieces of data for each question.

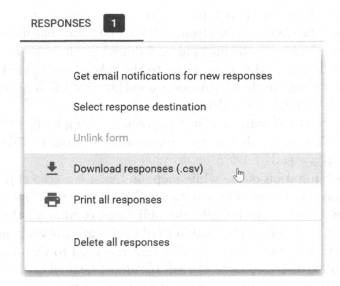

FIGURE 3.11: Google Form download CSV responses.

```
"Timestamp","Are you happy with our service?","How likely are you to return to our site?"
"2019/07/25 6:32:04 pm CET","Yes","10"
"2019/07/25 6:32:09 pm CET","No","5"
```

FIGURE 3.12: Sample Google Form CSV file.

Example 9: Reading from a CSV file

Although this is a very small sample of a CSV file, the process is the same regardless of the records utilized. As commas are used to separate each row, and quotation marks are used for each value, it can easily be processed by a PHP script.

Example code: read_csv.php
Sample Code 9 begins processing the CSV file by making a call to the *fopen()* function on line 2. The PHP file assumes that the CSV file being read in is beside the PHP script on the web server. Otherwise, a complete path to the CSV file must be entered. The *r* flag indicates that we wish to read from the file. The *fopen()* call is placed inside a simple *if statement* to ensure that a connection can be made to the file. This is done by checking the file reference does not equal *false*.

On line 3, after a connection has been made a *while* loop is used to iterate over each of the individual lines in the file. A call is made to the *fgetcsv()* function. This function accepts a reference to the file we wish to read the CSV contents from, followed by *1000* that indicates the max length of a line in the file. This is followed by the *delimiter* for the file. The delimiter is the name given to the token that is used to split individual columns in the file. As we are working with CSV files, we will use a simple comma as the delimiter.

Similar to the *if statement* in the previous example, the *while* loop has a guard to ensure that it will stop reading in from the file when a value returned equals *FALSE*.

For each iteration of the while loop, on line 4, an *echo* statement is used to print the contents of the data variable that contains one complete row. A key is passed to identify the individual column on the line we wish to display. A full stop is used in PHP to concatenate each individual string together as one complete string that is echoed to the browser. As we are printing to a web page, HTML tags must be used to break to the next line. On line 7, after the file has been processed, the reference to the file is closed.

```php
1  <?php
2  if (($file = fopen("data.csv", "r")) !== FALSE) {
3      while (($data = fgetcsv($file, 1000, ",")) !== FALSE) {
4          echo $data[0] . " --- " . $data[1] . " --- " . $data[2] .
5              '<br>';
6      }
7  fclose($file);
8  }
9  ?>
```

SAMPLE CODE 9: read_csv.php — Reading a CSV file using PHP.

Output

Figure 3.13 shows the result of the PHP reading from the CSV file and outputting the content to the browser. In this output, the first column that is stored at position 0 is printed. This is followed by position 1 and position 2 of the row.

Example 10: Reading from a text file

Reading from a text file is very similar to reading in from a CSV file. The main difference between a CSV file and a plain text file is

Timestamp --- Are you happy with our service? --- How likely are you to return to our site?
2019/07/25 6:32:04 pm CET --- Yes --- 10
2019/07/25 6:32:09 pm CET --- No --- 5

FIGURE 3.13: CSV file contents output to a browser.

the possible lack of formatting. Each individual line in the text file is treated as one individual record. The record is not further subdivided into individual columns.

Example code: read_text.php
In Sample Code 10, an *if statement* is first created on line 2. This is used to ensure that a connection can be made to the text file. If the file cannot be found, then it will return *FALSE*. Otherwise, the process of reading the individual lines from the file can begin.

On line 3, a *while* loop is used to iterate over each individual line in the file. The *feof()* function is used to check for an end of file character. If this is not found, then the loop will continue to iterate over each individual line. The ! at the beginning of this is used to state that *while not the end of file* then continue looping. Inside of this while loop, an individual line variable is created. The contents for this variable are read in using the *fgets()* function on line 4. This function is used to get a line from a file pointer. This function is passed a reference to the file that was opened. On line 5, a simple echo statement is used to print the line to the browser. This is followed by a *br* tag to break to the next line in the browser. On line 7, the *fclose()* function is called to close the reference to the file.

```php
1  <?php
2  if (($file = fopen("textfile.txt", "r")) !== FALSE) {
3      while (!feof($file)) {
4          $line = fgets($file);
5          echo $line . '<br>';
6      }
7  fclose($file);
8  }
```

SAMPLE CODE 10: read_text.php — Reading from a plain text file using PHP and printing to a web browser.

Output

Figure 3.14 shows the three lines that have been read in from the text file and output to the browser. As the *br* tag was used to break the lines, each individual line in the text file is output in the same format in the browser.

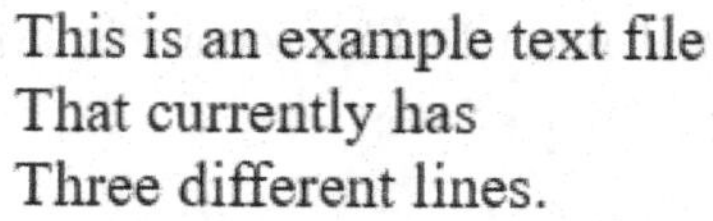

> This is an example text file
> That currently has
> Three different lines.

FIGURE 3.14: Three individual lines that are read in from a text file are output to the browser.

3.4   USER IP ADDRESS

The IP address of a user can provide a wealth of knowledge about a user and the environment they are using to get to your application. An IP address can also be considered a unique way of identifying an individual user.

Although it is possible to use IP addresses to pin down what user has been frequenting on your website, it is also important to remember that most Internet Service Providers (ISPs) do not provide a fixed IP address for all users. Often as a user reconnects to the Internet, they are provided with a new IP address. This is also the case for large companies where a number of different users in the company are all working from the same network. Internally they all may have different IP addresses, but externally they are all given the same IP address.

Although a useful method for identifying general user groups, they should not be used as the sole method of differentiating between users of a website. The IP address of a user is still useful to a developer to gather some basic information about the user or collection of users.

Getting the IP address of the user can be done using two main methods, the first of these is by using a server-side programming language to access the IP and the second is by using a service that implements this feature. The benefit of using a service is that all work is automatically performed, and the IP address can easily be accessed using JavaScript.

Example 11: User IP address — Web browser URL call

In this example, we will use IPify[6]. This is one of the many third-party services that offer developers the ability to retrieve a user's IP address.

Example code
This approach is based on a single *GET* request to a URL. When this URL is called, the IP address of the user is displayed. When the URL *https://api.ipify.org?format=json* is opened using a web browser, a simple JSON document is returned.

Output
Figure 3.15 shows the JSON document returned when the URL is entered in a web browser. This document contains a simple key-value pair where *ip* is the key, and the value is the user's IP address.

```
{"ip":"193.1.39.1"}
```

FIGURE 3.15: IP address in JSON format.

Example 12: User IP address — JavaScript *GET* request
In the previous example, the IP address was returned via a *GET* request that was performed when the URL is entered in to a web browser. To perform this same process automatically, a JavaScript *GET* request can be used.

This example contains one file and one library:

1. jQuery — This is used to perform the *GET* request to the service.

2. ipify.org — This service accepts a *GET* request and returns the IP address of the user.

Example code: get_ip.php

Sample Code 11 describes the process of integrating this functionality into an application. On line 1, jQuery is included. On line 4, a

---

[6]https://www.ipify.org

short-hand method of the document *ready* function is added to surround a *getJSON()* request to the web service. An additional parameter titled *format* is passed via the URL. This parameter is used to tell the web service which format we would like to get our response in. In this example, we are passing the format parameter and setting it to *JSON*. This call will return a JSON structured document containing the IP address of the visitor.

On line 5, once a call is made to the service, the IP address will be stored in a local variable titled *ip*. One simple use for this is variable is during the process of collecting data from a user, an additional column can be placed inside of the database to store the IP address of the user along with collected data.

```
1   <script src="https://code.jquery.com/jquery-3.5.1.min.js">
2     </script>
3   <script>
4   $(function() {
5       $.getJSON("https://api.ipify.org?format=json",
6           function(json) {
7               var ip = json.ip;
8               console.log(ip);
9       }
10      );
11  });
12  </script>
```

SAMPLE CODE 11: get_ip.php — Getting the user's IP address using a third-party service.

Example 13: User IP address — User Yes/No selection and IP address

This example contains three files and one library:

1. create.sql — To create the yesnolog database table.

2. yesno_ip.html — This file presents the user with a Yes/No option and also gathers their IP address.

3. ajax.php — This file receives the result along with the IP address and saves the data to a database table.

4. jQuery — This is used to retrieve the JSON and access elements using the jQuery selector.

Example code: create.sql

```
1  CREATE TABLE `yesnolog` (
2          `id` INT(11) NOT NULL AUTO_INCREMENT,
3          `articleid` INT(11) NOT NULL DEFAULT '0',
4          `result` INT(11) NOT NULL DEFAULT '0',
5          `ipadd` VARCHAR(50) NOT NULL DEFAULT '0',
6          PRIMARY KEY (`id`)
7  );
```

SAMPLE CODE 12: create.sql — Create the *yesnolog* table.

Example code: yesno_ip.html

In Sample Code 13, a *Yes/No* option is presented to the user using a HTML *radio* button. On line 1, a reference to the jQuery CDN is included. This is followed by two *input* fields, one for *Yes* and one for *No* on lines 3 and 4, respectively.

To trigger the IP gathering process, when the user clicks either of the radio buttons, a click handler is attached to the radio button with the name set to *answer* on line 6. Inside of this handler on line 7, the jQuery selector is used to select the value from the radio button using the *val()* function. This value is passed to the *saveAnswer()* function on line 8.

An additional variable is added to the page titled *ip* on line 10 that will be treated as a global variable to store the user's IP address. We will use this later when storing the data that has been entered by the user. Inside of the document, a *document ready* function is added on line 11 that will run only when the document has completed loading. Once loading has finished, the jQuery function to collect the IP address will run.

After a radio button is clicked a call is made to the *saveAnswer()* function on line 20. This function makes a *POST* request to the *ajax.php* page. In request takes four variables. The first is titled *type* that is used to define the *type* of *POST* we are about to perform, the second is *articleid* that is used for storing the *ID* of the article the user is viewing, and the third is *result* that is used to store the result of the user selecting the option *Yes* or *No*. The last variable passed is the *ip* variable that contains the value from the global variable containing the IP address that was gathered through the initial call to the web service. After the *POST* has been performed a call is made to the *.done()* function on line 23 that contains a simple alert statement to notify the user.

```
1   <script src="https://code.jquery.com/jquery-3.5.1.min.js">
2       </script>
3   <input type="radio" name="answer" value="Yes"> Yes  <br>
4   <input type="radio" name="answer" value="No">  No   <br>
5   <script>
6   $( "input:radio[name=answer]" ).click(function() {
7       var val = $(this).val();
8       saveAnswer(val);
9   });
10  var ip = '';
11  $(function() {
12      $.getJSON("https://api.ipify.org?format=json",
13      function(json) {
14          ip = json.ip;
15      }
16      );
17
18  });
19  var ip = 0;
20  function saveAnswer(answer){
21      $.post( "ajax.php", { type: "yesno", articleid: "1221",
22          result: answer, ip:ip })
23      .done(function( data ) {
24          alert('Thank you!');
25      });
26  }
27  </script>
```

SAMPLE CODE 13: yesno_ip.html — Yes/No option presented to the user that gathers the user's IP address.

Output

Figure 3.16 shows the Yes/No radio buttons being presented to the user.

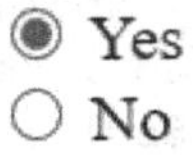

◉ Yes

○ No

FIGURE 3.16: Yes/No option presented to the user.

Example code: ajax.php

To handle the data, a second page titled *ajax.php* is added. At the top of this page on line 2, the *type* variable is first caught. A simple *if statement* is used to direct the request that was made to the correct function on line 3. A call is made to the PHP function titled *yesNoLog()* on line 4. Inside of this function on lines 7–9, the three variables are extracted from the PHP *POST* that has been sent using JavaScript. Each of these is placed in local PHP variables.

After gathering the data, a *try-catch* statement is added on line 10. Inside this, a connection to the database is created on line 15. Using the connection, a new *INSERT* statement is created with question marks for the associated values on line 16. To match values to the question marks that are added, on lines 20, 21 and 22 *bindParam()* function calls are made. Finally a call to the *execute()* function is performed on line 23. In the event of an error occurring during the database INSERT, on line 24, a *catch* is added to catch any error messages and display them to the browser.

```
1   <?php
2   $type = $_POST['type'];
3   if($type == 'yesno'){
4       yesNoLog();
5   }
6   function yesNoLog(){
7       $articleid = $_POST['articleid'];
8       $result = $_POST['result'];
9       $ip = $_POST['ip'];
10      try {
11          $host = 'localhost';
```

```
12    $dbname = 'bookexamples';
13    $user = 'sampleuser';
14    $pass = '3C9038A509BE6145AAD6827B4568AD918BC3DAC0';
15    $DBH = new PDO("mysql:host=$host;dbname=$dbname",
16        $user, $pass);
17    $sql = "INSERT INTO `yesnolog` (`articleid`,
18        `result`, `ipadd`) VALUES (?, ?, ?);";
19    $sth = $DBH->prepare($sql);
20    $sth->bindParam(1, $articleid, PDO::PARAM_INT);
21    $sth->bindParam(2, $result, PDO::PARAM_STR);
22    $sth->bindParam(3, $ip, PDO::PARAM_STR);
23    $sth->execute();
24  } catch(PDOException $e) {echo $e;}
25 }
26 ?>
```

SAMPLE CODE 14: ajax.php — Saving radio button selection and IP address to a database table.

Output

Figure 3.17 shows the resulting message displayed to the user after clicking Yes or No. As the process of inserting the record to the database is done via JavaScript, no output is visible to the user.

FIGURE 3.17: Message displayed to the user after selecting Yes or No.

3.5 FINDING THE USER AGENT

With the advent of smartphones and other devices, many different web browsers are available. During the development of a website, it is important to ensure that a site has been thoroughly tested using different versions of browsers. Although a website may be viewable in one environment does not mean that it is perfect for all environments. Typically many of the tools that are used to enhance the experience of a user such as JavaScript, can often perform uncharacteristically in a different browser.

Example 14: Finding the user agent

This example consists of two files and one library:

1. user_agent.html — This file is used to get the user's IP address with JavaScript

2. user_agent.php — This file is used to get the user's IP address with PHP.

3. jQuery — This is used to get the IP address of the user using JavaScript.

One method of finding more information is through the use of the *user agent*. A number of different libraries currently exist that allow developers to integrate user agent identification in their application. The jQuery library comes with useful functions to aid this development process.

Example code: user_agent.html

In Sample Code 15, on line 1, the jQuery library is first included in the PHP script using the *script* tag. On line 4, the user agent is retrieved. On line 5, a simple *console.log()* can be used to view the *UserAgent* variable.

```
1  <script src="https://code.jquery.com/jquery-3.5.1.min.js">
2    </script>
3  <script>
4      var agent = navigator.userAgent;
5      console.log(agent);
6  </script>
```

SAMPLE CODE 15: user_agent.html — User agent retrieved using jQuery.

Output

Figure 3.18 provides an example of a user agent being printed to the browser console.

FIGURE 3.18: User agent printed to the console.

Example code: user_agent.php

An alternative method to JavaScript is using the PHP code to check the user agent. Sample Code 16 shows a simple call being made to the $_SERVER array that contains a reference to the *HTTP_USER_AGENT*.

```php
1  <?php
2  echo $_SERVER['HTTP_USER_AGENT'];
3  ?>
```

SAMPLE CODE 16: user_agent.php — Retrieving the user agent using PHP.

Output

Figure 3.19 shows an example of the PHP user agent variable.

Mozilla/5.0 (Windows NT 10.0; Win64; x64) AppleWebKit/537.36 (KHTML, like Gecko) Chrome/71.0.3578.98 Safari/537.36

FIGURE 3.19: user_agent.php — User agent retrieved using PHP.

3.6 USER GEOGRAPHIC LOCATION

Any application that is built and served on the Internet is often not just used by a small collection of users. The global nature of the Internet opens opportunities for future business that may have been an oversight during the initial development of a website. Identifying who the target audience are for an application can often be very interesting, as although you are serving one audience, you may find traffic appearing to your application from another geographic audience.

A number of different services exist on the web that gather information about the user currently viewing the page. When a check is performed by dropping the latitude and longitude in a Google Map[7], it will show that we are not getting the pin-point location of the user. We are generally getting an approximate idea of where the user is. Although people consider the IP address a unique identifier, there is no physical address attached to the IP address that can be looked up by third-party services.

Example 15: geolocation-db.com

To aid the process of development, the geolocation-db.com API can be used. This API allows a single IP address to be passed to the service via a *GET* request. Information about the geographic location associated with the IP address is returned in a JSON structured document.

This example contains one file and two libraries:

1. geo.html — This file is used to place a call to the service.

2. jQuery — This is used to select individual span tags and to update their values.

3. geolocation-db.com — This service provides geographical information based on a single IP address.

Example code: geo.html

In Sample Code 17 a call is first made to include jQuery on line 1. On lines 3–8, individual *span* tags are used as placeholders for the variables that will be retrieved from the API. No value is needed when the *span*

---

[7]https://www.google.com/maps

tags are first created. An important element is the unique *ID* for each *span* tag.

Once the *span* tags have been added, the next step is to make an AJAX call to the *geolocation-db.com* URL on line 10. Instead of using JSON, JSONP is used. This is JSON but with padding. This differs from a traditional request as cross-domain calls are not an issue. When the call is made, on success, an object titled *location* is available. This object contains the country name, state, city, latitude, and longitude of the user. In addition to this, the IP address of the user is available. These attributes are available by adding the object *location* followed by a period, followed by the variable name of interest. On lines 15–20, the jQuery selector is used to select each individual *span* tag that was created earlier. The *.html()* function is called on the selector to update the value of the *span* tag to be the value from the current variable selected in the location object, e.g., *country_name*.

```
1   <script src="https://code.jquery.com/jquery-3.5.1.min.js">
2     </script>
3   <div>Country: <span id="country"></span></div>
4   <div>State: <span id="state"></span></div>
5   <div>City: <span id="city"></span></div>
6   <div>Latitude: <span id="latitude"></span></div>
7   <div>Longitude: <span id="longitude"></span></div>
8   <div>IP: <span id="ipv4"></span></div>
9   <script>
10  $.ajax({
11      url: "http://geolocation-db.com/jsonp",
12      jsonpCallback: "callback",
13      dataType: "jsonp",
14      success: function( location ) {
15          $('#country').html(location.country_name);
16          $('#state').html(location.state);
17          $('#city').html(location.city);
18          $('#latitude').html(location.latitude);
19          $('#longitude').html(location.longitude);
20          $('#ipv4').html(location.IPv4);
21      }
22  });
23  </script>
```

SAMPLE CODE 17: geo.html — Retrieving information about a user's location.

Output

Figure 3.20 shows an example of geographical information that is gathered and displayed in *span* tags.

> Country: Ireland
> State: Leinster
> City: Blanchardstown
> Latitude: 53.3881
> Longitude: -6.3756
> IP: 193.1.39.1

FIGURE 3.20: Example geographical information.

Example 16: ipstack.com

Another service that offers the ability to gather information from a user's IP address is IpStack.[8] Unlike the previous service that allowed for anonymous API calls, for this service a user must provide a valid API key. This key is used as the unique identifier for your project and is typically associated with billing when the number of requests exceeds that of the basic free package.

This example consists of one file and two libraries:

1. geo.html — This page is used to make a request to the ipstack.com web service.

2. jQuery — This library is used to make an AJAX request to ipstack.com

3. ipstack.com — The web service that provides information about the provided IP address.

When a free API key is received from the service, it can be added to the URL, e.g., *http://api.ipstack.com/193.1.39.1?access_key= XXXXXXXXXXXXXXX* where the Xs are replaced with the unique API key. The IP address that is added to this can be any IP address that we wish to explore. If this URL is opened in a web browser, a JSON document will be output.

---

[8]https://ipstack.com

Output

Figure 3.21 shows the output after a call is made to the ipstack.com web service. Although it is difficult to read, it is a valid JSON document.

```
{"ip":"193.1.39.1","type":"ipv4","continent_code":"EU","continent_name":"Europe","country_code":"
IE","country_name":"Ireland","region_code":"L","region_name":"Leinster","city":"Blanchardstown","
zip":"D15","latitude":53.3881,"longitude":-6.3756,"location":
{"geoname_id":2966110,"capital":"Dublin","languages":
[{"code":"ga","name":"Irish","native":"Gaeilge"},
{"code":"en","name":"English","native":"English"}],"country_flag":"http:\/\/assets.ipstack.com\/f
lags\/ie.svg","country_flag_emoji":"\ud83c\uddee\ud83c\uddea","country_flag_emoji_unicode":"U+1F1
EE U+1F1EA","calling_code":"353","is_eu":true}}
```

FIGURE 3.21: Geographical information shown in JSON format in a browser.

Example code: geo.html

In Sample Code 18, a reference to the jQuery CDN is included on line 1. Two variables are created on lines 4 and 5, one that contains the IP address we are interested in finding more information about and the other contains the unique API key for our ipstack.com account.

A jQuery AJAX call is performed on line 6 to the API URL. The IP address and access key variables are added to create the complete URL that will be called. JSONP is used as the method for the call that allows for cross-origin requests. When the request has been completed, the function beside the success attribute is called. This contains a single object reference titled *json* that contains the response from the server. Inside of this object on line 11, the *location* is referenced. Inside of this *location* object, individual attributes can be called, such as the *capital*. A complete listing of these along with error codes can be found in the official documentation.[9]

```
1  <script src="https://code.jquery.com/jquery-3.5.1.min.js">
2    </script>
3  <script>
4  var ip = '193.1.39.1'
5  var access_key = '34dd357a733f2142f58b1bada9f9f394';
6  $.ajax({
7      url: 'http://api.ipstack.com/' + ip + '?access_key=' +
8          access_key,
9      dataType: 'jsonp',
```

---

[9]https://ipstack.com/documentation

```
10  success: function(json) {
11      console.log(json.location.capital);
12  }
13 });
14 </script>
```

SAMPLE CODE 18: geo.html — Making an AJAX request to the ipstack.com web service.

Output

```
Dublin
```

FIGURE 3.22: Current location associated to the IP address is printed to the console.

3.7 TIME SPENT ON PAGES

A simple but effective measure to identify the interactions a user has with a web application is by recording the amount of time a user has spent on a page or sections of a page. For this example, the TimeMe.js[10] library is used. This can be downloaded from https://github.com/jasonzissman/TimeMe.js. The zip file should then be extracted providing access to the *timeme.js* JavaScript file.

Example 17: TimeMe.js implementation

The TimeMe.Js API provides a collection of tools that allow a developer to identify how much time is being spent on a web page. If the user changes to a different tab, minimizes the window, or stops having keyboard or mouse interactions, the timer will stop.

This example consists of one library and one file:

1. time.php — This page contains an instance of the TimeMe.js library.

2. TimeMe.js — This library provides the ability to record the interactions a user has with the webpage. Available from their website.[11]

---

[10]http://timemejs.com

[11]https://github.com/jasonzissman/TimeMe.js/

Example code: time.php

In Sample Code 19, on line 1, a reference to the *timeme.js* file that contains the main library is added. On line 3, the initialization of the timer is performed. Inside the initialization code on line 4, a simple reference name is added to uniquely identify the page where the timer is used. On line 5, the time out period, e.g., when the timer should stop after a period of idleness is added.

To aid future analysis of data, on line 7, a trigger is added to execute after a period of time has elapsed. In this example, the trigger is set to 4 seconds.

```
1   <script src="timeme.js"></script>
2   <script type="text/javascript">
3       TimeMe.initialize({
4           currentPageName: "my-home-page", // current page
5           idleTimeoutInSeconds: 3 // seconds
6       });
7       TimeMe.callAfterTimeElapsedInSeconds(4, function(){
8           console.log("The user has been using the page for
9               4 seconds!");
10      });
11  </script>
```

SAMPLE CODE 19: time.php — Example timer with elapsed time.

Output

In Figure 3.23 the output is printed to the console when 4 seconds has elapsed.

The user has been using the page for 4 seconds!

FIGURE 3.23: Output to the console after four seconds.

By identifying when the elapsed time has occurred, data from the current page, such as input field values can be retrieved and stored in a database at a specific time interval if required. This is often a useful process as users can fill out a form or search field but not complete the process of pressing the submit button. In this case, without the timer to trigger a logging process, the data would be lost.

3.8   TRACKING INDIVIDUAL DIV TAGS

Each individual area of a web application is typically broken down into individual *div* tags. Each different region of an application may denote one key feature, e.g., a specific *div* tag may be dedicated to content, where another *div* tag is designated as a search function.

Example 18: Tracking a div tag with TimeMe.js

This example consists of one library and one file:

1. time.php — This page contains an instance of the TimeMe.js library.

2. TimeMe.js — This library records the interactions a user has with the webpage.

Similar to the previous example, for the TimeMe.js to be used, a the TimeMe.js JavaScript file must be downloaded and place beside the current script.

Example code: time.php

In the Sample Code 20, on line 8, a derivative of the main time tracking tool can be used to focus on the time spent on a single area of interest. In this example the *trackTimeOnElement* function is used and is focused on the *area-of-interest-1 div* tag. On line 9, the *setInterval()* function is used to repeat the code inside every 100 miliseconds.

On line 10, a new variable is created titled *timeSpentOnElement* that has the value set to be the time spent on the textitarea-of-interest-time-1 *span* tag. On line 12, the *document.getElementById()* function is used to retrieve the *area-of-interest-time-1* and set the content to be the time spent on the element. The *timeSpentOnElement.toFixed()* function is called and the value 5 is passed. This indicates how many decimal points should be included when the time is printed.

```
1   <script src="timeme.js"></script>
2   <script type="text/javascript">
3       TimeMe.initialize({
4           currentPageName: "my-home-page", // current page
5           idleTimeoutInSeconds: 5, // stop recording time due to
            ↪  inactivity
6       });
7       window.onload = function(){
8           TimeMe.trackTimeOnElement('area-of-interest-1');
9           setInterval(function(){
10          var timeSpentOnElement =
            ↪  TimeMe.getTimeOnElementInSeconds
11              ('area-of-interest-1');
12          document.getElementById('area-of-interest-time-1').
13              textContent = timeSpentOnElement.toFixed(5);
14      }, 100);
15  }
16  </script>
17  <div class="area-of-interest" id="area-of-interest-1">
18      Interact with this element<br/><br/>
19      Interaction: <span id="area-of-interest-time-1"></span>
        ↪  seconds.
20  </div>
```

SAMPLE CODE 20: time.php — Recording the amount of time spent on a single *div* tag.

Output
Figure 3.24 shows the output in the web browser describing the amount of time a user has spent on an individual *div* tag.

Interact with this element

Interaction: 1.49000 seconds.

FIGURE 3.24: Number of seconds a user has spent on a *div* tag.

3.9 LOGGING TIMES

Although it is useful to see in real-time the amount of time a user is spending on a particular part of a page, for future analysis, it is useful to store this information in a database. Before this is done, to modularize the code, a custom function is first created that triggers when a user navigates away from the current page.

Example 19: Calling a custom function on unload

To do this, we will make a custom function that will get called once the user has navigated away from the current page. All of the timers that were active on the page will be stopped, and the values will be gathered and stored in a database table. If the user moves to an internal page in the application or manually types in the URL for a different website, this function will trigger.

Example code: time.php

In Sample Code 21, a JavaScript *addEventListener* is first bound to the *window* on line 2. The event type that is added is titled *beforeunload*. This event is triggered whenever the user attempts to navigate to a different page. In this function on line 3, a custom function is called titled *timingDataStore()*. The function definition is included on line 8. In the event listener on line 4, the return type is set to *undefined*. This ensures the user will not be prompted when the page is redirecting.

```
1  <script>
2  window.addEventListener('beforeunload', function (e) {
3      timingDataStore();
4      return undefined
5  });
6
7  // Customer logging function
8  function timingDataStore(){
9      console.log("goodbye...")
10 }
11 </script>
```

SAMPLE CODE 21: time.php — Calling a JavaScript function when a user leaves a page.

Output

Figure 3.25 shows the output that is printed to the console when the user navigates away from the current page. To see this message, in the Google developer console, click the cog on the right-hand side, and then click the option to *Preserve log*.

```
goodbye...                                                    logging1.html:9
```

FIGURE 3.25: Message printed to the console when the user navigates away from the current page.

Example 20: Saving to a database table

In the previous example, although we can find out when the user has navigated away, no timing is recorded in a database table. In this example, the process of saving the records to a database table is described.

This example consists of three files and two libraries:

1. timinglog.sql — timinglog create table SQL.

2. timing.php — Gathers the timing logs from the browser.

3. ajax.php — Used to receive the timing data and store it in a database table.

4. jQuery — This is used to perform a JavaScript *POST* request to the *ajax.php* page.

5. TimeMe.js — This is used to record the timings between the user and the application.

Example code: timinglog.sql
Sample Code 22 outlines the SQL for a database table titled *timinglog* that is required. This contains an *ID* column to identify each record along with an automatically added time stamp column titled *timelogged*. The *user* field can contain any additional information to identify a user in the form of a username, *ID* or IP address. The *pageID* column is used to hold the unique *ID* for any given page in our application.

To aid future retrieval, two sample key-value pair attributes were added. In the case of this example, *att1* would be the overall time spent on a page and *att2* can be used for an additional variable if required.

The *timing1* and *timing2* columns are used to store the values recorded for each.

```
1   CREATE TABLE `timinglog` (
2     `id` INT NOT NULL AUTO_INCREMENT,
3     `timelogged` TIMESTAMP NOT NULL DEFAULT CURRENT_TIMESTAMP,
4     `user` VARCHAR(50),
5     `pageID` VARCHAR(50),
6     `att1` VARCHAR(50),
7     `timing1` VARCHAR(50),
8     `att2` VARCHAR(50),
9     `timing2` VARCHAR(50),
10    PRIMARY KEY (`id`)
11  );
```

SAMPLE CODE 22: timinglog Database table.

Example code: timing.php

In Sample Code 23, on line 1, a reference to the jQuery CDN is included. On line 5, a reference to the local TimeMe.js library is added. On line 9, a unique name is given to the current page where the code is running. This will be used later to identify where the records have come from. On line 12, the event listener is added that will trigger when the user navigates away from the current page. On line 13, the core call to the *timingDataStore()* function is included. On line 17, the definition for the *timingDataStore()* function is added. To find out how long the user has been on the current page, a call is made to the *getTimeOnCurrent-PageInSeconds()* function on line 18.

Before any further progress is made on this function, a call is made to the *console.log()* on line 20 to output the information to the developer console in the web browser. This ensures we correctly gather the time and can, therefore, exclude any issues with the TimeMe.js library. After the data is gathered and an event has been triggered, it indicates the user has navigated away from the current page. An AJAX request is performed on line 23 to the *ajax.php* page to store the data in a database table. In this, we first gather the time, and then we perform an AJAX *POST* request to the data handling page.

The name of this page is *ajax.php*. The *POST* consists of first the *type* of request we are sending. In this case we are sending *timelog* as the value, followed by the *key-pair* attributes. The first of these is *pageTitle* that has the value set to the TimeMe.js page *ID*. This is followed by two attributes, the first will be the total time spend on the page and the second is a placeholder for an additional key-value pair if required in the future. Although this example just shows two attributes, it is possible to extend this to send multiple attributes and values at the same time.

On line 28, when the *POST* has been performed, a callback to the .done() function is performed, presenting the text *Bye!* to the user.

```
1  <script
2    src="https://code.jquery.com/jquery-3.5.1.min.js"
3    integrity="sha256-9/aliU8dGd2tb60SsuzixeV4y/faTqgFtohetphbbj0="
4    crossorigin="anonymous"></script>
5  <script src="timeme.js"></script>
6  <script type="text/javascript">
7  // Initialize library and start tracking time
8  TimeMe.initialize({
9  currentPageName: "my-home-page", // current page
10 idleTimeoutInSeconds: 3 // seconds
11 });
12 window.addEventListener('beforeunload', function (e) {
13     timingDataStore();
14     return undefined;
15 });
16 // Custome logging function
17 function timingDataStore(){
18     var timeSpentOnPage = TimeMe.getTimeOnCurrentPageInSeconds();
19
20     console.log('Time on Page:' + timeSpentOnPage);
21
22     // Send data to the server here
23     $.post( "ajax.php", { type: "timelog", pageTitle:
24         TimeMe.currentPageName,
25                         att1name: 'totaltime', att1:
26                             timeSpentOnPage,
27                         att2name: 'interest', att2: '0' })
28     .done(function( data ) {
29     alert("Bye!");
30     });
31 }
32 </script>
```

SAMPLE CODE 23: timing.php — Calling the *timingDataStore()* function to make a AJAX *POST* to the database.

Example code: ajax.php

On the server-side, we have a page titled *ajax.php*. The first step in this page is to decipher the type of request that we are sending by retrieving the *type* variable on line 2. In this example the JavaScript is sending the value *timelog*, so we will then use a simple *if statement* on line 3 to check the *type* variable and call the PHP *timeRecordLog()* function on line 4. Inside the *timeRecordLog()* function on line 6, we will first extract each piece of data from the *POST* that was performed. These include the *pageTitle, attribute 1* — name and value and *attribute 2* — name and value as shown on lines 7–11.

A connection to the MySQL database using the PDO object is performed on line 19. The *INSERT* statement is added on line 21. For each parameter, a question mark is placed on the right-hand side of the statement. These are filled in using the *bindParam()* functions on lines 25–29. The final step in this process is to *execute()* the SQL statement to *INSERT* in the database on line 30. A *try catch* statement always surrounds the database connection as if something goes wrong during the connection process or the *INSERT* statement, the catch will handle the error preventing the script from crashing.

```php
1   <?php
2   $type = $_POST['type'];
3   if($type == 'timelog'){
4       timeRecordLog();
5   }
6   function timeRecordLog(){
7       $pageID = $_POST['pageTitle'];
8       $att1name = $_POST['att1name'];
9       $att1time = $_POST['att1'];
10      $att2name = $_POST['att2name'];
11      $att2time = $_POST['att2'];
12
13  try {
14
15      $host = 'localhost:3306';
16      $dbname = 'bookexamples';
17      $user = 'sampleuser';
18      $pass = '3C9038A509BE6145AAD6827B4568AD918BC3DAC0';
19      $DBH = new PDO("mysql:host=$host;dbname=$dbname",
20       $user, $pass);
21      $sql = "INSERT INTO `timinglog` (`pageID`, `att1`, `timing1`,
22       `att2`, `timing2`)
```

```
23              VALUES (?,?,?,?,?);";
24       $sth = $DBH->prepare($sql);
25       $sth->bindParam(1, $pageID, PDO::PARAM_STR);
26       $sth->bindParam(2, $att1name, PDO::PARAM_STR);
27       $sth->bindParam(3, $att1time, PDO::PARAM_STR);
28       $sth->bindParam(4, $att2name, PDO::PARAM_STR);
29       $sth->bindParam(5, $att2time, PDO::PARAM_STR);
30       $sth->execute();
31
32  } catch(PDOException $e) {echo $e;}
33  }
```

SAMPLE CODE 24: ajax.php — Recording timer values to the *timinglog* database table.

Output

Figure 3.26 shows the output of five timings that have been recorded to the database when the user navigated away from the current page. We can see that the *timing1* column contains the total time spent on the page.

id	timelogged	user	pageID	att1	timing1	att2	timing2
1	2020-06-23 12:04:59	0	my-home-page	totaltime	2.073	interest	0
2	2020-06-23 12:06:07	0	my-home-page	totaltime	3.148	interest	0
3	2020-06-23 12:27:38	0	my-home-page	totaltime	2.352	interest	0
4	2020-06-23 12:27:44	0	my-home-page	totaltime	2.073	interest	0
5	2020-06-23 12:27:50	0	my-home-page	totaltime	3.256	interest	0

FIGURE 3.26: Sample timings logged to the database table.

3.10   WHERE A USER CAME FROM

Example 21: Using the HTTP_REFERER variable

Another method that exists to gather data is from the functions that exist in the PHP library. The most notable of these is the *HTTP_REFERER* variable. This variable allows you to find out what page in an application a user came from to get to the current page.

Example code: ref.php

To gather the data, a PHP start tag is added, followed by the

HTTP_REFERER variable on line 2. A simple *echo* statement is added
to print the value to the browser. Sometimes, however, this variable may
not be set, causing the script to provide a warning message. To prevent
this, the sample code can be wrapped up in a PHP *isset()* function to
see if it exists before it is printed.

```php
1  <?php
2  if(isset($_SERVER['HTTP_REFERER'])){
3      echo $_SERVER['HTTP_REFERER'];
4  }
5  ?>
```

SAMPLE CODE 25: ref.php — PHP HTTP_REFERER being printed
to the web browser.

Output

Figure 3.27 shows the output after navigating from one page to another. The page listed is the previous page viewed by the user.

http://localhost/bookexamples%20-%20tidy/examples/ch3/loggingtimes/

FIGURE 3.27: Output from calling the PHP REFERRER variable.

3.11   SOCIAL MEDIA CONTENT HARVESTING

Social media offers a data analyst an additional insight into the real-
time changes in user opinions. Social media platforms such as Facebook
and Twitter allow users to enter their thoughts and add additional key
identifiers such as hashtags and @ mentions that can be used to identify
what company they are addressing and their sentiment towards them.
In this section, we will look at the process of creating a tool to allow us
to scrape the content of specific Twitter pages.

When selecting a social media data source for analysis, the first hur-
dle that must be addressed is if authentication is required to view the
content. Many different components of a social media site are publicly
available without requiring the need to log in. Other sources, such as
Facebook groups, may be set to private, requiring a user account to be

logged in and also to be accepted to the group before the extraction process can begin.

Example 23: Twitter library-based feed extraction

This example requires one file and one library:

1. twitteroauth — This is the main library that is used to interface with the Twitter API.

2. twitter_auth.php — This is the sample application that will use the library to perfrom the API requests.

In this section the process of integrating with the Twitter API using one of the many available libraries is described. In this section, we will review the *twitteroauth*[12] library.

To install this library on our local server, we will use *composer*.[13] From the command prompt, use the *cd* command to enter the folder where the project is located.

Once inside of the folder, we can begin the process of initializing *composer*. This is done by running the *composer init* command. After running this command, the name of the project, a description for the project, the type of project, the license, and the author of the project must be entered. The stability of the project must be defined. In this example, we have set it to *dev*.

Finally, the development dependencies are defined. In this example, we can choose *no*. At the end of this process, we will be asked to confirm the *composer.json* file content that will be created in the project folder. Figure 3.28 shows a sample *composer.json* file.

Once the *composer.json* file has been created, we can begin the process of adding in the additional library that we require. To do this, the following command is entered into the command prompt at the root of our project folder.

```
composer require abraham/twitteroauth
```

This process will begin the download and installation of the library to the project as shown in Figure 3.29.

---

[12]https://github.com/abraham/twitteroauth
[13]https://getcomposer.org

```
"name": "kylegoslin/twitterlib",
"description": "Sample project",
"type": "project",
"license": "gnu",
"authors": [
    {
        "name": "Kyle Goslin",
        "email": "kylegoslin@itb.ie"
    }
],
"minimum-stability": "dev",
"require": {}
```

FIGURE 3.28: Sample composer.json contents for a new project.

```
Using version dev-master for abraham/twitteroauth
./composer.json has been updated
Loading composer repositories with package information
Updating dependencies (including require-dev)
Package operations: 1 install, 0 updates, 0 removals
  - Installing abraham/twitteroauth (dev-master 9350ad1): Cloning 9350ad14d5 from cache
Writing lock file
Generating autoload files
```

FIGURE 3.29: Composer library installation console output.

To access the Twitter API, a number of different web endpoints are created. Each different endpoint is an individual URL that takes in a variety of different parameters. As the Twitter API is a commercial tool, different plans such as the *Standard* and *Premium* plans are available. In this example, we will be using the *Standard* plan. The API component that we will be focusing on is the *Search API* that can be found in the API documentation.[14]

Before we can begin with this process of interacting with the API, a Twitter account is required. In addition to this, a new application must be registered with Twitter outlining the intent of the application. To register this application, the *app console* on the Twitter web page can be used.[15]. On this page, an option can be seen to *Create an app.*

---

[14]https://developer.twitter.com/en/docs/tweets/search/api-reference/get-search-tweets

[15]https://developer.twitter.com/en/apps

During this process, basic information about the application is added. The essential element that is added during this process is the callback URL. The purpose of this callback URL is to allow the Twitter OAuth process to send validation information back to a page on our server.

After the application has been registered, the unique *keys* and *tokens* that have been created for the application can be seen. These are unique to the application and serve as an identifier to the Twitter server for the project. These tokens will be added to the code aiding the authentication process.

The standard search API has a number of limits imposed on it. These include only allowing 180 requests to be performed in a 15-minute window by a user and 450 by an application.[16]

Example code: twitter_auth.php

After the library has been installed, we can begin the process of creating a new PHP file that will interact with the library. The first line that is added to this file is the autoload for the PHP libraries we are using, as shown in Sample Code 26 line 2.

After the library is imported into the project, we can add the *consumer key, consumer secret key* and the *callback* URL for the application on lines 4–7. This provides our authentication with the server. The callback is called once the authentication is completed and provides validation status information to us.

We can create a new instance of the library, along with our unique credentials. After this has been performed, we will make a call to the Twitter API using the *oauth()* function on line 8 to receive a unique request token that will be sent with all of the requests we make to the API in the future.

Once the unique access token has been generated, we can begin the process of making requests to the server. In this example, we will make requests to the search API on line 12. A *GET* request is performed to the server, passing the name of the API feature that we would like to use. Each different component of the API will have a different collection of available parameters. These parameters allow us to fine-tune the results that are returned to us. In the example below, we are searching for tweets by passing the query parameter *q* with a value set to *Dublin*.

---

[16]https://developer.twitter.com/en/docs/tweets/search/api-reference/get-search-tweets.html

One of the more interesting parameters that are available is the *result_type*. This allows us to specify what type of results should be returned. These include *mixed* which provides popular and real-time responses, *recent* showing only recent results and *popular* that returns only the most popular results. To add in this parameter, a simple comma is added.

The results variable will contain the complete response from the server. On line 15, to iterate over the results, a *for each* statement can be used. This is passed the results object, followed by a reference to the statuses. We can iterate over each individual tweet and extract the desired attributes. In the example, we are extracting the time the tweet was created and the text that is contained inside the tweet.

```php
<?php
require_once 'vendor/autoload.php';
use Abraham\TwitterOAuth\TwitterOAuth;
define('CONSUMER_KEY', '1wUmYQ6c2GQFh7j7CIYhyaJ6R');
define('CONSUMER_SECRET', 'yPHBqqT9o1lppggiscju0yAjutRclS6s
OVyshOrFXKTgFE20F3');
define('OAUTH_CALLBACK', 'https://www.kylegoslin.ie/test.php');
$connection = new TwitterOAuth(CONSUMER_KEY, CONSUMER_SECRET);
$request_token = $connection->oauth('oauth/request_token',
                                    array('oauth_callback' =>
                                    OAUTH_CALLBACK));
$results = $connection->get("search/tweets",
                           ["q" => "Dublin",
                           "result_type"=> "popular"]);
foreach($results->statuses as $tweet){
    echo $tweet->created_at . '-'. $tweet->text . '<br>';
}
```

SAMPLE CODE 26: twitter_auth.php — Twitter library accessing and iterating over Tweets

Output

Figure 3.30 shows a sample output from calling the Twitter search API. In this results the date is first printed followed by a single dash and then the text from the individual tweet.

Mon Nov 04 19:27:08 +0000 2019-Dublin, we can't wait to experience the energy of tonight with you. https://t.co/Hny0T0ZlFA

Sun Nov 03 19:08:16 +0000 2019-Cheers Dublin ♥ https://t.co/5z8JyWkYQb

Mon Nov 04 15:26:21 +0000 2019-#RIPGayByrne - so supportive of Irish artists. He came to see my first solo show in Dublin for no other reason than... https://t.co/hx9uyYiH0C

Mon Nov 04 13:12:07 +0000 2019-🙎 INSTORE ALBUM SIGNINGS 🌐 Manchester, Birmingham, Belfast and Dublin. To gain entry, you MUST purchase a copy of... https://t.co/SD5L6biphJ

Mon Nov 04 15:43:45 +0000 2019-Such sad news. #GayByrne brought wisdom, mischief & deep curiosity into my Dublin home as a child. His... https://t.co/AMkfSrX6fL

Mon Nov 04 18:30:31 +0000 2019-A boil water notice has been issued for a second time for people living in parts of counties Dublin, Kildare and Me... https://t.co/mrkpwpel5k

Mon Nov 04 20:47:27 +0000 2019-Paris, Rome and Dublin didn't even make the top ten. Time to get a long weekend booked. 👀🌍 https://t.co/Bs7qaEJrlp

Mon Nov 04 19:25:58 +0000 2019-Fans in a frenzy as Christina Aguilera stops into Dublin pub before 3Arena gig https://t.co/gevVentalX

Mon Nov 04 15:25:51 +0000 2019-Follow a behind the scenes account from the road over on https://t.co/RvV5p7vUkn - the first two tour blogs are fro... https://t.co/COdZb7MUiB

Mon Nov 04 17:00:30 +0000 2019-Brussels is the youngest capital city in the EU, followed by Paris and Dublin. In contrast, Lisbon is the capital c... https://t.co/31eh2alWJf

Mon Nov 04 17:29:15 +0000 2019-To be in with a chance of winning a pair of tickets to our Irish premiere screening of #LastChristmasMovie and fest... https://t.co/LVxknJSqXj

Mon Nov 04 14:47:56 +0000 2019-Very sad news from Dublin. A legend - the legend - of Irish broadcasting is no more #GayByrne https://t.co/kYCnQLE1N7

Sun Nov 03 19:39:39 +0000 2019-New mural of Lizzo in Dublin 🌿 https://t.co/ZAg6RmI6wT

FIGURE 3.30: Twitter API search results.

3.12 SUMMARY

This chapter introduced the concept of using passive data gathered from the user's areas of interest and their local browser environment without the need for direct user intervention. Simplistic data sources in the form of cookies and sessions were explored that contain short term data left by the user and application. To further extract insights, additional services were used to find the geographic location and IP address of the user. Server-side PHP was then explored to identify where a user came from. The time spent on areas of interest in an application was then described. To persist the data, the process of saving data to a database table was then explored.

Alternative sources of data were explored in the format of gathering data using authenticated API calls, as many users provide a wealth of knowledge to services such as Twitter. Chapter 4, next, describes the process of creating custom dashboards to aid the process of discovering insights and monitoring responses.

Custom Dashboards

Chapter 3 previously outlined mechanisms that can be implemented to collect passive data. In this chapter, both passive and active data sources become the core focus of the data analysis process. Campaigns are introduced as the primary method of differentiating between collections of data. These steps are performed using a custom dashboard, providing easy access to visualization tools and data sources of interest.

4.1 INTRODUCTION

When working with data, a key component is the ability to gather data from any device or environment and provide this data in a meaningful way to the data analyst. This chapter will review the process of creating a custom dashboard that provides a workspace for data to be collected and analyzed. This dashboard can be considered the primary portal for the analyst to review data and initiate new data collection processes.

This dashboard consists of a user login portal, allowing users to identify to the system and a register page that allows new users to become active. After a user has logged into the system, a core dashboard allows the user to select the analysis tools and visualizations that have been implemented. To aid the development process Bootstrap[1] is used as the core library during the layout of visual components.

---

[1]https://getBootstrap.com

4.2 USER LOGIN

Example 1: User login page

This example consists of six files:

1. create_dashboard.sql — This file is used to create the database table that is used during the login and registration.

2. bootstrap.js — The core Bootstrap JavaScript file. Available from their website[2].

3. bootstap.min.css — The core Bootstrap CSS file. Available on the Bootstrap website.

4. jquery.min.js — The minified version of the jQuery library. Available on their website[3].

5. index.php — This file is the main user interface for the login process. Bootstrap is used to theme this page.

6. login.php — This page is dynamically called using jQuery. The username and password hash are passed to this page and verified against the credentials stored in the database.

Example code: create_dashboard.sql
To begin the login process, a database table that contains the accounts is created titled *dashboard_accounts*, as shown in Sample Code 1. This table contains an *ID* column that is an auto-incremented primary key. The two core columns in this table are they *username* and the *password* columns. When working with passwords, it is always important to remember that the password should never be stored in the database in plain text. In the case where unauthorized access to the database is made, the same username and password combinations could be used on other systems. It is a common practice to store the password in a *hash* based format. Hashing is the process of passing a password through a hashing algorithm that will return a fixed-length string of symbols and letters. However, it

---

[2]https://getbootstrap.com/docs/4.0/getting-started/download/
[3]https://jquery.com/download/

is possible to take the hash and work backward to retrieve the password if no additional security measures are implemented, such as adding *salt*.

```
1   CREATE TABLE `dashboard_accounts` (
2           `id` INT NOT NULL AUTO_INCREMENT,
3           `username` VARCHAR(100),
4           `password` VARCHAR(100),
5           `email` VARCHAR(100),
6           PRIMARY KEY (`id`)
7   );
```

SAMPLE CODE 1: Main *dashboard_accounts* table for the system.

Example code: index.php

The user login page is the first page seen by a user before they can access the dashboard. In this section, the complete login page is described. The overall layout for this page is based on Bootstrap. Sample Code 2 begins with a reference to the jQuery[4] library on line 4. This is included as it will be used to gather the username and password that have been entered by the user for validation later. Popper[5] is included on line 5. This is a tooltip positioning engine for pop-overs and drop-down menus available from the Bootstrap library. To utilize this functionality, the core Bootstrap library is included on line 8.

The style for the login page is kept very minimal. On lines 10–16, the input fields are styled to stretch to the width of the available space. Padding is added to move the text from the left-hand side of the input field. The margin is set to *8px* and the *display* is set to *inline-block*. A small *1px* border is added to the input fields that is solid light-gray. On lines 17–25, the style for the main login button is added. The color is set to *white* and the *padding* and *margin* is set. As this is a button, when the user places the mouse pointer over the button, the cursor will change to a *pointer*. On line 27, when a mouse is placed over the button, the opacity of the button will change to 0.8 from the initial 1.0.

On line 30, the *viewport* is added as the main visible area for the user. This helps scale the content the user will see with the initial scale set to 1.

---

[4]https://www.jquery.com
[5]https://popper.js.org

The main body of HTML contains a *div* tag with the *class* set to *container* on line 34. Inside this the *nav* bar is added on line 35. This *nav* bar has the *bg-light* colour with rounded edges. More of these colors are are available on the Bootstrap website.[6] On line 36, a single link is added with the *class* set to *navbar-brand*. This is the main focus for the title. The *href* points to the *index.php* page with the visible text set to *Feedback Dashboard*.

On line 38, the *main* tag is added with the role set to *main*. Inside this main, a single *div* tag is added with the class set to *jumbotron* on line 39. This provides a space for the main content to be displayed. Inside the jumbotron, a *div* tag is added with the class set to *mx-auto* on line 40, allowing us to center the component.

On line 42, a simple piece of text is added to instruct the user to enter their username and password. A form tag is wrapped around two input fields with the *ID* set to *login* on line 43. This is followed by two HTML *input* fields on lines 45 and 47 that were styled earlier using CSS. This *ID* will be used later to attach a listener for the form submission process. A single *span* tag is added with the *ID* set to *message* on line 49 that is used as a default display location for error messages that can occur when the form values are incorrect, e.g., the wrong username or password.

```
1   <head>
2   <link rel="stylesheet" href="Bootstrap.min.css" crossorigin=
3   "anonymous">
4   <script src="jquery.min.js"></script>
5   <script src="https://cdnjs.cloudflare.com/ajax/libs/popper.js/
6   1.12.3/umd/popper.min.js"
7           crossorigin="anonymous"></script>
8   <script src="Bootstrap.js" crossorigin="anonymous"></script>
9   <style>
10  input[type=text], input[type=password] {
11      width: 100%;
12      padding: 12px 20px;
13      margin: 8px 0;
14      display: inline-block;
15      border: 1px solid #ccc;
16  }
17  button {
18      background-color: grey;
19      color: white;
20      padding: 14px 20px;
```

---

[6]https://getBootstrap.com/docs/4.3/utilities/colors

```
21       margin: 8px 0;
22       border: none;
23       cursor: pointer;
24       width: 100%;
25  }
26  button:hover {
27       opacity: 0.8;
28  }
29  </style>
30  <meta name="viewport" content="width=device-width,
31      initial-scale=1, shrink-to-fit=no">
32  </head>
33  <body>
34  <div class="container">
35  <nav class="navbar navbar-expand-lg navbar-light bg-light rounded">
36      <a class="navbar-brand" href="index.php">Feedback Dashboard</a>
37  </nav>
38  <main role="main">
39      <div class="jumbotron">
40      <div class="mx-auto" style="width:300px">
41          <h1>Login</h1>
42          <p> Please enter your username and password to login.</p>
43          <form id="login">
44          <label><b>Username</b></label>
45          <input type="text" id="username"/>
46          <label><b>Password</b></label>
47          <input type="password" id="password"/>
48          <button type="submit">Login</button>
49          <span id="message"></span>
50          </form>
51
52      </div>
53      </div>
54  </main>
55  </div>
56  </body>
```

SAMPLE CODE 2: index.html — Login page for the dashboard created using Bootstrap.

In Sample Code 3, the core functionality of the login page is performed using JavaScript. The first component is a form *submit* listener that is appended to the *login* form on line 58. Instead of a traditional form *POST* that requires the page to be refreshed, the form *POST* is performed using JavaScript. The *preventDefault()* function is called on line 59, during the form submission to prevent any redirection of the page. After this has been performed the jQuery selector is used to select the *username* on line 60 and *password* on line 61. The *val()* function is used to extract the values from the fields. These values are placed into two local variables, *un* and *pw*.

To validate the details that have been entered are correct, a call is made to the jQuery *POST* function to send the *username* and *password* variables to a second PHP page titled *login.php* on line 62. The *type* of request being sent to this page is described as a *login*. This allows the single PHP page to be re-purposed for other tasks in the future. Once the call has been made to the PHP page the *data* variable is returned on line 64. The variable will contain a flag titled *success* if the login credentials were correct. The location of the web browser is redirected to the *dashboard.php* page on line 67.

In the case where the username or password was incorrect, on line 70, the message *span* tag is used to hold the error message. This is done by passing a string to the *text()* function that can be called on the *span* tag. To aid debugging, two *console.log()* functions are added on lines 68 and 72.

```
57  <script>
58  $( "#login" ).submit(function( event ) {
59      event.preventDefault();
60      var un = $("#username").val();
61      var pw = $("#password").val();
62      $.post( "login.php", { type:"login", username: un, password:
63       pw })
64          .done(function( data ) {
65              alert(data);
66              if(data == 'success'){
67                  $(location).attr("href", "dashboard.php");
68                  console.log('success');
69              } else {
70                  $('#message').text('Login failed, please check
71                   your username and password.');
72                  console.log('failed');
73              }
74          });
75  });
76  </script>
```

SAMPLE CODE 3: index.html — JavaScript form listener with redirection to the correct page on successful login.

121
122
123
124
125
126
127
128
129
130
131
132
133
134 }▶
135 }▶
136 $(
137
138

139 }▶
140

ows the completed dashboard login page.

d

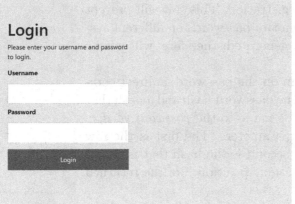

: Custom dashboard for the login page.

ode: login.php

ite the login details, the *login.php* page is used. When the
orm submission is performed on the login page, the *username*
rd are sent across via a *POST*. In Sample Code 4, before
e login process, the *type* parameter is first checked on line
t type of request was being made. When the *type* is set to
vin() function is called.

e *login()* function on lines 7 and 8, the *username* and *pass-*
t extracted from the *POST* and placed into local variables.
inection is made to the local database to get the record for
e that was provided. In the SQL, a *LIMIT 1* clause is ap-
ily return a single record from the database. This is shown
where the *username* is left as a question mark, on line 19
e is added using the *bindParam()* function. The statement
on line 20.

S⌄

C
Fi
08
th
th
us
er

6.

In
T.
vi
al

ie returned record, the *password* is hashed using the *bcrypt* algo-
During the registration process of the user, the password that is
l from the user is passed to the password hashing function that
irn a 60 character hash string that is stored in the database.
mple of a string for the password *MySamplePassword* would
10tLUrTdYnlSI3B/dsYBtga.1JtDXxEKn.Dyqux5LmRvjwHCS
). *Salt* can be added, which is a small additional piece of text
ɔ the user's password during registration. This salt will prevent
match ever being found between two passwords on different sys-
the salt is different. The hash generated, therefore, will not be
e each time.
ve are using a hashing algorithm on the password, a direct com-
can not be performed between the password hash and a hash that
l in the database. A call must be made to the *password_verify()*
on line 22 that takes in two parameters. The first is the raw
d entered by the user, and the second is the hash that is stored
ecord returned from the database at position 2 of the returned

n the login is successful, a session is started on line 25, and the
the user's record is stored in the session variable *ID* on line 26,
by the username in the *username* variable on line 27. When the
successful, the word *success* is returned back to the JavaScript
that performed the *POST*. This triggers the original JavaScript
led the *login.php* page to redirect to the main *dashboard.php*
the case where the password is not valid, the *else* statement is
d, and the text *Password is not valid* is returned to the user.

```
 $_POST['type'];
e == 'login'){
in();

n login(){
ername = $_POST['username'];
ssword = $_POST['password'];
 {
 $host = 'localhost';
 $dbname = 'bookexamples';
 $user = 'sampleuser';
 $pass = '3C9038A509BE6145AAD6827B4568AD918BC3DAC0';
```

://www.php.net/manual/en/function.password-hash.php

```
H = new PDO("mysql:host=$host;dbname=$dbname", $user,
ass);
l = "SELECT * FROM dashboard_accounts WHERE username
LIMIT 1";
h = $DBH->prepare($sql);
h->bindParam(1, $username, PDO::PARAM_STR);
h->execute();
s = $sth->fetch();
sult = password_verify ($password,$res[2]);
$result){
  echo 'success';
  session_start();
  $_SESSION['id'] = $res[0];
  $_SESSION['username'] = $res[1];
  $_SESSION['valid'] = True;
lse {
  echo 'Password is not valid';

(PDOException $e) {echo $e;}
```

ODE 4: login.php — Accepts the username and password
he user for validation.

REGISTRATION

n, we will review the process of creating a new user account
1. The interface for this is similar to that of the login process.

2: User registration page

file titled *register.php* is created. This file will provide the
ut fields to enter their username, email, and password. This
tains two files and three libraries:

rap.js — The core Bootstrap JavaScript file. Available from
ebsite[8].

ap.min.css — The core Bootstrap CSS file. Available on the
rap website.

tbootstrap.com/docs/4.0/getting-started/download/

uery.min.js — The minified version of the jQuery library. Avail-
le on their website[9].

gister.php — This is the main registration page for the dash-
oard.

ax.php — This is used to receive the registration details via a
uery *POST* and save them to the database.

le code: register.php
Code 5 shows the HTML for the registration page titled *regis-*
This page will contain the Bootstrap HTML to layout the page
ith the JavaScript to trigger the registration process.
he top of this file on line 2, a reference to the Bootstrap CSS file
ed. This is followed on line 3 by a reference to the jQuery library.
5, a reference to *Popper.js* is included as it is a dependency for
ap. On line 9, the core Bootstrap JavaScript file is included. On
the *meta* tag is added as the main *view port* for the registration

main style for the registration page is added. The input fields
most styling, on lines 13–19, setting the width to be 100% of
lable space. Padding and a margin are added to align the text
ally across the input field. The method of display is set to *inline-*
line 17. A simple border is added of *1px* with a light gray color
18. The registration button also has a small amount of styling.
in change visible is the cursor on line 26. This is changed to a
when the mouse is placed over the register button. The opacity
utton is also changed on line 30, by setting it to 0.8 from the
.0 when a mouse hovers over it. On line 35, a *div* tag is added
class set to *container*. Inside of this, a *nav* bar tag is added
theme set to *bg-light* with rounded *edges* on line 36.
r the navigation bar has been added, the next step is to add the
ntent for the page to allow the user to enter their details. The
g is added on line 40 as a wrapper around all the content. Inside
on line 41, a *div* tag is added with the class set to *jumbotron*.
aponent allows for easy scaling. Inside of this, on line 42, another
is added with the *class* set to *mx-auto* that will automatically
aorizontally. Inside of this, two simple pieces of text are added.

is added on line 45 as a unique method of identifying this

ut fields are added to gather the *username, e-mail address*
d from the user on lines 46–53. A second input field is added,
user to verify their password. The IDs for the password are
nd *password2* for simple reference later during comparison.
t element is the *ID* attribute associated with each element,
be used later when processing the form with JavaScript.
re added that allow a simple piece of text to be specified
of the input fields. To allow the registration to begin, a
ɔn is added on line 54. A simple *span* tag is added titled
line 55, which is used as a placeholder for error messages
cur during validation. When the page first loads, this *span*
have any value.

```
stylesheet" href="Bootstrap.min.css" crossorigin=
>
="jquery.min.js"></script>
="https://cdnjs.cloudflare.com/ajax/libs/popper.js/
popper.min.js"
ssorigin="anonymous">

="Bootstrap.js" crossorigin="anonymous"></script>
"viewport" content="width=device-width,
ale=1, shrink-to-fit=no">

text], input[type=password] {
100%;
: 12px 20px;
 8px 0;
: inline-block;
 1px solid #ccc;


und-color: grey;
white;
: 14px 20px;
 8px 0;
 none;
 pointer;
100%;
```

Line numbers right column: 28, 29 }, 30, 31 //, 32 //, 33 $s, 34 $s, 35 $s, 36 $r, 37 $1, 38 $ρ, 39 $r, 40 fɔ, 41, 42, 43, 44 }, 45 $1, 46 $ρ, 47 $r, 48, 49 ?>

```
city: 0.8;

>


ass="container">
v class="navbar navbar-expand-lg navbar-light bg-light
unded">
class="navbar-brand" href="#">Feedback Dashboard</a>
av>
ole="main">
ass="jumbotron">
ass="mx-auto" style="width:300px">
>Register</h1>
 Register for a new account</p>
rm id="register">
 <label><b>Username</b></label>
 <input type="text" id="username"/>
 <label><b>E-mail Address</b></label>
 <input type="text" id="email"/>
 <label><b>Password</b></label>
 <input type="password" id="password1"/>
 <label><b>Repeat Password</b></label>
 <input type="password" id="password2"/>
 <button type="submit">Register</button>
 <span id="message"></span>
orm>
```

E CODE 5: register.html — User registration page HTML part

ample Code 6, a custom modal is shown. This modal is hidden
.e application is launched and only becomes visible when a new
ord has successfully been inserted in the database. On line 61,
que *ID* provided to the modal is set to *nowRegistered*. On line
.itle of the modal is set to *Success*. On lines 74-75, the main text
o the user can be seen. On line 79, a *href* is added with a link
.dex.php page that contained the original login page.

```
61   <div class="modal" id="nowRegistered" tabindex="-1" role=
62   "dialog">
63     <div class="modal-dialog" role="document">
64       <div class="modal-content">
65         <div class="modal-header">
66           <h5 class="modal-title" style="width:100%">Success</h5>
67           <button type="button" class="close" data-dismiss="modal"
68           aria-label="Close"
69                   style="width:100px">
70             <span aria-hidden="true">&times;</span>
71           </button>
72         </div>
73         <div class="modal-body">
74           <p>You are now registered.</p>
75           <p>Click to login!</a></p>
76         </div>
77         <div class="modal-footer">
78
79           <a href="index.php" class="btn btn-primary"
80           role="button">Login!</a>
81         </div>
82       </div>
83     </div>
84   </div>
```

SAMPLE CODE 6: register.html — User registration page HTML part 2.

After the HTML components have been added, form validation is required. Sample Code 7 outlines this validation. To provide the best user experience when the form is submitted, the natural redirection process of the page will be suppressed. To do this, we will first use the jQuery selector on line 86 to select the *register* form and append a submit handler function. Whenever the form is submitted, this function will be called.

Inside this function, a variable is added titled *valid* on line 87. This is used as a flag to show if the form fields are valid or not before any further processing, e.g., sending the data to the database. The second component is the call to the *event.preventDefault()* on line 88. This will prevent the default redirection process of the page.

The jQuery selector is used to select the *username* field on line 90. The value is extracted using the *val()* function. On line 91, a check is performed to see if the *un* variable is blank. In the case where nothing was typed into the *username* field, the input field would be blank, allowing the *if statement* to run. Inside this *if statement*, the jQuery selector is used again on line 109 to select the *message* span tag that was created earlier and append the message *Username blank* followed by a HTML *br* tag. This is added as the *message* span tag contains a long string that will be printed directly to the user's browser when an error occurs. By adding in the line break, each error message will be visible on a separate line.

In addition to these basic checks, the values of *password1* on line 102 and *password2* on line 103 are compared with each other and they must match. This is to prevent human error when entering passwords. On line 108, a simple *if statement* can be used with a != between the two values identifying that if they are not equal to each other to show the error message.

```
85   <script>
86   $( "#register" ).submit(function( event ) {
87       var valid = true;
88       event.preventDefault();
89       // Username
90       var un = $("#username").val();
91       if(un == "" ){
92           $('#message').append('Username blank.<br>');
93           valid = false;
94       }
95       // Email
96       var email = $("#email").val();
97       if(email == "" ){
98           $('#message').append('E-mail blank. <br>');
99           valid = false;
100      }
101      // Password
102      var pw1 = $("#password1").val();
103      var pw2 = $("#password2").val();
104      if(pw1 == "" || pw2 == ""){
105          $('#message').append('Password blank.<br>');
106          valid = false;
107      }
108      if(pw1 != pw2){
109          $('#message').append('Sorry your passwords do not match.
110          <br>');
111          valid = false;
112      }
113      // If valid, then perform the post request
```

```
114    if(valid == true){
115        $.post( "ajax.php", { type:"register", username: un,
116           password: pw1, email: email })
117        .done(function( data ) {
118        if(data == 'registered'){
119           // Show modal
120            $("#nowRegistered").modal();
121
122        } else {
123            $('#message').text('Sorry registration failed.');
124        }
125        });
126    }
127
128    });
129    </script>
```

SAMPLE CODE 7: register.html — JavaScript registration page validation part 3.

At any stage during the registration process, if any of the fields are not correct the *valid* variable will be set to *false*. This is used to keep track of the form fields and see if the submission process can continue on to the next section. Before we perform the *POST* operation, an *if statement* on line 114 is used to ensure that the *valid* variable is equal to *true*. After this, on line 115, a jQuery *POST* is performed to the *ajax.php* page. The *username, password,* and *email* are sent to the second page. On successful *INSERT* on the second page, the Bootstrap modal will be shown by calling the *modal()* function on line 120, otherwise the message *span* tag will be used again to show this error message on line 123.

Example code: ajax.php

In Sample Code 8, the page titled *ajax.php* that is responsible for inserting new records in the database can be seen. At the top of this page on line 2 the *type* variable is received. On line 3, if the *type* variable is equal to *register* then a call is made to the custom *registerNewUser()* function.

Inside the *registerNewUser()* function on line 7, the three variables that were sent across via the *POST* are set into local variables *username, password,* and *email* on lines 7–9. The *password* variable is passed into the PHP *password_hash()* function on line 10. This function takes two parameters. The first one is the password the user has provided, and the second is the type of hash that we would like to produce. In this example, we are working with the *bcrypt* algorithm. It is important to remember that the user's password should never be stored in plain-text in a database.

On line 18, a simple SQL *INSERT* statement is built up to insert into the database that contains the table titled *dashboard_accounts*. The three columns we are inserting into are specified, followed by the *VALUES* keyword and three question marks. These three question marks are used as unnamed placeholders. The values are not put directly into the SQL as this is unsafe. The three values are bound onto the statement using the *bindParam()* function on lines 22–24. The number at the start of each denotes the position to insert. This is followed by the value we want to add, and the data type that is roughly associated with it. As the *username, password,* and *email* are all strings, *PARAM_STR* is used as the data type for each.

```php
<?php
$type = $_POST['type'];
if($type == 'register'){
    registerNewUser();
}
function registerNewUser(){
    $username = $_POST['username'];
    $password = $_POST['password'];
    $email = $_POST['email'];
    $hashed_password = password_hash($password, PASSWORD_BCRYPT);
    try {
        $host = 'localhost:3306';
        $dbname = 'bookexamples';
        $user = 'sampleuser';
        $pass = '3C9038A509BE6145AAD6827B4568AD918BC3DAC0';
        $DBH = new PDO("mysql:host=$host;dbname=$dbname", $user,
         $pass);
        $sql = "INSERT INTO `dashboard_accounts` (`username`,
        `password`, `email`)
                                            VALUES (?,?,?);";
        $sth = $DBH->prepare($sql);
        $sth->bindParam(1, $username, PDO::PARAM_STR);
        $sth->bindParam(2, $hashed_password, PDO::PARAM_STR);
        $sth->bindParam(3, $email, PDO::PARAM_STR);
        $sth->execute();
```

```
26        echo 'registered';
27    } catch(PDOException $e) {echo 'failed' . $e;}
28 }
29 ?>
```

SAMPLE CODE 8: ajax.php — Register new user function.

When the *INSERT* runs successfully, the term *registered* will be returned to the browser. This result will be returned to the JavaScript caller on the *register.php* page triggering a Bootstrap modal to open. A *PDOException* is fired if any errors occur during the registration. The error message will be suppressed, and the word *failed* will be returned.

Output

Figure 4.2 shows the completed register page. Figure 4.3 describes the modal that is presented to the user once they have successfully registered. This modal provides the user with a link to bring them back to the login page.

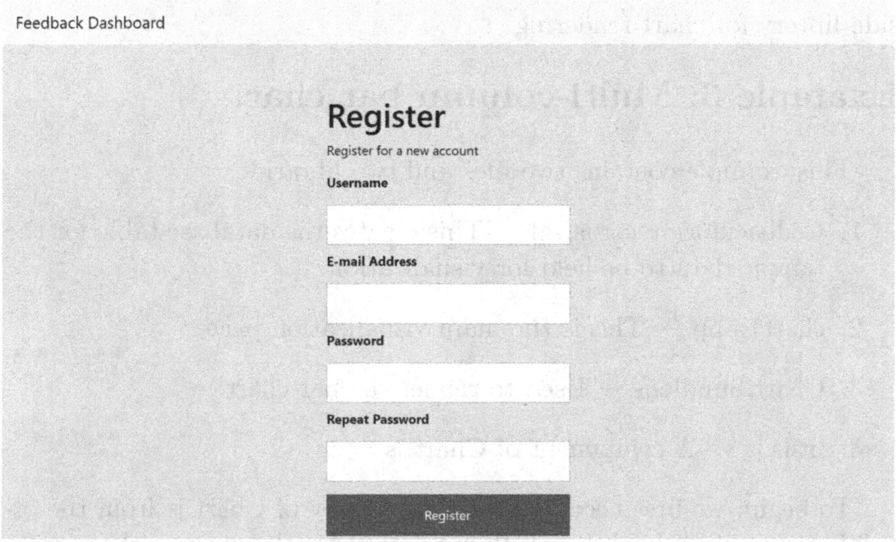

FIGURE 4.2: Completed dashboard register page.

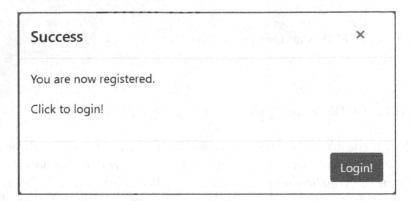

FIGURE 4.3: Bootstrap modal shown when the registration was successful.

4.4   MULTI-COLUMN BAR CHART

In the previous examples, a focus was placed on creating the dashboard to allow for the registration and login of users. Once logged into the system, data that has been collected will be presented to the user in chart format. In these examples, Charts.js is used as the main client-side library for chart rendering.

Example 3: Multi-column bar chart

This example contains two files and two libraries:

1. feedbackformrecords.sql — This creates the database table for the sample data to be held for visualization.

2. chart1.php — This is the main visualization page.

3. Chart.bundle.js — Used to render the bar chart.

4. utils.js — A component of Chart.js

To begin, we first need to download a copy of Chart.js from the official repository.[10] In the GitHub repository for the project, there are a number of variations to choose from. These are available as sometimes a developer may only want the source code while other times, they may

---

[10]https://github.com/chartjs/Chart.js/releases/tag/v3.0.0-alpha

want the minified (or shrunk) version of the code for a deployed application in other times. In our case, we want the code and also the collection of examples to showcase the functionality. This will allow us to view the existing chart samples in context. For this example we download the *Chart.js.zip* file as shown in Figure 4.4.

⊕ Chart.esm.js	335 KB
⊕ Chart.esm.min.js	157 KB
⊕ Chart.js	386 KB
⊕ Chart.js.zip	351 KB
⊕ Chart.min.js	173 KB
ⓘ Source code (zip)	
ⓘ Source code (tar.gz)	

FIGURE 4.4: List of download options for Charts.js.

After the zip file has downloaded, unzip the contents of the zip file and place the entire Chart.js folder into the *htdocs* of the web server for convenience. When accessing the examples, this can be done by typing *http://localhost* into our web browser and then navigating into the *Chart.js* folder. Inside the Chart.js folder, there is a number of different JavaScript files with an additional folder titled *samples*, as shown in Figure 4.5. The JavaScript files will be kept beside the charts that we will create to make the chart functionality available to us.

> samples
> Chart.esm.js
> Chart.esm.min.js
> Chart.js
> Chart.min.js
> LICENSE.md

FIGURE 4.5: Contents of Chart.js zip file.

Inside of this *samples* folder as shown in Figure 4.6, there is a file titled *index.html*. When this is opened through a web browser, as shown in Figure 4.7, complete running examples can be chosen. Unlike working on smaller pieces of code, when generating charts, there are many different elements that are required for the chart to function correctly. When creating a custom chart, it is best practice to begin with a sample chart that utilizes sample data. This ensures minimal modifications need to be made for the sample chart to be used with alternative data or parameters.

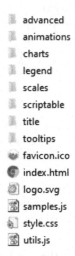

advanced
animations
charts
legend
scales
scriptable
title
tooltips
favicon.ico
index.html
logo.svg
samples.js
style.css
utils.js

FIGURE 4.6: Contents of Chart.js folder.

Chart.js | Samples

Simple yet flexible JavaScript charting for designers & developers

Website   Documentation   GitHub

Bar charts	Line charts	Area charts	Other charts
Vertical	Basic	Boundaries (line)	Bubble
Horizontal	Multi axis	Datasets (line)	Scatter
Multi axis	Stepped	Stacked (line)	Scatter - Multi axis
Stacked	Interpolation	Radar	Doughnut
Stacked groups	Line styles		Pie
Floating	Point styles		Multi Series Pie
	Point sizes		Polar area
			Radar
			Combo bar/line

FIGURE 4.7: index.html containing a list of working samples.

Example code: feedbackformrecords.sql
Before generating a chart, a new database table is set up. In Sample Code
9, a sample database table can be seen. The *FeedbackFormId* contains
an integer used to identify what form the data has come from. The
FeedbackElementID is a second attribute used to further narrow down
exactly what component a user has used, e.g., input field or clicked a
button. To record a user's rating between one and ten, an attribute titled
Score is added. This will contain the numeric rating a user has given.

```
1  CREATE TABLE `feedbackformrecords` (
2      `id` INT NOT NULL AUTO_INCREMENT,
3      `FeedbackFormId` INT,
4      `FeedbackElementID` INT,
5      `Score` INT,
6      PRIMARY KEY (`id`)
7  );
```

SAMPLE CODE 9: Sample feedback records with score attribute.

Example code: chart1.php

Sample Code 10 begins on line 5 with reference to the *Chart.bundle.js*
file that contains the core JavaScript to render the graph. After this on
line 6, a reference is made to the *utils.js* file that contains additional utilities for drawing the graph. This graph is a Chart.js demo with additional
PHP to gather the data to be rendered.

On line 16 and 17 a *div* with the *ID* set to *container* is added and
a canvas with the *ID* set to *canvas*. The *canvas* is where the drawing
operations will take place, and the *container* is the single identifiable *div*
tag for the entire bar chart. The width of the *container div* tag can be
changed to suit the application needs. In the code below, the *container
div* is taking up 50% of the page width.

Following this code, on line 20, the color helper is included. On line
21, the main object used to hold the data for the chart is created. Inside
this on line 22, the labels attribute is created. This is an array of different
names that will appear across the horizontal axis of the bar chart.

On line 24, the *datasets* array is created. This array contains the
values that will appear for each label. This bar chart expects a comma-
separated values inside the array. A sample data point array would be:

data [6, 40, 10, 11, 12, 1, 90, 9, 3, 10]. The first element inside of this array, 6, would be the value then associated with the *Score 1* label on the bar chart.

As hard-coding the values into the bar chart would not be dynamic, we will instead replace the values inside the *data[]* array with a call to a PHP function on line 31 that will dynamically call the database to return the values. This PHP function that takes a single parameter in the form of the *ID* of the records we are interested in plotting. In this example, 1 is passed.

```
1   <!doctype html>
2   <html>
3   <head>
4       <title>Bar Chart</title>
5       <script src="Chart.bundle.js"></script>
6       <script src="utils.js"></script>
7       <style>
8       canvas {
9           -moz-user-select: none;
10          -webkit-user-select: none;
11          -ms-user-select: none;
12      }
13      </style>
14  </head>
15  <body>
16  <div id="container" style="width: 50%;">
17      <canvas id="canvas"></canvas>
18  </div>
19  <script>
20  var color = Chart.helpers.color;
21  var barChartData = {
22      labels: ["Score 1", "Score 2", "Score 3", "Score 4", "Score 5",
23      "Score 6", "Score 7", "Score 8", "Score 9", "Score 10"],
24      datasets: [{
25          label: 'Customer Satisfaction',
26          backgroundColor: color(window.chartColors.blue).alpha(0.5).
27          rgbString(),
28          borderColor: window.chartColors.blue,
29          borderWidth: 1,
30          data: [
31              <?php getSatisfactionScores(1); ?>
32          ]
33      }]
34  };
```

```
35   window.onload = function() {
36       var ctx = document.getElementById("canvas").getContext("2d");
37       window.myBar = new Chart(ctx, {
38           type: 'bar',
39           data: barChartData,
40           options: {
41               responsive: true,
42               legend: {
43                   position: 'top',
44               },
45               title: {
46                   display: true,
47                   text: 'Customer Satisfaction'
48               }
49           }
50       });
51
52   };
53   </script>
54   </body>
55   </html>
```

SAMPLE CODE 10: chart1.php — Simple Chart.js bar chart part 1.

Inside of the *getSatisfactionScores()* function shown in Sample Code 11, on line 57, we are taking in the *formID* and then passing this to the database query in the form of an unnamed placeholder. On line 65, the SELECT statement will gather the unique *score* labels, e.g., 1–10 followed by the *count* for each *score*. This is done by making a call to the SQL *count()* function and passing the *score* column.

A question mark is used to mark where the *formID* value will be placed. The value is passed to this position using the *bindParam()* function on line 69. Once the query has run, ten results will be returned. The *foreach()* statement on line 73 is used to loop over these results and print out the *score* label and the associated *count* number. This is done by running a *echo* statement on the current row at position 1 as shown on line 74.

```
56   <?php
57   function getSatisfactionScores($formID){
58       try {
59           $host = 'localhost:3306';
60           $dbname = 'bookexamples';
```

```
61    $user = 'sampleuser';
62    $pass = '3C9038A509BE6145AAD6827B4568AD918BC3DAC0';
63    $DBH = new PDO("mysql:host=$host;dbname=$dbname", $user,
64     $pass);
65    $sql = "SELECT score, count(score) FROM
66                    feedbackformrecords
67                    WHERE FeedbackFormId = ? GROUP BY score";
68    $sth = $DBH->prepare($sql);
69    $sth->bindParam(1, $formID, PDO::PARAM_INT);
70    $sth->execute();
71    $res = $sth->fetchAll();
72
73    foreach ($res as $row){
74        echo $row[1] . ', ';
75    }
76  } catch(PDOException $e) {echo $e;}
77 }
78 ?>
```

SAMPLE CODE 11: chart1.php — Simple Chart.js bar chart part 2.

Output

The final resulting bar chart can be seen in Figure 4.8. As this bar chart is pulling data directly from the database, and not dependent on a static file, so whenever a user submits data into the database the result data will be visible when the chart is reloaded.

4.5   BINARY BAR CHART

A simple form of data is binary feedback, whereby, a question is asked, and the answer is stored in the form of 1 for a *yes* and 0 for a *no*. Typically a user will be asked questions, and they will respond by ticking a box or clicking a radio button. Unlike the previous example that showed data on a range between one and ten, this data has only two variations. Although it may seem limited, it is the only way of accurately gathering information about specific questions such as:

- Do you earn over 50k?

- Are you married?

- Do you have kids?

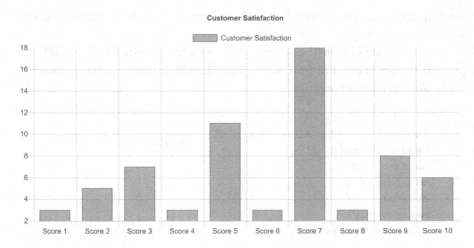

FIGURE 4.8: Bar chart showing the count of each score.

These questions can have a definitive *yes* or *no* answer attached to them. When graphing this type of data, both data collections for the *yes* and the *no* are shown. This helps derive quick insights from the data such as checking whether three-quarters of the people said *yes*, then there would likely be one quarter who said *no*.

Example 4: Binary bar chart

This example contains two files:

1. survey.sql — This file contains the SQL to create the survey database table.

2. chart2.php — This file contains the main visualization.

3. Chart.bundle.js — This provides the ability to create the bar chart.

4. utils.js — An additional file that is used by Chart.js.

Example code: survey.sql
Sample Code 12 shows a sample database table titled *survey*. Like previous examples, an *ID* is added which is the primary key and also auto-incremented. Every time a new survey has been completed, the data will be entered into this table. However, it is possible to have additional

descriptive data about who took the survey and when, it will be left out of this example.

The *FeedbackFormId* column references the feedback campaign attached to this data and four additional data columns: *married, haskids, ownscar,* and *makesover50k*.

```
1  CREATE TABLE `survey` (
2      `id` INT NOT NULL AUTO_INCREMENT,
3      `FeedbackFormId` INT,
4      `married` INT,
5      `haskids` INT,
6      `ownscar` INT,
7      `makesover50k` INT,
8      PRIMARY KEY (`id`)
9  );
```

SAMPLE CODE 12: Example *survey* database table SQL.

Example code: chart2.php

In Sample Code 13, on lines 5 and 6, the additional JavaScript files that allow us to create the bar chart are imported. On lines 8–12, the browser is set not to allow selections. On line 16, the *container div* tag is added to hold the new chart.

Three different arrays are set up to hold the data for the chart. On line 21, The first of these titled *lab* array is to be used to hold each of the labels which will be added to the chart. On line 22, the *Data1* is added, which is responsible for holding all of the 0 data, e.g., *no*. On line 23, the *Data2* is added which is responsible for holding all the 1 data, e.g., *yes*.

After the arrays have been set up in JavaScript, they next have to be populated with data. To do this a custom PHP function titled *getData()* is called on line 24. This function takes in the name of the column we would like to add to the chart. On line 29, the color of the *No* bar which will be added is set to *red*. This is followed by the *Yes* bar being set to *blue* on line 35. On line 46, the graph is initialized by passing a reference to the canvas in the form of a reference titled *ctx*. On line 48, the data is passed into the graph.

```
1   <!doctype html>
2   <html>
3   <head>
4       <title>Bar Chart</title>
5       <script src="Chart.bundle.js"></script>
6       <script src="utils.js"></script>
7       <style>
8       canvas {
9           -moz-user-select: none;
10          -webkit-user-select: none;
11          -ms-user-select: none;
12      }
13  </style>
14  </head>
15  <body>
16      <div id="container" style="width: 75%;">
17          <canvas id="canvas"></canvas>
18      </div>
19      <script>
20          var color = Chart.helpers.color;
21          var lab =  new Array();
22          var data1 = [];
23          var data2= [];
24          <?php getData('married'); ?>
25          var barChartData = {
26               labels: lab,
27          datasets: [{
28              label: 'No',
29              backgroundColor: color(window.chartColors.red).
30              alpha(0.5).rgbString(),
31              borderColor: window.chartColors.red,
32              borderWidth: 1,
33              data: data1,
34          }, {
35          label: 'Yes',
36              backgroundColor: color(window.chartColors.blue).
37              alpha(0.5).rgbString(),
38              borderColor: window.chartColors.blue,
39              borderWidth: 1,
40              data: data2,
41          }]
42      };
43      window.onload = function() {
44          var ctx = document.getElementById("canvas").
45          getContext("2d");
```

```
46          window.myBar = new Chart(ctx, {
47              type: 'bar',
48              data: barChartData,
49              options: {
50                  responsive: true,
51                  legend: {
52                      position: 'top',
53                  },
54                  title: {
55                      display: true,
56                      text: 'Chart.js Bar Chart'
57                  }
58              }
59          }); };
60  </script>
61  </body>
62  </html>
```

SAMPLE CODE 13: chart2.php — Sample binary data bar chart.

In Sample Code 14, the core of this bar chart generation process is the custom PHP function that is used to gather the data. This function begins on line 64 as a simple function definition with one variable being passed into it titled *column*. This is the name of the database column that we wish to gather the data from.

Inside of this function, on line 70, a connection to the database is first made, and the SQL statement is created on line 72. In this query, the *SELECT* statement selects the *column* that was passed to the function. The SQL *count()* function is then used to count the number of records for the defined column. This allows the one function to be used to return information about any column in the database table.

A *for each* statement on line 80 is used to iterate through each of the rows returned from the database. Once the query has run, a collection of counted records will be returned. Before the data is used by the chart, on line 83 and 86, a PHP *echo* is used to place modified JavaScript code on the page for both the count of *Yes* records if we are viewing 1 records and 0 if we are working with the count of *No* records. These *echo* statements generate JavaScript array values that are read in by the chart.

```
63  <?php
64  function getData($column){
65      try {
```

```
66        $host = 'localhost:3306';
67        $dbname = 'bookexamples';
68        $user = 'sampleuser';
69        $pass = '3C9038A509BE6145AAD6827B4568AD918BC3DAC0';
70        $DBH = new PDO("mysql:host=$host;dbname=$dbname",
71         $user, $pass);
72        $sql = "SELECT $column, count($column) FROM survey WHERE
73                             FeedbackFormId = 1
74                             GROUP BY $column";
75        $sth = $DBH->prepare($sql);
76        $sth->execute();
77        $res = $sth->fetchAll();
78        // add the label
79        echo 'lab.push("'.$column.'");';
80        foreach ($res as $row){
81            // its is 0 add to first column
82            if($row[0] == 0){
83                echo " data1.push('".$row[1]."');";
84            } //if it is 1 add to the second column
85            else if($row[0] == 1){
86              echo "data2.push('".$row[1]."');";
87            }
88        }
89    } catch(PDOException $e) {echo $e;}
90 }
91 ?>
```

SAMPLE CODE 14: chart2.php — Example PHP to retrieve the records for a single column by name.

Output

In Figure 4.9 we can see the result of calling the *getData()* function to gather the values for the *married* column. Both have a count of *Yes* and a count for *No*.

4.6 DYNAMIC DASHBOARD

Although we looked at gathering data and placing results into individual database tables, there was no complete solution. In the following sections, we will introduce the concept of *campaigns*. Each campaign is

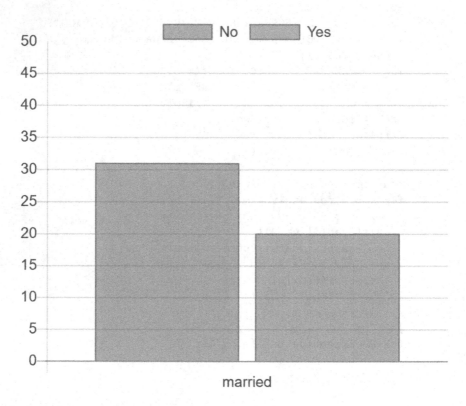

FIGURE 4.9: Two-column bar chart for binary data.

considered one complete data gathering and analysis solution that will be presented on a dashboard.

Example 5: Basic dashboard

To view data, a dashboard is designed to allow users to dynamically select different data sources and render visualizations. This example includes Bootstrap, Popper.js, jQuery, and jQueryUI.

1. camps.sql — This contains the *dashboard_camps* table and the *dashboard_camp_elements* table that are used for storing data about an individual campaigns.

2. dashboard1.php — A sample dashboard that is styled using Bootstrap.

3. Bootstrap — The JavaScript and CSS is used to provide a layout to the dashboard.

4. dashboard.css — This contains additional CSS for the dashboard layout.

5. Popper.js — This is used as a tooltip positioning engine for Bootstrap.

6. jQuery/jQueryUI — This library is used to provide modals and for selecting individual tags using the jQuery selector.

Example code: camps.sql

Before beginning with the process of editing the HTML for the dashboard, a new database table is created titled *dashboard_camps*, as shown in Sample Code 15. This will be used as the main location for storing an individual campaign in the system. Each campaign will contain a date when it was first created and a brief description that is used as the method of describing the campaign to the user. The core identifier used for an individual campaign is the *campid*. Unlike other fields, the campid is not auto-incremented as legacy labels and IDs may have already been created. In the case where they are not, a simple integer can be used for each unique campaign.

```
1  CREATE TABLE `dashboard_camps` (
2        `id` INT NOT NULL AUTO_INCREMENT,
3        `datemade` DATETIME NOT NULL DEFAULT CURRENT_TIMESTAMP,
4        `campname` VARCHAR(100),
5        `campid` INT,
6        PRIMARY KEY (`id`)
7  );
```

SAMPLE CODE 15: Example *dashboard_camps* database table.

Each individual campaign can contain a number of different campaign elements, e.g., total sales data that is an integer that is stored in a database table X with column name Y. As the data may not be stored in a database, the method used to store these data sources should remain flexible. To achieve this a second database table titled *dashboard_camp_elements* is created. This table will contain all the data about the individual data sources a single campaign may have. The table consists of a unique primary key titled *ID*, followed by the *campID* that is linked to the *campID* in the previous table. The *description* column is used to provide a brief description to the user as to what the element is used for.

The *datatype* column is used to define the data type, e.g., int, string, boolean, etc. This is used as a flag for the developer in future steps when this data is going to be used. The final column titled *datasource* contains a reference to where the element being visualized is stored, e.g., in a MySQL database table or a CSV file that was uploaded to the server. The *options* column is used to hold specific data about the columns that should be retrieved from the data source. The final column is the *chart* that contains a description of the type of chart that the data source is associated with, e.g., a bar chart or line chart. Although these two examples are used for the dashboard, additional chart types can easily be added.

```
1  CREATE TABLE `dashboard_camp_elements` (
2      `id` INT NOT NULL AUTO_INCREMENT,
3      `campID` INT,
4      `desc` VARCHAR(500),
5      `datatype` VARCHAR(100),
6      `datasource` VARCHAR(100),
7      `options` VARCHAR(500),
8      `chart` VARCHAR(50),
9      PRIMARY KEY (`id`)
10 );
```

Output

Figure 4.10 describes a sample database table containing values for each of the attributes.

To create a dashboard, Bootstrap offers a sample dashboard layout that can be used for the basic configuration. Figure 4.11 shows an example of the Bootstrap theme with very minimal modifications to remove unnecessary links and data. This sample can be seen live at *https://getBootstrap.com/docs/4.0/examples*.

id	campID	desc	datatype	datasource	options	chart
14	1	sales	int	mysql	select Score, count(Score) from feedbackform...	barchart
20	1	products	int	csv	products.csv,0,1	linechart
21	2	products	int	csv	products.csv,0,1	barchart

FIGURE 4.10: Database table with sample data sources and configuration options.

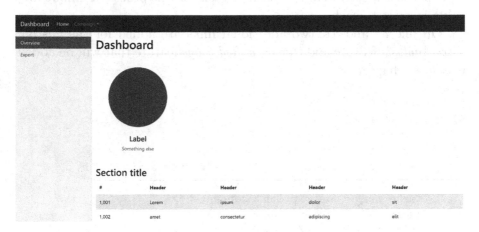

FIGURE 4.11: Sample Bootstrap dashboard.

Example code: dashboard1.php

In Sample Code 16, a new file titled *dashboard1.php* is created. This will be the main portal when a user has logged into the system. At the top of this page inside the *head* tag on lines 4–8, the default tags are added, including the *viewport, description, author,* and *title* for the page. This is followed by the CSS that is used for the core Bootstrap theme on line 9. A custom CSS file titled *dashboard.css* is also added on line 12 that can be modified to suit any application theme. On lines 12–15, jQuery, Popper.js, Bootstrap, and jQueryUI are included.

Once the libraries have been imported, the *header* for the dashboard is included on line 20. This header contains a *nav* tag that has the *class* set to *navbar* including the *navbar-dark* theme that is fixed to the top of the page.

On line 22, a link is included with the *class* set to *navbar-brand* which is a reference to the main text focused on the page. In this example, the word *Dashboard* is used as the title. A *div* tag is added with the *class* set to *collapse navbar-collapse* on line 23. This adds an additional item to the nav bar that can be used as a drop-down menu. In this example it is used to display the word *Home*. On line 26, a link to the homepage or the start page of the dashboard is placed in the *href* tag.

On line 28, a navbar item titled *Campaign* is added that will be used as the root of the campaign. This contains three options on lines 32–34, *Add New Visualization, Build New Campaign* and *Add Campaign Elements*. As each of these items are children of the *Campaign* navbar item, the *class* of each is set to *dropdown-item*. Three separate modals will open when each item is clicked. To trigger this process a unique *href* value is given to each.

On line 38 and 41, two additional links are added for the custom *Text Analysis* feature and the *View Red Flags* feature that will be added in a later chapter.

```
1   <!doctype html>
2   <html lang="en">
3       <head>
4           <meta charset="utf-8">
5           <meta name="viewport" content="width=device-width,
            ↪   initial-scale=1, shrink-to-fit=no">
6           <meta name="description" content="">
7           <meta name="author" content="">
8           <title>Dashboard</title>
9           <link rel="stylesheet" href="Bootstrap.min.css">
10          <link rel="stylesheet"
            ↪   href="https://code.jquery.com/ui/1.12.1/themes/base/
11          jquery-ui.css">
12          <link href="dashboard.css" rel="stylesheet">
13          <script src="jquery-3.1.0.min.js"></script>
14          <script src="popper.min.js"></script>
15          <script src="Bootstrap.min.js"></script>
16          <script
            ↪   src="https://code.jquery.com/ui/1.12.1/jquery-ui.js">
17          </script>
18      </head>
19      <body>
20          <header>
21              <nav class="navbar navbar-expand-md navbar-dark
                ↪   fixed-top bg-dark">
22                  <a class="navbar-brand" href="#">Dashboard</a>
23                  <div class="collapse navbar-collapse"
                    ↪   id="navbarsExampleDefault">
24                      <ul class="navbar-nav mr-auto">
25                          <li class="nav-item active">
26                              <a class="nav-link" href="#">Home <span
                                ↪   class="sr-only">(current)</span></a>
27                          </li>
```

```
28        <li class="nav-item dropdown">
29            <a class="nav-link dropdown-toggle"
              ↪  href="#" id="dropdown01"
              ↪  data-toggle="dropdown"
30               aria-haspopup="true"
              ↪  aria-expanded="false">Campaign</a>
31            <div class="dropdown-menu"
              ↪  aria-labelledby="dropdown01">
32                <a class="dropdown-item" id="addViz"
                  ↪  href="#addAtt" data-toggle="modal"
                  ↪  >Add New Visualisation</a>
33                <a class="dropdown-item"
                  ↪  href="#buildCamp"
                  ↪  data-toggle="modal" >Build New
                  ↪  Campaign</a>
34                <a class="dropdown-item"
                  ↪  href="#addElements"
                  ↪  data-toggle="modal" >Add Campaign
                  ↪  Elements</a>
35            </div>
36        </li>
37        <li class="nav-item dropdown">
38            <a class="nav-link dropdown-toggle"
              ↪  href="#" id="dropdown01"
              ↪  data-toggle="dropdown"
39               aria-haspopup="true"
              ↪  aria-expanded="false">Text
              ↪  Analysis</a>
40            <div class="dropdown-menu"
              ↪  aria-labelledby="dropdown02">
41                <a class="dropdown-item"
                  ↪  href="#selectRanges"
                  ↪  data-toggle="modal" >View Red
                  ↪  Flags</a>
42            </div>
43        </li>
44     </ul>
45   </div>
46 </nav>
47 </header>
```

SAMPLE CODE 16: dashboard1.php — Simple Bootstrap dashboard — part 1.

To add extra options, on line 48, an additional *div* is added with the class set to *container-fluid*. Inside this, a *nav* tag is added with the *class* set to *small*, with a *light* theme. Two options are added on lines 53 and 58 in the form of two *li* tags with the *class* set to *nav-item*. Although currently unused, a *href* can be set here.

In Sample Code 17, a tag titled *main* is added that represents the center of the dashboard. Inside of this tag a *div* tag is added with the *ID* set to *output* on line 66. As visualizations are created, they will be appended into this *div* tag.

```
48  <div class="container-fluid">
49      <div class="row">
50          <nav class="col-sm-3 col-md-2 d-none d-sm-block bg-light
51          sidebar">
52              <ul class="nav nav-pills flex-column">
53                  <li class="nav-item">
54                      <a class="nav-link active" href="#">Overview
55                      <span class="sr-only">(current)</span>
56                      </a>
57                  </li>
58                  <li class="nav-item">
59                      <a class="nav-link" href="#">Export</a>
60                  </li>
61              </ul>
62          </nav>
63          <main role="main" class="col-sm-9 ml-sm-auto col-md-10
64          pt-3">
65          <h1>Dashboard</h1>
66          <div id="output">
67          </div>
68          <section class="row text-center placeholders">
69          </section>
70      </div>
71  </div>
```

SAMPLE CODE 17: dashboard1.php — Simple Bootstrap dashboard — part 2.

Output
Figure 4.12 shows the dashboard with a custom navigation bar.

FIGURE 4.12: Bootstrap default dashboard with a nav bar.

Example 6: Select campaign elements

When the Campaign menu on the dashboard is clicked, followed by the *Add New Visualization*, a modal is required to present the user with a list of campaigns and campaign attributes.

This example includes Bootstrap, Popper.js, jQuery, and jQueryUI.

1. dashboard2.php — This is a modification to the original dashboard to present the user with campaign options.

2. ajax.php — This file is used to retrieve campaign elements and data from the database.

3. Bootstrap — The JavaScript and CSS is used to provide a layout to the dashboard.

4. dashboard.css — This contains additional CSS for the dashboard layout.

5. Popper.js — This is used as a tooltip positioning engine for Bootstrap.

6. jQuery/jQueryUI — This library is used to provide modals and for selecting individual tags using the jQuery selector.

Example code: dashboard2.php

In Sample Code 18, to create the modal, a *div* tag is added with the class set to *modal fade* on line 2. This modal is uniquely identified by the *ID* that is set to *addAtt*. By default, the modal is hidden on the page until it has been opened by the user. The *role* of the *tag* is set to *dialog*. The *aria-labelledby* is set to *addAtt*, that is similar to creating a name to link a label to the *div*. Inside this *div*, a second *div* on line 4 is added with the *class* set to *modal-dialog*. This contains a *div* tag on line 6 with the *class* set to *modal-header* that is displayed at the top of the modal. In this header, on line 7, a *title* is added with the text *Select Campign*. On line 8, a *button* tag is used on the right-hand side of the modal to provide the user an option to close the modal if required.

In the body of the modal, a row is added on line 14 that contains a *div* tag with the *class* set to *col-4* on line 15. Inside this, a *list-group* is added for structure on line 16. After this, on line 19, a second *div* is added with the *class* set to *col-8* that provides a wider window for the content to be displayed. A *list-group* is again added for structure on line 20. On lines 27 and 28, two buttons are added to the end of the modal. The first of these is the *Close* button, allowing the user to dismiss the modal followed by the *Add Vizualization* button. When this button is clicked, the selected element is used as the starting point for the call that is made to the *addViz()* JavaScript function that is responsible for adding the visualization to the dashboard. The modal does not have any content specified in this list. The list of campaigns and campaign attributes is added later using JavaScript.

```
1   <!-- Select Campaign Modal -->
2   <div class="modal fade" id="addAtt" tabindex="-1" role="dialog"
3        aria-labelledby="addAtt" aria-hidden="true">
4     <div class="modal-dialog" role="document">
5       <div class="modal-content">
6         <div class="modal-header">
7           <h5 class="modal-title" id="addAtt">Select Campaign</h5>
8           <button type="button" class="close" data-dismiss="modal"
              ↪  aria-label="Close">
9             <span aria-hidden="true">&times;</span>
10          </button>
11        </div>
12        <div class="modal-body">
13        <!--- List of camps-->
14        <div class="row">
15            <div class="col-4">
```

```
16          <div class="list-group" id="list-tab-camp"
            ↪  role="tablist">
17          </div>
18        </div>
19        <div class="col-8">
20            <div class="list-group" id="list-tab-att"
              ↪  role="tablist">
21              Click on a campaign for attributes
22            </div>
23        </div>
24      </div>
25    </div>
26    <div class="modal-footer">
27      <button type="button" class="btn btn-secondary"
        ↪  data-dismiss="modal">Close</button>
28      <button onclick="addViz()" type="button" class="btn
        ↪  btn-primary">Add Visualisation</button>
29    </div>
30  </div>
31  </div>
32 </div>
```

SAMPLE CODE 18: dashboard2.php — List of campaigns modal.

In Sample Code 19, on line 35, the jQuery selector is used to select
the menu item with the *ID* set to *addViz*. When this is clicked, on line 36,
a jQuery *POST* is performed to the *ajax.php* page. The *type* being sent
to the page is set to *getcamp*. This function returns a variable titled *data*
on line 37 that contains the list of campaigns marked up in HTML. On
line 37 the *list-tab-camp* element is selected and the HTML is set using
the *html()* function and passing in the *data* variable that was returned.

When each campaign is clicked, a list of elements is available for
visualization. On line 41 to perform this action, a listener is bound to
the *div* tag with the *ID* set to *list-tab-camp*. On *shown.bs.tab*, e.g., a
person clicking on one of the campaigns, this function will then trigger.
On line 42, a variable title *data* is added that will contain the HTML for
the selected tab element. On line 43, the campaign *ID* is extracted from
the data variable using the *attr()* function and passing in the name of
the element of interest. In this case, the *cid*.

To retrieve a list of elements that make up the individual campaign,
on line 45, a *POST* is made to the *ajax.php* passing the *type* of request
as the *getformfields*. The *cid* for the individual campaign is also passed

to return only the relevant elements. On line 46, when the function is complete, the result will be returned inside a function with a variable titled *data* that is appended to the *list=tab-att* using the *html()* function on line 47.

```
33  <script>
34  // Add list of camp elements to the modal
35  $("#addViz").click(function() { console.log("Called add viz");
36      $.post( "ajax.php", { type: "getcamp"} )
37      .done(function( data ) {
38          $('#list-tab-camp').html(data);
39      });
40  });
41  $('div[id="list-tab-camp"]').on('shown.bs.tab', function (e) {
42      var data = e.target; // HTML of just selected tab
43      var cid = $(data).attr('cid'); // get the ID
44      // get list of attributes for campaign
45      $.post( "ajax.php", { type:"getformfields", cid: cid})
46      .done(function( data ) {
47          $('#list-tab-att').html(data);
48      });
49  })
50  </script>
```

SAMPLE CODE 19: dashboard2.php — JavaScript for listing campaigns on the dashboard modal.

Example code: ajax.php
To retrieve a list of campaigns and campaign elements, the *ajax.php* page is modified. In Sample Code 20, on line 3, if the *type* is set to *getcamp* a list of campaigns are returned by calling the *getCamp()* PHP function on line 4. A second *type* attribute titled *getformfields* is added on line 6, for retrieving a campaign elements based on the *cid*.

When the campaign modal first opens, a list of campaigns is retrieved from the *dashboard_camps* table. The two pieces of information of interest are the *campid* and the *campname*. During each iteration of the *foreach* statement on line 22, a new *href* link is created. The *class* is set to *list-group-item ist-group-item-action*. Custom attributes are added into the link to aid the movement of basic campaign data such as the *cid* attribute. The list-camp is set to be the *ID* of the campaign. The *data-toggle* attribute is set as a *list* on line 24. For the user, the text shown is the *campid* followed by a single dash followed by the *campname* that is extracted from the row.

For each campaign in the modal that has been selected, an AJAX request is made to the *ajax.php* page making a call to the *getFormFields()* function.

```php
1   <?php
2   $type = $_POST['type'];
3   if($type == 'getcamp'){
4       getCamp();
5   }
6   else if($type == 'getformfields'){
7       getFormFields();
8   }
9   function getCamp(){
10      try {
11          $host = 'localhost:3306';
12          $dbname = 'bookexamples';
13          $user = 'sampleuser';
14          $pass = '3C9038A509BE6145AAD6827B4568AD918BC3DAC0';
15          $DBH = new PDO("mysql:host=$host;dbname=$dbname",
16           $user, $pass);
17          $sql = "select campid, campname from dashboard_camps;";
18          $sth = $DBH->prepare($sql);
19          $sth->execute();
20          $res = $sth->fetchAll();
21
22          foreach($res as $row){
23           $id = $row['campid'];
24           echo '<a class="list-group-item list-group-item-action"
25            cid="'.$id.'"
26           id="list-camp-'.$id.'" data-toggle="list" href=
27           "#list-camp-'.$id.'"
28           role="tab" aria-controls="camp-'.$id.'">CID:' .
29            $row['campid'] . '-
30            '.$row['campname'].'</a>';
31          }
32
33      } catch(PDOException $e) {echo $e;}
34  }
```

SAMPLE CODE 20: ajax.php — Retrieving a list of campaigns — part 1

In Sample Code 21, on line 37, the function is defined. This function is responsible for returning a list of data about the elements that make up a single campaign. These Include the text-based description that was given to the element, the *dataType* that was being processed, information about the data source, e.g., if it was a CSV file or SQL and the type of chart that will be used to render the data on the dashboard.

On line 38, the *cid* that has been passed is stored in a local variable. On line 46, the SQL to select the campaign elements is added. A question mark is used for the *campID* attribute as it is dynamically passed to the function and then appended using the *bindParam()* function on line 49. On line 53, a *for each* statement is added that iterates over the results. On lines 54–58, for each record, the *ID*, description, data type, data source, and chart type are gathered and placed into local variables. On line 61, for each record a complete HTML link is created. Each of the attributes is placed into the link to aid future retrieval during the graph generation process.

```
35    // return a list of form fields
36    // for a given cid
37    function getFormFields(){
38        $cid = $_POST['cid'];
39        try {
40            $host = 'localhost:3306';
41            $dbname = 'bookexamples';
42            $user = 'sampleuser';
43            $pass = '3C9038A509BE6145AAD6827B4568AD918BC3DAC0';
44            $DBH = new PDO("mysql:host=$host;dbname=$dbname",
45             $user, $pass);
46            $sql = "select * from dashboard_camp_elements where
47             campID=?;";
48            $sth = $DBH->prepare($sql);
49            $sth->bindParam(1, $cid, PDO::PARAM_STR);
50            $sth->execute();
51            $res = $sth->fetchAll();
52
53            foreach($res as $row){
54                $elementID = $row['id'];
55                $desc = $row['desc'];
56                $dataType = $row['datatype'];
57                $src = $row['datasource'];
58                $chart = $row['chart'];
59                // print out each individual attribute as a new button
60                // inside of the tab panel.
```

```
61    echo'<a chart="'.$chart.'" datasource="'.$src.'"
62      elementid="'.$elementID.'"
63      elementtitle="'.$desc.'" cid="'.$cid.'"
64      class="list-group-item list-group-item-action"
65      id="list-camp-e" data-toggle="list" href="#"
66      role="tab"
67      aria-controls="camp">'.$desc.' - ('.$dataType.') -
68      '.$src.'</a>';
69    }
70  } catch(PDOException $e) {echo $e;}
71 }
72 ?>
```

SAMPLE CODE 21: ajax.php - Retrieving a list of form fields - part 2

Output
Figure 4.13 shows the *Select Campaign* modal. This modal has a list of the active campaigns on the left. When the campaign is selected, a list of the associated elements is shown on the right of the modal. This contains information about the element description, the format of the data, and the source of the data.

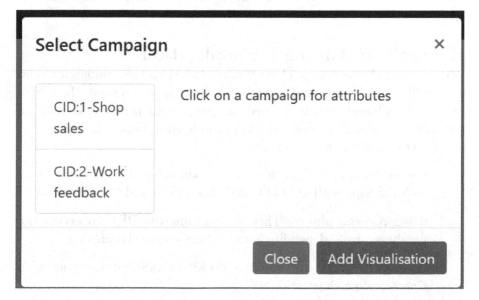

FIGURE 4.13: Select campaign modal with two available campaigns.

Figure 4.14 describes a list of campaigns on the left followed by a list of campaign elements that can be visualized on the right. Once an item has been selected in the right menu, the *Add Visualization* option can be selected.

FIGURE 4.14: Viewing a list of campaigns with a single campaign element selected.

Example 7: Adding a visualization

When any of the campaign elements are clicked on the campaign modal they will become blue, indicating they have been selected. To add a visualization based on this selected campaign element, a call is made to the *addViz()* function when the *Add Visualization* button is clicked.

This example contains four files:

1. dashboard3.php — This file contains the original dashboard HTML/JavaScript with an additional function to add visualizations.

2. data_processor.php — This file contains the PHP to access the database or file depending on the data source chosen.

3. line.php — This contains the HTML/JavaScript to generate a Charts.js line chart.

4. barchart.php — This contains the HTML/JavaScript to generate a Chart.js bar chart.

Example code: dashboard3.php

In Sample Code 22, the *addViz()* function is described that is added inside the *script* tag at the bottom of the dashboard3.php file. On line 2, a simple *console.log()* is performed to indicate to us that the function has correctly been called. On lines 3–6, the *list-tab-att* items are searched for where the status is set to *a.active* indicating that it has been selected. For the selected campaign item, the *elementID, chart, datasource,* and *elementtitle* are extracted. These were placed in the individual items earlier during generation.

On line 11, a check is performed to see what type of chart is required. On line 11, if the *type* is equal to *barchart*, the jQuery selector is used to select the *output div* tag and append a new *div* tag. The contents of this *div* tag are gathered by dynamically calling the *barchart.php* page via the *load()* function and passing in the *source, ID,* and *title* variables. On line 16, the same process is repeated for the line chart.

```
1   function addViz(){
2       console.log('add viz called');
3       var elementid = $("#list-tab-att a.active").
4        attr('elementid');
5       var chartType = $("#list-tab-att a.active").
6       attr('chart');
7       var dataSource = $("#list-tab-att a.active").
8       attr('datasource');
9       var vizTitle = $("#list-tab-att a.active").
10      attr('elementtitle');
11      if(chartType == 'barchart'){
12          $('#output').append(($('<div>').load("bar.php?source="
13              +dataSource+"&id="
14              +elementid + "&title="+escape(vizTitle))));
15      }
16      else if(chartType =='linechart'){
17          $('#output').append(($('<div>').load("line.php?source="
18          +dataSource+"&id="
19              +elementid + "&title="+escape(vizTitle))));
20      }
21  }
```

SAMPLE CODE 22: dashboard3.php — addViz() function to add a new visualization based on the current selected campaign element.

Example code: data_processor.php
Both the *barchart.php* and *line.php* file require use of a file titled
data_processer.php. This file is used as the main method of gathering
data from different data sources.

In Sample Code 23, on line 2, the *getData()* function is defined that
takes in the *ID* of the element to chart along with the *sourceType* that
references where the data is currently stored. On line 3, if the source type
is a MySQL database, then a query to the database is made. The query
is gathered by making a call to the *getDataSourceOptions()* function on
line 11 and passing the *ID* of the element to be visualized. For each
row that is returned the *row[0]* that contains the X value is added to
the JavaScript *lab* array by calling the *push()* function on line 16 and
passing the term. On line 17, the *Y* value to be displayed to modify the
height of the bar is gathered from the *row[1]* and pushed to the *data1*
JavaScript array.

On line 23, if the *sourceType* variable is set to *csv*, then a call to
the *getDataSourceOptions* is made on line 24. This function takes in the
ID of the elements to be graphed. The data that will be plotted must
follow the same structure of X and Y. Where X is the label and Y is the
value to be plotted. During the process of adding a CSV to the system,
the two columns are defined, and then the file name is described. In the
database table, these values take the form of *filename.csv, 1, 2* where 1
is the X column and 2 is the Y column of the CSV file to be plotted.

To break the values apart for processing, a call is made to the *ex-
plode()* function on line 25 that takes in a delimiter followed by the
string to process. In this example, the delimiter is a comma. A call to
fgetcsv() is made on line 27 to open a connection to the file and gather
the contents. As the file is a CSV, the delimiter is once again specified
as a comma here. The *label* for the chart is stored in the *lab* JavaScript
array.

The values for this are extracted from the *data* variable that contains
the individual columns in the CSV file. On lines 30 and 31, a reference
to *col1* and *col2* is provided to identify the two columns of interest and
extract their values. The first of these is the label and the second is the
value associated to the label. These are printed using an *echo* statement
that contains the javaScript to add to the *lab* and *data1* JavaScript
arrays. The JavaScript *push()* function is used to add the values to the
associated arrays.

```php
1  <?php
2  function getData($id, $sourceType){
3      if($sourceType =='mysql'){
4          try {
5              $host = 'localhost:3306';
6              $dbname = 'bookexamples';
7              $user = 'sampleuser';
8              $pass = '3C9038A509BE6145AAD6827B4568AD918BC3DAC0';
9              $DBH = new PDO("mysql:host=$host;dbname=$dbname",
10              $user, $pass);
11             $sql = getDataSourceOptions($id);
12             $sth = $DBH->prepare($sql);
13             $sth->execute();
14             $res = $sth->fetchAll();
15             foreach ($res as $row){
16                 echo " lab.push('".$row[0]."');";
17                 echo " data1.push('".$row[1]."');";
18             }
19
20         } catch(PDOException $e) {echo $e;}
21
22     }
23     else if($sourceType =='csv'){
24         $dataSourceOptions = getDataSourceOptions($id);
25         $op = explode(',',$dataSourceOptions);
26         if (($file = fopen('samplefiles/'.$op[0], "r")) !== FALSE)
27          {while (($data = fgetcsv($file, 1000, ",")) !== FALSE)
28             {$col1 = $op[1];
29                 $col2 = $op[2];
30                 echo " lab.push('".$data[$col1]."');";
31                 echo " data1.push('".$data[$col2]."');";
32         }
33         fclose($file);
34         }
35     }
36
37
38  }
39  function getDataSourceOptions($id){
40      try {
41          $host = 'localhost:3306';
42          $dbname = 'bookexamples';
43          $user = 'sampleuser';
44          $pass = '3C9038A509BE6145AAD6827B4568AD918BC3DAC0';
45          $DBH = new PDO("mysql:host=$host;dbname=$dbname",
```

```
46        $user, $pass);
47        $sql = "SELECT options FROM dashboard_camp_elements
48         WHERE id = ?";
49        $sth = $DBH->prepare($sql);
50        $sth->bindParam(1, $id, PDO::PARAM_INT);
51        $sth->execute();
52        $res = $sth->fetch();
53        return $res[0];
54      } catch(PDOException $e) {echo $e;}
55  }
```

SAMPLE CODE 23: data_processor.php — Get data from a data
source depending on the data source type.

Example code: line.php
A file titled *line.php* is created to visualize line charts. On line 2, the
data_processor.php file is included that will provide access to the data
source as described earlier. On lines 11 and 12, the two JavaScript files
required by Charts.js are included. Both these files must be in the current
directory. On lines 14–18, the *canvas* is set to not allow selections. On
line 22, a *div* is added that will be used for holding the visualization. On
line 27, a random number is generated and placed into a local variable
titled *uniqueID*. This is used as the *ID* for the graph. On lines 38 and
30, the *ID* is set into the *container* and the canvas. On line 36 a call is
made to the PHP function titled *getData()* that was described earlier.
The *ID* and the *sourceType* are passed to this function.

On line 38, the *config* variable is added that contains the *type* of graph
to be rendered. the *labels* is set to be the *lab* array that was generated.
Inside the *datasets* array on line 43, the *data* for the graph is set to be
the *data1* array that was generated.

```
1   <?php
2   include('data_processor.php');
3   $id = $_GET['id'];
4   $title = $_GET['title'];
5   $sourceType = $_GET['source'];
6   ?>
7   <!doctype html>
8   <html>
9   <head>
10      <title>Line Chart</title>
11      <script src="Chart.bundle.js"></script>
```

```
12      <script src="utils.js"></script>
13      <style>
14      canvas{
15          -moz-user-select: none;
16          -webkit-user-select: none;
17          -ms-user-select: none;
18      }
19      </style>
20  </head>
21  <body>
22  <div id="container" style="width:50%"; class="ui-widget-
23  content">
24  <canvas id="canvas"></canvas>
25  </div>
26  <script>
27  var uniqueID = Math.floor((Math.random() * 1000) + 1);
28  document.getElementById("container").setAttribute("id",
29   "container"+uniqueID);
30  document.getElementById("canvas").setAttribute("id",
31   "canvas"+uniqueID);
32  var lab =   new Array();
33  var data1 = new Array();
34  <?php
35  // Get the data for the graph
36  getData($id,$sourceType);
37  ?>
38  var config = {
39      type: 'line',
40      data: {
41          labels: lab,
42          datasets: [{
43              label: "",
44              backgroundColor: window.chartColors.red,
45              borderColor: window.chartColors.red,
46              data: data1,
47              fill: false,
48          }]
49      },
```

SAMPLE CODE 24: line.php — Used when adding a visualization —
part 1.

In Sample Code 25, on line 84, the chart reference *ctx* and the *config*
are passed to to create a new *chart* object. On lines 85 and 86, the *drag-gable()* and the *resizable()* functions are called on the container allowing

it to be moved on the screen. These functions are components of the jQueryUI library that is added as part of the original dashboard.

```
50      options: {
51          responsive: true,
52          title:{
53              display:true,
54              text: unescape('<?php echo $title;?>')
55          },
56          tooltips: {
57              mode: 'index',
58              intersect: false,
59          },
60          hover: {
61              mode: 'nearest',
62              intersect: true
63          },
64          scales: {
65              xAxes: [{
66                  display: true,
67                  scaleLabel: {
68                      display: true,
69                      labelString: 'Month'
70                  }
71              }],
72              yAxes: [{
73                  display: true,
74                  scaleLabel: {
75                      display: true,
76                      labelString: 'Value'
77                  }
78              }]
79          }
80      }
81  };
82  var ctx = document.getElementById("canvas"+uniqueID).
83  getContext("2d");
84  window.myLine = new Chart(ctx, config);
85  $("#container"+uniqueID).resizable();
86  $("#container"+uniqueID).draggable();
87  </script>
88  </body>
89  </html>
```

SAMPLE CODE 25: line.php — Used when adding a visualization — part 2.

Example code: bar.php

In Sample Code 26 and 27, the *bar.php* file can be seen. This file has the exact same JavaScript as the *line.php* file. The only modification that needs to be made is on line 52, the *type* is set to *bar*.

```php
1   <?php
2   include('data_processor.php');
3   $id = $_GET['id'];
4   $title = $_GET['title'];
5   $sourceType = $_GET['source'];
6   ?>
7   <!doctype html>
8   <html>
9   <head>
10  <script src="Chart.bundle.js"></script>
11  <script src="utils.js"></script>
12  <style>
13  canvas {
14      -moz-user-select: none;
15      -webkit-user-select: none;
16      -ms-user-select: none;
17  }
18  </style>
19  </head>
20  <body>
21  <div id="container" style="width:50%"; class="ui-widget-content">
22      <canvas id="canvas"></canvas>
23  </div>
24  <script>
25  var uniqueID = Math.floor((Math.random() * 1000) + 1);
26  document.getElementById("container").setAttribute("id",
27   "container"+uniqueID);
28  document.getElementById("canvas").setAttribute("id",
29   "canvas"+uniqueID);
30  var color = Chart.helpers.color;
31  var lab =  new Array();
32  var data1 = new Array();
33  <?php
34  // Get the data for the graph
35  getData($id, $sourceType);
36  ?>
37  var barChartData = {
38      labels: lab,
39      datasets: [{
```

```
40        label: '',
41        backgroundColor: color(window.chartColors.red).
42        alpha(0.5).rgbString(),
43        borderColor: window.chartColors.red,
44        borderWidth: 1,
45        data: data1
46    }]
47
48  };
49  var ctx = document.getElementById("canvas"+uniqueID).
50  getContext("2d");
51  window.myBar = new Chart(ctx, {
52      type: 'bar',
53      data: barChartData,
```

SAMPLE CODE 26: bar.php — Used when adding a visualization — part 1.

```
54      options: {
55          responsive: true,
56        scales: {
57              yAxes: [{
58                  ticks: {
59                      beginAtZero: true
60                  }
61              }]
62        },
63        legend: {
64            display:false,
65        },
66        title: {
67            display: true,
68            text: unescape('<?php echo $title;?>')
69        }
70  }
71  });
72  $("#container"+uniqueID).resizable();
73  $("#container"+uniqueID).draggable();
74  </script>
75  </body>
76  </html>
```

SAMPLE CODE 27: bar.php — Used when adding a visualization — part 2.

Output

Figure 4.15 outlines the final dashboard that contains two different visualizations. The first of these is a bar chart and the second is a line chart. As the setup of the chart was dynamic, to add in further chart types requires minimal modification.

Dashboard

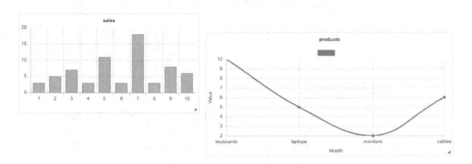

FIGURE 4.15: Example dashboard with two visualizations added.

Example 8: Adding a new campaign

The backbone of each visualization is the campaign. To add new campaigns into the system, a menu item titled *Build New Campaign* is available in the *Campaign* drop-down menu. When this is selected, a new modal is created that allows the user to enter the unique *ID* for the campaign, followed by a description. To do this, a new modal is first created.

This example consists of two files:

1. dashboard4.php — This is the original dashboard with an additional Bootstrap modal.

2. ajax.php — This file is used to dynamically insert a new campaign into the database.

Example code: dashboard4.php

In Sample Code 28, on line 2, a *div* tag is added with the *ID* set to *buildCamp*. On line 9, the title for the modal is set to *Create new campaign*. On lines 21 and 22, two input fields are added with the IDs set to *newcid* and *newdesc*, respectively. On line 28, a close button is added, followed by another button on line 30 that is responsible for triggering the campaign to be added to the database. The *ID* of this button is set to *addNewCamp*.

```
1   <!-- Build new camp modal -->
2   <div class="modal fade" id="buildCamp" tabindex="-1"
3    role="dialog"
4                          aria-labelledby="buildCamp"
5                          aria-hidden="true">
6     <div class="modal-dialog" role="document">
7       <div class="modal-content">
8         <div class="modal-header">
9           <h5 class="modal-title" id="buildCamp">Create new
10           Campaign</h5>
11          <button type="button" class="close" data-dismiss="modal"
12           aria-label="Close">
13            <span aria-hidden="true">&times;</span>
14          </button>
15        </div>
16        <div class="modal-body">
17        <!--- List of camps-->
18        <div class="row">
19        <div class="col-5">
20          <div class="list-group" id="list-tab-camp" role="tablist">
21          Campaign ID <input type="text" id="newcid"><br>
22          Description  <input type="text" id="newdesc"><br>
23          </div>
24        </div>
25        </div>
26        </div>
27        <div class="modal-footer">
28          <button type="button" class="btn btn-secondary"
29           data-dismiss="modal">Close</button>
30          <button id="addNewCamp" type="button" class=
31          "btn btn-primary"
32                  data-dismiss="modal">Add New Campaign</button>
33        </div>
34      </div>
35   </div>
```

```
36   </div>
37    <!---- END NEW CAMP MODAL -->
```

SAMPLE CODE 28: dashboard4.php — Additional add new campaign modal.

In Sample Code 29, on line 3, a jQuery listener is bound to the *addNewCamp* button. On line 5 and 6, when the button is clicked, the jQuery selector is used to grab the *newcid* and the *newdesc* values from the modal. On line 7, these variables are *POST* to the *ajax.php* page under the *type* titled *addnewcamp*. A simple *alert()* is used to output the response after calling the *ajax.php* page.

```
1   <script>
2   // example 3 changes
3   $("#addNewCamp").click(function() {
4       alert("called");
5       var newcid = $("#newcid").val();
6       var newdesc = $("#newdesc").val();
7       $.post( "ajax.php", { type: "addnewcamp", newcid:newcid,
8        newdesc:newdesc} )
9           .done(function( data ) {
10               alert(data);
11      });
12
13  });
14  </script>
```

SAMPLE CODE 29: dashboard4.php — Add new campaign button click listener.

Example code: ajax.php

Sample Code 30 outlines the *ajax.php page*. On line 1, the type is first caught. On line 2, if the *type* is equal to *addnewcamp*, a call is made to the *addNewCamp()* function. On lines 6 and 7, the new *ID* and description are first extracted from the *POST* and placed in local variables. On line 13, a new connection to the database is created. On line 15, the SQL *INSERT* statement is created placing two question marks for the values. The values are bound by calling the *bindParam()* function on lines 18 and 19. On line 20, the *INSERT* statement is executed.

```php
$type = $_POST['type'];
if($type == 'addnewcamp'){
    addNewCamp();
}
function addNewCamp(){
    $newcid = $_POST['newcid'];
    $newdesc = $_POST['newdesc'];
    try {
        $host = 'localhost:3306';
        $dbname = 'bookexamples';
        $user = 'sampleuser';
        $pass = '3C9038A509BE6145AAD6827B4568AD918BC3DAC0';
        $DBH = new PDO("mysql:host=$host;dbname=$dbname",
         $user, $pass);
        $sql = "INSERT INTO `dashboard_camps` (`campname`,
         `campid`) VALUES (?,?);";
        $sth = $DBH->prepare($sql);
        $sth->bindParam(1, $newdesc, PDO::PARAM_STR);
        $sth->bindParam(2, $newcid, PDO::PARAM_INT);
        $sth->execute();
        echo 'Added';
    } catch(PDOException $e) {echo 'failed' . $e;}
}
```

SAMPLE CODE 30: ajax.php — Add a new campaign PHP.

Output

Figure 4.16 shows the output after clicking *Add New Campaign.*

Example 9: Add new campaign element

The most complicated modal that is shown to the user is the modal that is designed to allow the user to specify a new campaign element. A campaign element is a single field in a campaign. This example consists of three files:

1. dashboard5.php — The original dashboard with a new modal for adding campaign elements.

2. ajax.php — This file is responsible for inserting a new campaign element record into the database.

FIGURE 4.16: Two text fields allowing the user to create a new campaign.

3. listOfFiles.php — This file is used to retrieve a list of files that can be used as a data source.

Example code: dashboard.php

In Sample Code 31, on line 2 a new *div* tag is created. The *ID* for this *div* is set to *addElements*. The *role* is set to *dialog*.

On line 19, an input field is added, allowing the user to enter the campaign *ID*. On line 21, another input field is added, allowing the user to enter a column name. As data can come in any format, on line 24, a *select* field is added, allowing the user to specify if the content is int, text, or decimal. On line 30, another field is added, allowing the user to determine if the content is coming from a CSV file or a MySQL database.

On line 35, a *select* is added, allowing the user to select if they want a bar chart or a line chart to appear on the dashboard. A *div* titled *dataSourceOptions* is added. When this modal loads, no content is shown in this *div* tag. When the user selects MySQL, a text area will be shown in this *div*. When the user selects CSV, then a list of files will be shown to select from.

```
1   <!-- ADD NEW CAMP ELEMENT -->
2   <div class="modal fade" id="addElements" tabindex="1"
3   role="dialog"
4       aria-labelledby="addElements" aria-hidden="true">
5    <div class="modal-dialog">
6      <div class="modal-content" style="width:900px">
7        <div class="modal-header">
8          <h5 class="modal-title" id="addElements">Create New
9          Campaign Element</h5>
10         <button type="button" class="close" data-dismiss="modal"
11          aria-label="Close">
12           <span aria-hidden="true">&times;</span>
13         </button>
14       </div>
15       <div class="modal-body">
16       <div class="container">
17         <div class="row">
18           <div class="col-sm">
19             <b>  Campaign ID</b><br> <input type="text"
20              id="addElementCid"><br>
21             <b>  Custom Column Name </b><br><input type="text"
22              id="addElementCol"><br>
23         <b>Data type</b><br>
24          <select id="addElementDataType">
25           <option>int</option>
26           <option>text</option>
27           <option>decimal</option>
28          </select><br>
29          <b>Data Source</b><br>
30           <select id="addElementSource">
31               <option value="csv">CSV File</option>
32               <option value="mysql">MySQL Column</option>
33           </select><br>
34          <b>Chart Type</b><br>
35          <select id="chartType">
36               <option value="barchart">Bar Chart (X and y)
37               </option>
38               <option value="linechart">Line Chart (X and Y)
39               </option>
40          </select><br>
41          </div>
42          <div class="col-sm">
43              <b> Select data source</b><br>
44              <div id="dataSourceOptions" style="width:300px;
45               height:200px; overflow: auto">
```

```
46                    </div>
47                    <div id="dataSourceAdditional">
48                    </div>
49                </div>
50
51          </div>
52              <div class="modal-footer">
53                  <button type="button" class="btn btn-secondary"
54                              data-dismiss="modal">Close</button>
55                  <button id="addNewCampElement" type="button"
56                    class="btn btn-primary"
57                              data-dismiss="modal">Add New Element
58                              </button>
59              </div>
60          </div>
61        </div>
62      </div>
63  </div>
64  </div>
```

SAMPLE CODE 31: dashboard5.php — Add new campaign element modal.

Sample Code 32 describes the Javascript that is used to track the data source the user is adding. On line 65, when the source, e.g., CSV or MySQL is selected on the form, the *on()* function will trigger. On line 66, if the selected source is equal to *mysql*, on line 67, the *dataSourceOptions div* tag is selected, and the content is updated to be a sample SQL query. On line, 71, if a CSV is selected, then the *dataSourceOptions div* tag is selected and the contents are set to be the output of loading the *listOfFiles.php* file. This PHP file is used for listing the contents of a directory.

```
65  $('#addElementSource').on('change', function() {
66      if(this.value == 'mysql'){
67          $('#dataSourceOptions').html('<textarea rows="6"
        ↪ cols="35" id="querybox">select Score, count(Score)
        ↪ from feedbackformrecords where FeedbackFormId=1 and
        ↪ FeedbackElementID = 1 group by Score;</textarea>');
68          $('#dataSourceAdditional').html('');
69      }
70      else if(this.value =='csv'){
71          $('#dataSourceOptions').load('listOfFiles.php');
```

```
72
73        $('#dataSourceAdditional').html('Column X: <input
          ↪  type="text" id="selectedColX" size="2"/>'
74                               +'Column Y: <input type="text"
                                 ↪   id="selectedColY"
                                 ↪   size="2"/><br>');
75      }
76      else if(this.value == 'textfile'){
77          $('#dataSourceOptions').load('listOfFiles.php');
78          $('#dataSourceAdditional').html('');
79      }
80
81
82  });
```

SAMPLE CODE 32: dashboard5.php — JavaScript to update the *dataSourceOptions div* tag.

In Sample Code 33, on line 83, if a button with the *ID* set to *addNew-CampElement* is clicked, the following code will run. On lines 84–87, the values from the input fields and select boxes are gathered. On line 91, the data source type that is selected is gathered.

As each different data source has a different combination of fields, a string titled *optionString* is added. This is used to hold the configuration for accessing the specified data source. For the data source of type CSV, on lines 96–99, the defined columns are gathered. These are set into the *optionsString* variable separated by commas. For the data type MySQL, on line 104 the *querybox* value is gathered and placed directly into the *optionsString*.

After the values have been gathered, on line 109, a *POST* is performed to the *ajax.php* page. The *type* of request being sent is set to *addElementToCamp*. Each of the attributes gathered is sent. When this function completes, an *alert()* statement with the content output of the *ajax.php* page is shown on line 116.

```
83  $("#addNewCampElement").click(function() {
84      var addElementCid = $("#addElementCid").val();
85      var addElementCol =  $("#addElementCol").val();
86      var dataType = $('#addElementDataType').val();
87      var chartType = $('#chartType').val();
88      var optionsString = '';
89
```

```
90      // get the data source type
91      var dataSourceType = $('#addElementSource :selected').val();
92
93      if(dataSourceType == 'csv'){
94          // Select CSV specific options
95          // filename
96          var selectedFile = $("#file:checked").val();
97          // column of interest
98          var selColX =  $("#selectedColX").val();
99          var selColY =  $("#selectedColY").val()
100         optionsString = selectedFile + ',' + selColX +','+
101           selColY;
102     }
103     else if(dataSourceType == 'mysql'){
104         var queryBoxContent = $('#querybox').val();
105         optionsString = queryBoxContent;
106     }
107
108
109     $.post( "ajax.php", { type: "addElementToCamp",
110      cid:addElementCid,
111                             customName: addElementCol,
112                              dataType:dataType,
113                              dataSourceType:dataSourceType,
114                  options:optionsString, chart:chartType} )
115         .done(function( data ) {
116             alert(data);
117         });
118 });
```

SAMPLE CODE 33: dashboard5.php — JavaScript click triggering the saving of a new campaign.

Example code: listOfFiles.php

To list available CSV files to the user, an AJAX call was made to a page titled *listOfFiles.php*. Inside this, file a reference to the *opendir()* function was used to open the *samplefiles* folder that was placed beside the PHP script. In reality, this folder can be placed anywhere as long as the path to the folder is correct. To find out what the current working directory is, a simple called to *echo getcwd();* will print out the exact directory path aiding the debugging process.

While in the folder, a while loop is used to loop over each individual file. A simple *if statement* is added to ensure that the *entry* or a single file does not contain a full stop or two full stops that would indicate a parent folder. For each individual file, an *input* field is added with the *type* set to *radio*. The *ID* of the field is set to file. The most essential element is the value that stores the internal reference to the file name. In this case, the value is set to be the value from the *entry* variable. The entry variable is printed again for the user to see, followed by a simple *br* tag to break onto the next line. After listing all the files, it is essential to close the connection to the directory using the *closedir()* function. In Sample Code 34, the complete code for *listofFiles.php* can be seen.

```php
<?php
if ($handle = opendir('samplefiles')) {
    while (false !== ($entry = readdir($handle))) {
        if ($entry != "." && $entry != "..") {
            echo '<input type="radio" id="file" name="file"
              value="'.$entry.'">' . $entry .'<br>';
        }
    }
    closedir($handle);
}
?>
```

SAMPLE CODE 34: listOfFiles.php — Retrieving a list of files from the *samplefiles* folder.

Example code: ajax.php

Sample Code 35 outlines the ajax.php page. On line 2, the *type* variable is first accessed and placed in a local variable. On line 3, if the variable is equal to *addElementToCamp*, on line 4 a call is made to the *addElementToCamp()* function. From lines 7–12 each variable in the *POST* is extracted and placed in local variables. On line 20 a new database connection is made. On line 23, the *INSERT* statement is created, with question marks for the values. On lines 28–33 each value is added to the statement using the *bindParam()* function. On line 34, the statement is finally executed.

```php
1  <?php
2  $type = $_POST['type'];
3  if($type =='addElementToCamp'){
4      addElementToCamp();
5  }
6  function addElementToCamp(){
7      $cid = $_POST['cid'];
8      $customName = $_POST['customName'];
9      $dataType = $_POST['dataType'];
10     $dataSourceType = $_POST['dataSourceType'];
11     $options = $_POST['options'];
12     $chart = $_POST['chart'];
13
14     try {
15         $host = 'localhost:3306';
16         $dbname = 'bookexamples';
17         $user = 'sampleuser';
18         $pass = '3C9038A509BE6145AAD6827B4568AD918BC3DAC0';
19
20         $DBH = new PDO("mysql:host=$host;dbname=$dbname",
21          $user, $pass);
22
23         $sql = "INSERT INTO `dashboard_camp_elements` (`campID`,
24                             `desc`, `datatype`, `datasource`,
25                                     `options`, `chart`)
26                                     VALUES (?,?,?,?,?,?);";
27         $sth = $DBH->prepare($sql);
28         $sth->bindParam(1, $cid, PDO::PARAM_STR);
29         $sth->bindParam(2, $customName, PDO::PARAM_STR);
30         $sth->bindParam(3, $dataType, PDO::PARAM_STR);
31         $sth->bindParam(4, $dataSourceType, PDO::PARAM_STR);
32         $sth->bindParam(5, $options, PDO::PARAM_STR);
33         $sth->bindParam(6, $chart, PDO::PARAM_STR);
34         $sth->execute();
35         echo 'New Element Added';
36     } catch(PDOException $e) {echo 'failed' . $e;}
37  }
38
39  ?>
```

SAMPLE CODE 35: ajax.php — Add elements to existing campaign.

Output

Figure 4.17 outlines the data source selection process. On the right-hand side of this, the data source options become visible when either MySQL or CSV is selected. In this example, CSV has been selected, and a list of files is returned on the right of the modal. The campaign *ID* will then be entered, followed by a name for the unique element. The X column is entered to indicate the row of interest and Y is entered to indicate the column of interest from the selected CSV file. The data type for the column of interest can be set, along with the type of chart we wish to create.

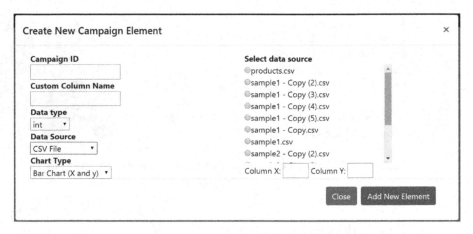

FIGURE 4.17: The process of adding a new campaign element and selecting the data source.

4.7 SUMMARY

This chapter described the process of creating a login page, register page, and dashboard. This dashboard served as the starting point for adding data visualizations in the form of charts. As data comes in various formats, the process of creating dynamic charts was explored. Although visualizations are useful for exploring data, additional processing is often required to gain a deeper insight into the data.

In Chapter 5, the process of working with text is explored, outlining methods of removing irrelevant terms and processing those of interest.

Working with Text

5.1 INTRODUCTION

When gathering data from users, there are times when a predefined collection of answers does not suit the user's need to express themselves. When this happens, providing the user with a text field where they can enter their text feedback can be useful. However, text-based feedback comes with constraints as typical metrics for analysis, such as calculating the sum of a database column, can not be performed.

To gather insights from text, additional processing is required to identify the relevance and importance of the text or terms. This chapter will review the processing methods that can be performed on the text and the metrics for identifying value and relevance.

5.2 NATURAL-LANGUAGE PROCESSING

The area of natural-language processing (NLP) goes back to the early 1950s. As text is one of our primary forms of communication, software that utilizes text became a natural area of interest for researchers. Text in raw form often needs to be further processed to condense and extract meaningful insights.

In a business setting, analysts would like a user to be as specific as possible when describing what issues they are having. However, users often use the wrong keywords or terminology when describing problems. In addition to this, unlike numeric data, text-based data can come in different forms. Examples of this include:

- a single word or a single sentence;

- large paragraphs of text out of context;

- unfavourable feedback that has no true reflection on the service or product.

Unlike other data formats, the punctuation and order in a sentence can impact the meaning. An example of this is seen in the following sentence: *I really hated how well the people at the front desk treated me. I am shocked!* When a simple analysis is performed on this sentence, for negative terms such as *hate*, the words surrounding this sentence *I really hated* may appear to be negative content directed toward the staff at the front desk. However, when the full context of the sentence is retained, we can see that it was a genuine compliment.

In each of the following sections, we will be working with text that may contain a single word, a single sentence, or a number of different sentences together. As this text has been entered by different users, no assumptions can be made about the format, content, or quality of the data. Some users may choose to use correct punctuation, while others may just create long sentences. These uncertainties are what add to the difficulty in processing text.

5.3   STOP WORDS

A single piece of text entered by a user contains two main varieties of terms: (1) terms that are useful to understand what the user is saying, or (2) terms that are used to join a sentence together.

Stop words are terms that are considered the glue in a sentence, example of stop words include: *as, the, it, on, which,* and *that*. Each of these terms does not describe anything particular to us. If these terms were removed from a piece of text, a person reading the text would still understand what the user is trying to say. Another example is the sentence *to be or not to be*, each term could be considered a stop word.

During analysis, these terms are often removed from the text before any further processing is performed. However, there is no official list of stop words. The length of the word does not necessarily mean that it is a stop word. However, stop words are frequently one and two characters long.

Issues often arise with stop words when the terms are essential. An example of this is the band name *The Who*. When stop words are removed, e.g., the term *The*, we would be left with the band titled *Who*. This can equally be seen with the band name *Take That*, both terms could be considered stop words. This further reinforces the reason as to why no official lists of stop words exist.

The InnoDB[1] storage engine for MySQL has a default collection of 36 different terms that it considers to be stop words. The Python NLTK library English stop word list contains 127 terms.[2]

The great variety in terms and the requirement of application-specific stop words often causes the need to have our own collection of stop words. This collection of terms can be appended to, or have terms removed, as tasks change.

When looking at a collection of terms, we often need to consider what case our text is in. An example of this is when our stop word list contains the term *the*, but the word in our sentence contains the word *The* with a capital *T*, we often find the need to take our text and convert it into a lower case during text processing to avoid missing the term.

Another consideration that needs to be made during the text processing stage is where the processing should be performed. We have a choice to perform these actions on the server-side using a language such as PHP that places the burden on the server, or we can choose to use a client-side language such as JavaScript and place the burden on the user's web browser.

Another interesting element of feedback is the use of swear words inside of text. Often swear words do not add any great taste to data, but we often have a choice of removing these swear words from the text (for the sake of the analyst). As we all know, there are many common swear words, but often the list of swear words expands as people become more creative with methods or slurs to add to their text. Like stop words, there is no official list of swear words, but there are a number of different locations where lists of swear words can be obtained. Such as:

- https://www.cs.cmu.edu/ biglou/resources/bad-words.txt

- https://en.wiktionary.org/wiki/Category:English_swear_words

As swear words can often be portrayed in a positive or negative sense, it may or may not be relevant to the task to remove them from the text. If they do appear, they may be an attempt of a person to convey a severe dissatisfaction with a service or experience.

---

[1] https://dev.mysql.com/doc/refman/8.0/en/innodb-storage-engine.html
[2] https://www.nltk.org

Example 1: JavaScript stop word function

As stop words can be removed on both the client-side and the server-side, in this section we describe a JavaScript-based approach.

Example code: stopwords.html

In Sample Code 1, on line 3, a reference to the jQuery content delivery network (CDN) is first included. This will be used for selecting *div* tags on the page later. On line 7, a variable is created titled *sampleSentence* that contains a sentence with stop words included. On line 8, a new function is created titled *stripStopWords()*. This function takes a single variable titled *input*. This variable is in a unprocessed state.

Inside of this function on line 9, a placeholder variable is added that will be used as the location where the cleaned data will be placed as stop words are removed from the original *input*. On line 10, a JavaScript array is created that contains each of the MySQL stop words as individual elements of the array. After this on line 15, the *input* variable that was passed into the function is split based on the spaces between the words and placed into an array titled *termArray*.

Once we have each individual term inside of the *termArray*, we then begin the process of detecting if the stop words are present inside of the input. This is done by using a *for loop* to iterate over each term inside of the term array. For each iteration of the *for loop* on line 17, a term is pulled from the *termArray* at position *i*. This variable *i* references the current position in the array. The term is taken and placed inside of a temporary variable titled *currentTerm*.

On line 18, a simple *if statement* is used to check if the term we are currently processing can be found inside of the stop word list. This is done by using the *indexOf()* function that is part of the JavaScript array. If a positive number is returned, this identifies the word was present, if a negative is returned, that means the word was not present.

In the case that the term was not present, on line 20, the *currentTerm* is appended on to the *cleaned* variable. It is important to remember to add a space before the current term is appended. Otherwise, all terms would appear together. At the very end of this function, on line 24, a simple *return* statement is added to return the cleaned string to the function caller.

On lines 27–32, at the bottom of the page, to provide an output in the web browser, two *div* tags are created, one that contains the *ID output1* and another with the *ID output2*. To test the function on line

33, first we will use the jQuery selector to select the *div* tag with the *ID output1* and append variable *sampleSentence* in its original form. After we have done this on line 35, we will then create a variable titled *cleaned*, that will be used to store the results after making a call to the *stripStopWords()* function that is passed the *sampleSentence* variable. Once the cleaned variable has a result, the output is appended to the second *div* tag with the *ID* set to *output2* on line 36.

```
1   <head>
2       <script
3       src="http://code.jquery.com/jquery-3.5.1.min.js"
4       crossorigin="anonymous"></script>
5   </head>
6   <script>
7   var sampleSentence = "what a great night I loved the food";
8   function stripStopWords(input){
9       var cleaned = '';
10      var stopwords = ["a","about","an","are","as","at","be","by",
11      "com","de","en",
12      "for","from","how","i","in","is","it","la","of","on","or",
13      "that","the","this","to","was","what","when","where","who",
14      "will","with","und","the","www"];
15      var termArray = input.split(" ");
16      for (i = 0; i < termArray.length; i++) {
17          var currentTerm = termArray[i];
18          if(stopwords.indexOf(currentTerm) >= 0){
19          } else {
20              cleaned += " " + currentTerm;
21          }
22
23      }
24      return cleaned;
25  }
26  </script>
27  <div id = "output1">
28      <b>Before Filter:</b>
29  </div>
30  <div id = "output2">
31      <b>After Filter:</b>
32  </div>
33  <script>
34  $('#output1').append(sampleSentence);
35  var cleaned = stripStopWords(sampleSentence);
```

```
36   $('#output2').append(cleaned);
37   </script>
```

SAMPLE CODE 1: stopwords.html — JavaScript stop word function.

Output
Once this has been performed, inside of the web browser we can see the original string and the string after it has been processed shown in Figure 5.1.

Before Filter: what a great night i loved the food
After Filter: great night loved food

FIGURE 5.1: Before and after stop-word removal with JavaScript.

In the *After Filter* result, we still retain the original descriptive terms that are core to the feedback, but the terms that do not add any value to the description have been removed. At any stage, if there were terms that we do not want to see as part of the output, we can simply add these custom stop words into the original stop word array.

Example 2: PHP stop-word function
In place of this client-side based filter, we can perform the same action on the server-side using PHP. As records are often retrieved from the database using PHP, it provides us with a good opportunity to perform this sanitization.

Example code: stopwords.php
In Sample Code 2, a new PHP page is created. On line 2, a new function is created titled *stripStopWords()*. This function takes a single parameter titled *input*, that contains the text to be processed.

On line 3, a variable title *cleaned* is added as a place holder for the final cleaned string after processing. On line 4, a PHP array is created that contains each of the individual stop words we wish to remove if present.

On line 8, the string input is broken into array format using the *explode()* function that takes in two parameters. The first is the delimiter used to break the string. As we are working with a string, this will be a single space. The second parameter is the *input* variable that has been sent to the function. This input is converted into lower case before the stop word detection process is started.

Two loops are used to begin processing. On line 9, the first loop that is placed on the outside and is used to iterate over each individual item inside the *inputArray*. Each term is placed into the *inputword* variable temporarily. A flag titled *isStopWord* is first set to *False* on line 10. As at the time of processing the term has not been identified as a stop word.

On line 11, a second internal loop is started that takes each individual term inside of the *stopwords* array and compares it to the *inputword* being processed. At any stage if the term is equal to a stop word then the *isStopWord* flag is set to *True* on line 13.

After the stop word loop has finished a simple if statement is used on line 16 to check if the *isStopWord* variable is set to *False*. If it still remains False then the input term is appended to the *cleaned* variable on line 17. After both loops have finished processing the *cleaned* string is returned back to the function caller on line 20.

To run this example a variable title *input* is created that contains a string on line 23. The input is printed to the web browser using an *echo* statement. On line 25, a call is made to the *stripStopWords()* function and the input variable is passed. The *result* variable is used to hold the cleaned string that is returned. On line 26, this string is printed to the console with the stop words removed.

```php
1   <?php
2   function stripStopWords($input){
3       $cleaned = '';
4       $stopwords = array("a","about","an","are","as","at","be",
5       "by","com","de","en", "for","from","how","I","in","is","it",
6       "la","of","on","or", "that","the","this","to","was","what",
7       "when","where","who", "will","with","und","the","www");
8       $inputArray = explode(' ', strtolower($input));
9       foreach ($inputArray as $inputword) {
10          $isStopWord = False;
11          foreach ($stopwords as $word) {
12              if($inputword == $word){
13                  $isStopWord = True;
14              }
15          }
16          if($isStopWord == False){
17              $cleaned .= ' ' . $inputword;
18          }
19      }
```

```
20      return $cleaned;
21  }
22
23  $input = 'I am really happy with the service';
24  echo 'Input:' . $input . '<br>';
25  $result = stripStopWords($input);
26  echo 'Result: '. $result;
```

SAMPLE CODE 2: stopwords.php — PHP stop word function.

Output

Figure 5.2 shows the input and output after stop word removal using PHP.

> Input: I am really happy with the service
> Result: am really happy service

FIGURE 5.2: stopwords.php — Before and after stop-word removal with PHP.

5.4   RED-FLAG MONITORING

Similar to stop words, red flags can be considered terms of interest in a piece of text. A red flag may be a term that is rarely mentioned, but when it is, it should be identified. This can be useful when working with larger collections of text as the size can make reading individual pieces of text a difficult process.

Example 3: Red-flag dashboard option

This example consists of four files and two libraries:

1. redflag_comments.sql — This is the create code for the database table that contains sample comments.

2. redflagterms.sql — This is the database table that contains the list of terms that are identified as red flags.

3. dashboard.php — The original dashboard with additional red flag modal.

4. redFlags.php — Additional file that is dynamically called using jQuery to render the selected records with highlighted red flag terms.

5. jQuery — This is used to select elements on the page and perform AJAX *POST* requests

6. jQueryUI — This is used to provide an interactive date picker.

A red flag may be a term that can be a cause of concern for a business. Before the process begins, we will create a sample collection of words that we consider red flags. The terms used in this example include *staff* and *breakfast*.

Example code: redflag_comments.sql
To begin, we will create a simple table titled *redflags_comments* that will contain our test data as shown in Sample Code 3. This table contains a *ID* column that is unique, and a column titled *mytime* that has a record of when the comment was left. A *comment* column is added to store the text gathered from users during the feedback process. An additional column titled *cid* is added. This will contain the *ID* number for this individual campaign.

```sql
1  CREATE TABLE `redflag_comments` (
2       `id` INT NOT NULL AUTO_INCREMENT,
3       `mytime` DATETIME NOT NULL DEFAULT CURRENT_TIMESTAMP,
4       `comments` TEXT,
5       `cid` INT,
6       PRIMARY KEY (`id`)
7  );
```

SAMPLE CODE 3: *redflag_comments* table SQL.

As each different campaign may have a different collection of terms that are considered red flags, a table titled *redflagterms* is created as shown in Sample Code 6. Each individual term is stored as a row in this table along with the the campaign *ID* in the *cid* column.

```sql
1  CREATE TABLE `redflagterms` (
2       `id` INT NOT NULL AUTO_INCREMENT,
3       `term` VARCHAR(50),
4       `cid` INT,
5       PRIMARY KEY (`id`)
6  );
```

SAMPLE CODE 4: redflagterms table.

To provide a working example, this database table will be filled with sample data as shown in Figure 5.3.

	timestamp	comments	cid
1	2018-08-05 10:24:29	The staff are horrible here, I am really not hap...	1
2	2019-08-05 10:24:51	The staff have been great, I am really not hap...	1
3	2019-08-05 10:25:09	I was five minutes late and they said i can not ...	1
4	2019-08-05 10:25:37	The breakfast was great.	1
5	2019-08-05 10:25:43	More coffee is needed at breakfast time. How ...	1
6	2019-08-05 21:09:23	breakfast was good but the staff are great	1

FIGURE 5.3: Sample comment records.

Example code: dashboard.php

Building on the dashboard that was described in Chapter 4, additional HTML and JavaScript is added to include a new option to show red flags in text. In Sample Code 5, to present the options to the user a Bootstrap modal is created. On line 2, the *ID* of the modal is set to *selectRanges*. On line 15, a *div* tag is added with the *class* set to *modal-body*. This is the main location where content will be placed. In this tag, we will provide the user with two different jQueryUI date pickers that will allow the user to choose a date range for the analysis process. On line 16, 21 and 26, *div* tags are added to create individual rows. On line 17, the text *Start Date:* is added inside a *div* tag with the class set to *col*. On line 18 and 23, input fields are added that will be converted into date pickers using jQueryUI. A third field is added on line 28, to allow the user to enter in the *CID* of interest. A *Show Red Flags* button is added on line 35. The *onclick* attribute is set to call the *showRedFlags()* JavaScript function described later.

```
1   <!---- Red Flag Modal -->
2   <div class="modal fade" id="selectRanges" tabindex="-1"
3    role="dialog" aria-labelledby="selectRanges"
4    aria-hidden="true">
5     <div class="modal-dialog" role="document">
6       <div class="modal-content">
7         <div class="modal-header">
8           <h5 class="modal-title" id="addAtt">Select Date Ranges
9           </h5>
10          <button type="button" class="close" data-dismiss="modal"
11           aria-label="Close">
```

```
12          <span aria-hidden="true">&times;</span>
13        </button>
14      </div>
15      <div class="modal-body">
16          <div class="row">
17              <div class="col-3">Start Date:</div>
18              <div class="col"><input type="text" id=
19              "startDate"></div>
20          </div>
21          <div class="row">
22              <div class="col-3">End Date:</div>
23              <div class="col"><input type="text" id=
24              "endDate"></div>
25          </div>
26          <div class="row">
27              <div class="col-3">CID:</div>
28              <div class="col"> <input type="text" id=
29              "selectedCID"></div>
30          </div>
31      </div>
32      <div class="modal-footer">
33        <button type="button" class="btn btn-secondary"
34        data-dismiss="modal">Close</button>
35        <button onclick="showRedFlags()" type="button"
36        class="btn btn-primary">Show Red Flags</button>
37      </div>
38    </div>
39  </div>
40 </div>
41 <!---- end red flag modal -->
```

SAMPLE CODE 5: dashboard.php — Select date ranges and campaign *ID* of interest.

In Sample Code 6, a short hand for the *document ready* function is added on line 43. On line 44, the jQuery selector is used to select the *startDate* input field. A call is made to the datePicker() jQueryUI function to convert the input field into a date picker. On line 45, the date format that is being used is set to *yy-mm-dd*. On line 47 and 48, the same process is repeated for the *endDate* input field.

On line 51, the *showRedFlags()* function is added. This is the main function that is called when the *Show Red Flags* button is clicked on the modal. In this function on line 52, the start date of interest is gathered followed by the end date on line 53. As there may be a number of campaigns running, on line 54 the unique *cid* of interest is extracted. On line 55, if the *redFlags div* tag is already on the dashboard it will be removed by using the jQuery selector to select the *redFlags div* tag followed by a call to the *remove()* function.

On line 56, the *output div* tag is selected using the jQuery selector. This is the main *div* tag in the center of the dashboard. A call is made to the *load()* function that dynamically retrieves the contents of a file. In this example, the *redFlags.php* page is called that is responsible for rendering the output. The *cid*, *start*, and *end* variables are passed via the URL to this page. The output of this page will be gathered and placed into the *output div* tag.

```
42   <script>
43   $( function() {
44       $( "#startDate" ).datepicker({
45           dateFormat: 'yy-mm-dd',
46       });
47       $( "#endDate" ).datepicker({
48           dateFormat: 'yy-mm-dd',
49       });
50   } );
51   function showRedFlags(){
52       var start = $('#startDate').val();
53       var end = $('#endDate').val();
54       var cid = $('#selectedCID').val();
55       $('#redflags').remove();
56       $('#output').append(($('<div>')
57       .load("redFlags.php?cid="+cid+"&start="+start+"&end="+end)));
58
59   }
60   </script>
```

SAMPLE CODE 6: dashboard.php — JavaScript to convert input field into date pickers and showRedFlags() function.

Output

In the dashboard, when the item called *Text Analysis* is clicked a menu titled *View Red Flags* becomes available, as shown in Figure 5.4. In Figure 5.5 the layout of the modal can be seen. When the user clicks on either of the input boxes, the date picker will then become visible, as shown in Figure 5.6. The values they select will be populated into the *input* fields.

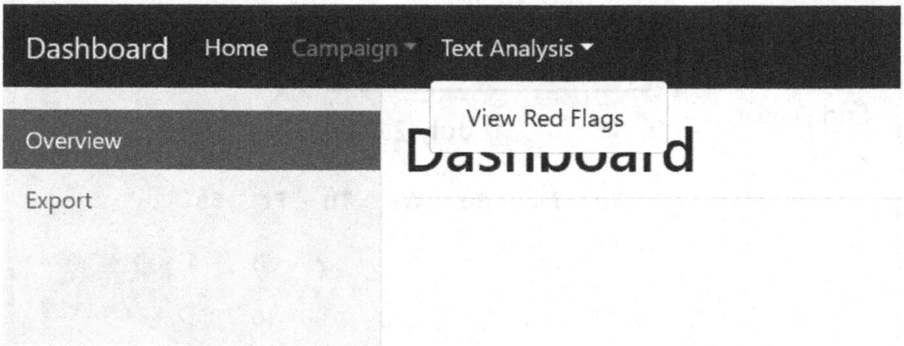

FIGURE 5.4: View red-flags menu option.

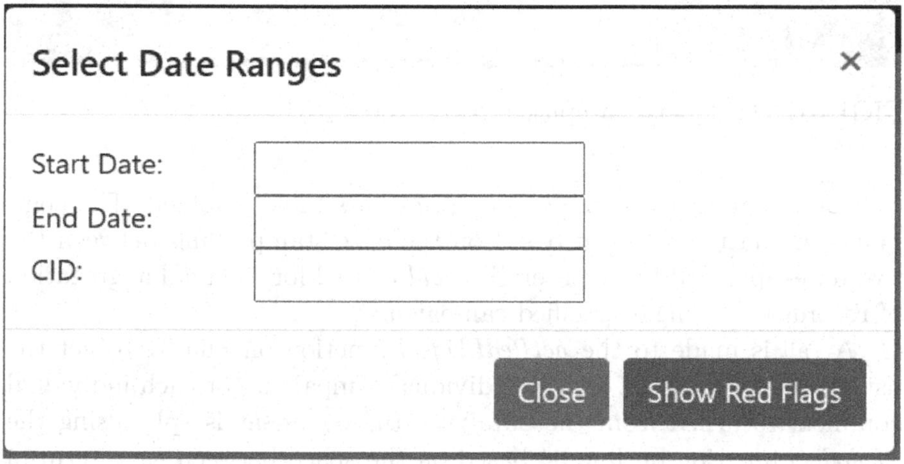

FIGURE 5.5: Select date and CID modal.

Example code: redFlags.php
The core of this process is held in the *redFlags.php* page. In Sample Code 7, at the top of this page on lines 2–4, the *start* date, *end* date, and *cid* are gathered from the *GET* request. A new *div* tag is output to the page on line 5. The *start* date, *end* date, and *CID* are echoed to the page on line 6. A call is made to the *getData()* function on line 9, that is responsible for gathering the data.

The *getData()* function is defined on line 12. Inside this function, on line 19, a connection is made to the database. On line 21, the SQL

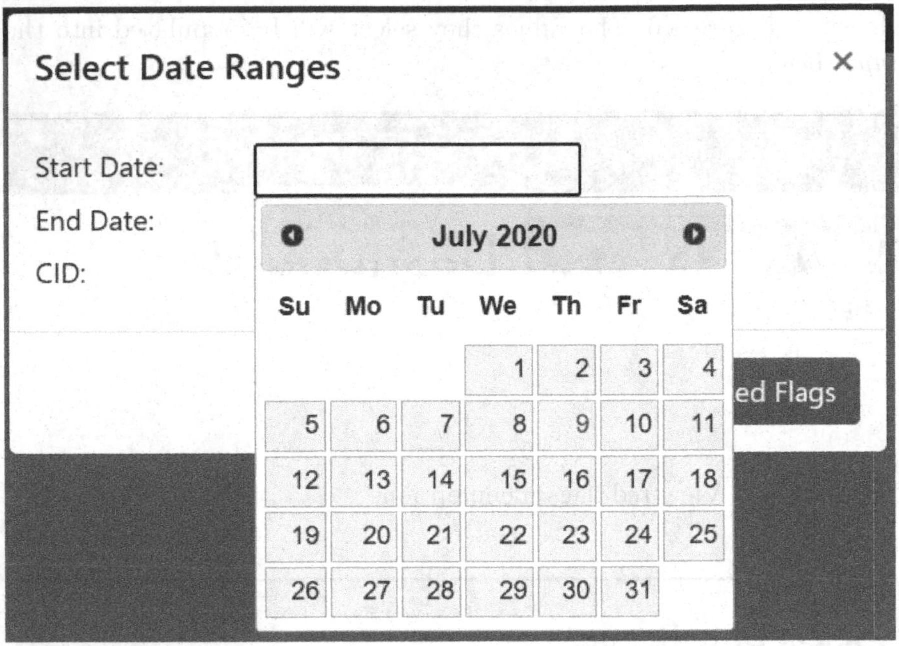

FIGURE 5.6: jQuery datepicker.

SELECT statement to the *redflag_comments* table is added. The comments are narrowed down based on the date stamp being between the two dates specified by the user. The *cid* is used for the final aggregation of records for a single specified campaign.

A call is made to the *getRedFlags()* function on line 31 to get the list of specific red flags for the individual campaign. For each individual comment returned from the database, the comment is split using the *explode()* function on line 34 based on the space between each term in the comment. Each individual term is put into lower case.

On line 39, a PHP variable titled *output* is added that will be appended to as each comment is iterated through. On line 37, a single *inputWord* from the comment is compared against the *redFlags* array. This is done by using the PHP *in_array()* function that checks to see if a given term exists in the provided array.

On line 39, If the term currently under analysis exists inside of the *redFlags* array, then the color of the term is set to *red* using a small amount of CSS styling. If the term is not, it is simply appended to the string. The final result is printed to the browser using a PHP *echo*.

```php
1   <?php
2   $start = $_GET['start'];
3   $end =   $_GET['end'];
4   $cid =   $_GET['cid'];
5   echo '<div id="redflags">';
6   echo '<b>Start:</b> ' . $start . ' - <b>End date:</b> ' . $end.'
7   - <b>CID:</b> '.$cid.'<br>';
8   echo '<hr>';
9   getData();
10  echo' </div>';
11
12  function getData(){
13     global $start,$end, $cid;
14     try {
15          $host = 'localhost:3306';
16          $dbname = 'test';
17          $user = 'root';
18          $pass = '3C9038A509BE6145AAD6827B4568AD918BC3DAC0';
19          $DBH = new PDO("mysql:host=$host;dbname=$dbname", $user,
20           $pass);
21          $sql = "SELECT * FROM redflag_comments WHERE mytime
22           BETWEEN ?
23           AND ? AND cid = ?";
24          $sth = $DBH->prepare($sql);
25          $sth->bindParam(1, $start, PDO::PARAM_STR);
26          $sth->bindParam(2, $end, PDO::PARAM_STR);
27          $sth->bindParam(3, $cid, PDO::PARAM_INT);
28          $sth->execute();
29          $res = $sth->fetchAll();
30          // Get the list of red flags from the database
31          $redFlags = getRedFlags($cid);
32          foreach ($res as $row){
33              $comment = $row[2];
34              $inputArray = explode(' ', strtolower($comment));
35              $output = '';
36              foreach ($inputArray as $inputWord) {
37                  $isFlag = in_array($inputWord, $redFlags);
38                  if($isFlag){
39                      $output .= '<span style="color:red"> ' .
40                       $inputWord . '</span> ';
41                  } else {
42                      $output .= ' ' . $inputWord;
43                  }
44              }
45              echo $output . '<br>';
```

```
46          }
47      } catch(PDOException $e) {echo $e;}
48  }
```

SAMPLE CODE 7: redFlags.php — Identifying red flag terms — part 1.

In Sample Code 8, to get a list of unique red flags for each campaign, a custom *getRedFlags()* function is created that takes a single parameter title *cid*. At the top of this function, an array titled *flags* is added on line 45. A connection to the database is performed on line 51.

On line 53, a *SELECT* statement is created to select data from the *redflagterms* table. The results are narrowed by returning those only with the *cid* equal to the one provided to the function. For each term, on line 59, they are appended to the *flags* array that is returned on line 63 and used as the source of red flags during the analysis of each comment.

```
44  function getRedFlags($cid){
45      $flags = array();
46      try {
47          $host = 'localhost:3306';
48          $dbname = 'test';
49          $user = 'root';
50          $pass = '3C9038A509BE6145AAD6827B4568AD918BC3DAC0';
51          $DBH = new PDO("mysql:host=$host;dbname=$dbname", $user,
52           $pass);
53          $sql = "SELECT term FROM redflagterms WHERE cid = ?";
54          $sth = $DBH->prepare($sql);
55          $sth->bindParam(1, $cid, PDO::PARAM_STR);
56          $sth->execute();
57          $res = $sth->fetchAll();
58          foreach ($res as $row){
59              array_push($flags, $row[0]);
60          }
61      } catch(PDOException $e) {echo $e;}
62
63      return $flags;
64  }
```

SAMPLE CODE 8: redFlags.php — Retrieving a lit of red-flag terms — part 2.

Dashboard

Start: 2018-01-08 - **End date:** 2020-01-01 - **CID:** 1

the staff are horrible here, i am really not happy.

the staff have been great, i am really not happy about the pool.

i was five minutes late and they said i can not have breakfast

the breakfast was great.

more coffee is needed at breakfast time. how can i work without it?

breakfast was good but the staff are great

FIGURE 5.7: Each comment is output with the red flag terms highlighted.

Output

In Figure 5.7 a list of comments that were stored in the database can be seen. Each red flag term is highlighted in red. The *Start date* and *End date* selected by the user are also shown along with the campaign *ID* shown as *CID*.

5.5 N-GRAMS

When working with text-based data, a common practice that is performed is the process of creating *n-grams*. Before this process is introduced, we will first begin with an overview of the structure of a document. A document D consists of P individual paragraphs. Each paragraph can contain S individual sentences, each of which contains W words. Each individual sentence, contains words from $W_0...W_y$.

Although documents can be viewed as a collection of independent terms, the context around these terms can provide valuable insight into how the term was used. When considering the sentence *I was shocked, the service was great!*, if term frequency was performed on this sentence,

TABLE 5.1: Sample n-grams with $N{=}2$

the staff
staff are
are horrible
horrible here
here i
i am
am really
really not
not happy

TABLE 5.2: Sample n-grams with $N{=}3$

the staff are
staff are horrible
are horrible here
horrible here i
here i am
i am really
am really not
really not happy

the weight for each term would be one as each term was present only once. If these terms were taken without context, the term *shocked* would be seen as a negative term as no additional context is provided.

As a solution to this, n-grams can be generated. N-grams take a sentence, S, as input that contains terms $W_0...W_y$. The n-gram algorithm takes a parameter, N, identifying how many terms should be included in an individual gram sequence. During the n-gram process, different values for N can produce vastly different results. Bi-grams are when the N is set to 2. For the sentence *the staff are horrible here I am really not happy*, Table 5.1 shows the output when $N = 2$.

Tri-grams is when $N = 3$. Unlike the previous examples, tri-grams include a large body of context. Table 5.2 shows the output when $N = 3$.

Example 4: Generating n-grams
The advantage of using n-grams during the data analysis process is the additional context around a term is retained. This is especially useful when the number of records exceeds that of a manual review process.

Example code ngram.php

Sample Code 9 describes a simple n-gram approach. The *sentence* variable on line 2 holds the sentence to be processed. To break the sentence into individual tokens, the *explode()* function is used on line 3. This function takes two quotation marks with a single space between them. This is the *delimiter* and is used as the token in which the sentence split on. The second variable that is passed is the *sentence* variable containing the text.

As we will be processing any number of grams, a variable titled *gram* is added on line 4. In the case of $N = 2$ for the sentence *This is a sample sentence* the *gram* variable will first contain the term *The* followed by a space and then the second term *staff* will be added. As the number to grams added will be equal to 2, the gram will be printed, and the variable will be cleared, allowing it to be reused for the next iteration.

This piece of code contains two loops, the first on line 6 loop will iterate over each individual term, while on a single term, Y number of grams will be added using the loop on line 8. A small internal variable titled *counter* on line 9 is used to keep track of the number of grams that have been added. When the counter is equal to the desired number of tokens, the *gram* variable is printed to the browser, followed by a *br* tag to break onto the next line. This variable is cleared, and then the loop is broken using the *break* statement on line 14. This will then allow the outside loop to progress on to the next term. This piece of code can be used for any number of gram sequences by modifying the *n* variable.

```php
1   <?php
2   $sentence = 'The staff are horrible here';
3   $tokens = explode(' ', $sentence);
4   $gram = '';
5   $n = 2;
6   for ($x = 0; $x <= sizeof($tokens) -1; $x++) {
7       $counter = 0;
8       for ($y = $x; $y <= sizeof($tokens) -1; $y++) {
9           $counter++;
10          $gram .= ' ' . $tokens[$y];
11          if($counter == $n){
12              echo $gram . '<br>';
13              $gram='';
14              break;
15          }
```

```
16       }
17   }
```

SAMPLE CODE 9: ngram.php — PHP N-gram algorithm.

Output

Figure 5.8 shows the n-gram output where N=2 for the sentence *The staff are horrible here.*

The staff
staff are
are horrible
horrible here

FIGURE 5.8: Sample n-gram output with $N=2$.

5.6 SENTENCE COMPLETION

When working with large quantities of user comments, often an overlap can be seen in specific words that are used together. An example of this can be seen with the word *staff* in the following comments:

1. The staff are great.

2. I had fun. The staff made the experience even better.

3. Good food, but the staff were nasty.

All three comments are outlining how the customer felt about the staff, however, the last comment was negative. This can be beneficial during analysis as comments about one topic, e.g., the staff, may prompt the start of an investigation to see why that one particular piece of negative feedback was left.

The issue that is presented however, is how to view this data. The small piece of information about the staff may be hidden in a larger paragraph or body of the text. The use of sentence completion can greatly enhance how text is analyzed, trimming the irrelevant text before the terms of interest occur, leaving only the relevant text. This is done by first starting with a single term, or set of terms that are considered the *stem* of the sentence.

Example 5: Sentence completion

This example contains two files:

1. create.sql — This file is used to create the *feedback_wild* database table.

2. completion.php — This files provides an example of sentence completon being used.

Example code: create.sql

To begin, Sample Code 10 starts with a simple SQL table titled *feedback_wild*. This table contains a column titled *feedback* that is used to hold sample records for the sentence completion process.

```
1   CREATE TABLE IF NOT EXISTS `feedback_wild` (
2     `id` INT NOT NULL AUTO_INCREMENT,
3     `mytime` datetime NOT NULL DEFAULT CURRENT_TIMESTAMP,
4     `feedback` text,
5     PRIMARY KEY (`id`)
6   );
```

SAMPLE CODE 10: feedback_wild database table.

Example code: completion.php

In Sample Code 11, a connection to the database is first made on line 7. A variable titled *rootWords* is added on line 9. This variable contains the term of interest. In this example, we are searching for the word *staff*. On line 10, a fragment of SQL is created. A percentage sign is added to the start and end of the *rootWords* variable and placed into a new variable titled *likeString*. The percentage sign indicates that the term can be found anywhere inside of a feedback record, e.g., start with, end with or in the middle of a sentence.

On line 11, a SQL query is created with a question mark for the value of the LIKE. An unnamed placeholder is used, shown as a question mark in the query. During the call to the *execute()* function on line 13, the prepared *rootWords* variable is passed in the form of the *likeString*.

Once the query has been executed, on line 14, a *while* loop is used to iterate over the records that have been identified. On line 15, the text data stored in the *feedback* column is placed into a local variable titled *record*. After this on line 16, the *strpos()* function is used to identify the index of where the first occurrence of the term *staff* was found.

On line 17, a call is made to the *substr()* function. This function takes three parameters. The first is the variable that contains the text we wish to process. The second is the starting index we wish to begin processing from. Finally, the third parameter contains the index number where we wish to stop at. In this example, this index is set to be the length of the *record* variable that is found using the *strlen()* function. The result of the *substr()* is printed to the browser using a simple *echo* statement.

```php
1   <?php
2   try {
3         $host = '127.0.0.1:3306';
4         $dbname = 'test';
5         $user = 'root';
6         $pass = '3C9038A509BE6145AAD6827B4568AD918BC3DAC0';
7         $DBH = new PDO("mysql:host=$host;dbname=$dbname", $user,
8          $pass);
9         $rootWords = 'staff';
10        $likeString = '%' . $rootWords . '%';
11        $stmt = $DBH->prepare("SELECT * FROM feedback_wild WHERE
12         feedback LIKE ?");
13        $stmt->execute([$likeString]);
14        while ($row = $stmt->fetch(PDO::FETCH_ASSOC)) {
15            $record = $row['feedback'];
16            $start = strpos($record, "staff");
17            echo substr($record ,$start, strlen($record)).'<br>';
18        }
19   } catch(PDOException $e) {echo $e;}
```

SAMPLE CODE 11: completion.php — Sentence completion for the term *staff*.

Output

Figure 5.9 shows an example of the term *staff* being found at the start and the middle of sentences. All text that was before the term of interest is disregarded, leaving only the term of interest followed by the rest of the sentence.

> staff are horrible here, I am really not happy.
> staff have been great, I am really not happy about the pool.
> staff are great

FIGURE 5.9: Result of searching for the word *staff* inside a feedback records.

5.7 WORD STEMMING

When processing terms, often they can have a different suffix depending on how the word is being used. For the term *house*, if this is used in a sentence, it is common to see variations such as *Houses, House,* and *Housing.* The issue with this, however, is if any calculations are being performed, e.g., counting the number of times the word was found, often the other variations of the term will be missed.

Example 6: Word stemming

To prevent this from happening, when working with collections of text *stemming* can be performed. This is the process of reducing the term back to the word stem. Many different approaches can be taken when stemming. One example of a stemming tool is the Porter Stemmer. In this example, we will be working with a PHP implementation of this algorithm.[3]

This example contains two files:

1. stemming.php — A sample instance of the Porter stemming being used.

2. PorerStemmer — An instance of the stemming algorithm.

Example code: stemming.php
In Sample Code 12, on line 2, the library is first added into the current page. The word to be stemmed is placed inside the *word* variable on line 3. This variable is passed to the *Stem* function on line 4. This function

---

[3]https://tartarus.org/martin/PorterStemmer/php.txt

returns the word stem that is printed to the page. The stemming process is completed for the terms *Houses, House,* and *Housing.* HTML *br* tags are used to break the output onto individual lines.

```php
1  <?php
2  require('PorterStemmer.php');
3  $word = 'Houses';
4  $stem = PorterStemmer::Stem($word);
5  echo $stem . '<br>';
6  $word = 'House';
7  $stem = PorterStemmer::Stem($word);
8  echo $stem . '<br>';
9  $word = 'Housing';
10 $stem = PorterStemmer::Stem($word);
11 echo $stem . '<br>';
```

SAMPLE CODE 12: stemming.php — Using the Porter Stemmer on three terms.

Output

Figure 5.10 shows the output of the stemming process. Although three different words were passed to the stemming algorithm, the same stem is returned after each call. This approach helps us identify that the three terms are all related.

Hous

Hous

Hous

FIGURE 5.10: Result after calling the stemming algorithm.

5.8 SYNONYMS

When reviewing feedback records, it can become apparent quickly that two reviews never contain a similar collection of phrases or terms. This can cause difficulty for any feedback processing that requires a match to be made between terms. An example of this can be seen when the term *chef* is used in one record and the term *cook* in another record. By developing a function to identify these synonyms, another dimension is added into the analysis process.

Example 7: BigHugeLabs.com API

In this example, we will outline the process of using the BigHuge-Labs.com API for synonyms of a given term. The first step in this process is to get an API key to access the service. They currently offer 500 requests per day for free. Additional calls to the service can be made for a modest fee. To get this key, an account is first created. Figure 5.11 describes the parameters needed to sign up for a key. A brief description of the application is added, followed by the URL where the requests will be coming from. As this is a test application, *localhost* was added for the URL.

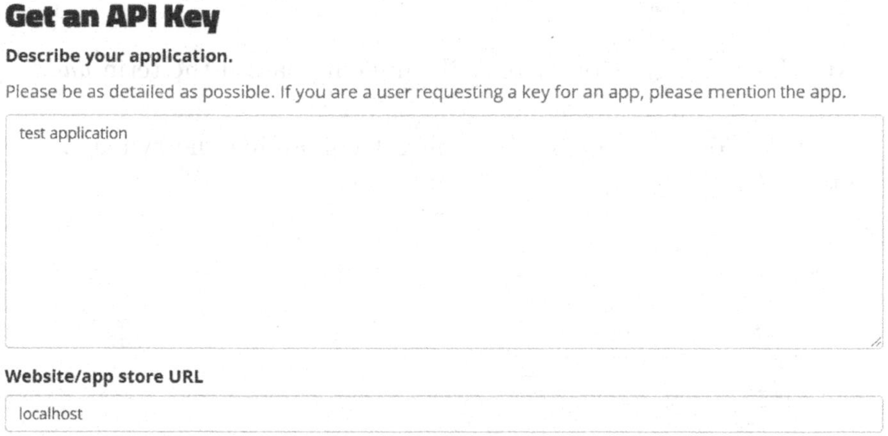

Get an API Key

Describe your application.

Please be as detailed as possible. If you are a user requesting a key for an app, please mention the app.

```
test application
```

Website/app store URL

```
localhost
```

FIGURE 5.11: BigHugeLabs.com API key creation process.

After the key creation has been completed, sample REST URLs are shown. Each of these passes the unique API key to the service along with a single word of interest. The difference in each API URL is the format in which the response is returned. Figure 5.12 shows the options available including plain text, XML or JSON.

Output

In Sample Code 13, the API URL is constructed. The first parameter that is passed is the unique API access key. The term *dad* is passed to the API as the term of interest. To aid the processing of the result */json* is appended to the end of the URL to retrieve the result in JSON format.

FIGURE 5.12: BigHugeLabs.com sample REST URLs.

```
https://words.bighugelabs.com/api/2/
0c7cc83b387027012538b959c8576cfb/dad/json
```

SAMPLE CODE 13: Complete API call being passed the term *dad*.

Sample Code 14 shows the result set containing the synonyms for the term *dad*.

```
1  {"noun":{
2    "syn":[
3      "dada",
4      "daddy",
5      "pa",
6      "papa",
7      "pappa",
8      "pop",
9      "begetter",
10     "father",
11     "male parent"
12   ]
13 }
14 }
```

SAMPLE CODE 14: Synonyms returned for the term *dad*.

When calculating the number of feedback records that contain the term *dad*, additional records can be included if any of the synonyms are found. Although a useful tool during analysis, some issues do exist. An example of this is the synonym for dad titled *pop*. As context is often removed during the processing of text, it can be difficult to identify if this is a reference to a person's *dad* or to the synonym for *soda* which is *pop*.

Example 8: PHP API request to Big Huge Lab's API

To provide access to the REST API from PHP we can use the *file_get_contents()* function. This allows us to pass the URL of the API that contains a single variable titled *term* that contains the term of interest.

Example code: syn.php

In Sample Code 15 on line 2, the term of interest is first defined. In this example, we are searching for synonyms of the term *dad*. On line 3, a call is made to the PHP *file_get_contents()* function. This function will make a *GET* request to the provided URL. The value of the variable *term* is substituted into the string. The contents of the page that is output is placed inside a local variable titled *result*.

The service will return JSON content. On line 5, to process the JSON, the result is passed to the *json_decode()* function. The *true* parameter is passed to ensure the result is returned as an associative array. On line 6, after the *decoded* variable is filled, we can pass a key to select the results from the array. The *noun* is the parent result. Inside this, the *syn* collection can be accessed.

Once we have accessed the *syn* results, a *foreach* statement is used to loop over each individual synonym on line 7. A simple *br* tag is added to break each result on to a new line when viewing the results in a web browser.

```php
1  <?php
2  $term = 'dad';
3  $result = file_get_contents("https://words.bighugelabs.com/api/2/"
4              ."0c7cc83b387027012538b959c8576cfb/$term/json");
5  $decoded = json_decode($result, true);
6  $syn = $decoded['noun']['syn'];
7  foreach($syn as $item){
8      echo $item . '<br>';
9  }
```

SAMPLE CODE 15: syn.php — Calling the BigHugeLabs API using PHP.

Output

Figure 5.13 shows the output after passing the term *dad* to the Big Huge Lab's synonym API.

dada
daddy
pa
papa
pappa
pop
begetter
father
male parent

FIGURE 5.13: Example synonyms returned from the Big Huge Labs API called via a *GET* request.

5.9 TERM WEIGHTING

In previous examples, text was gathered from the database and different tasks were performed directly on the text without any additional processing. One issue that can be seen with this approach is the scalability of the solutions. When working with a small number of records, the process of searching through the text can easily be performed and insights can be gathered. However, when hundreds or thousands of records are under analysis, any application of the data quickly becomes difficult as irrelevant text may become prominent in the results. For this reason, additional metrics to identify the importance of text can be applied.

Example 9: Term frequency

One simple approach that can be used to aid the analysis process is focused on applying weights to the individual terms. The most simplistic approach to this is to calculate the number of times each individual word has been found across all records. In this example, we will consider five individual records as shown in Table 5.3.

TABLE 5.3: Sample Records for Term Frequency

ID	Feedback
1	I was very happy with the product that I got in the mail. However, the package was handled badly.
2	I am very happy with the product that I got. I will come back again in the future.
3	There was a number of issues with the customer service of this company. I will take my business somewhere else. It was a bad experience.
4	I will never return. I was treated badly by the man on the front desk.
5	This is a great company, I will never go elsewhere.

Example code: tf.php

To calculate the term frequency for each word, a total count for each term across all records is performed.

In Sample Code 16, on lines 2–6 individual records are added as strings. On line 8, an array is created that will be used as the main storage place for the strings. On line 9–13, each individual string is added to the array. On line 14, a new array is created that will be used to hold all the individual terms. On line 15, a simple *foreach* statement is used to iterate over all the records. For each individual record, on line 17, the full stops and commas are removed from the string and replaced with spaces. On line 18, the *explode()* function is called to break the individual string into single terms every time a space is found.

On line 20, each individual term is added to the *allWords* array. Finally on line 24, a call is made to the *array_count_values()* function that will count the total occurrences of each term in the array. This output is printed to the browser using the *print_r()* function.

```
1  <?php
2  $doc1 = 'I was very happy with the product that I got in the
   ↪  mail. However, the package was handled badly.';
3  $doc2 = 'I am very happy with the product that I got. I will
   ↪  come back again in the future.';
4  $doc3 = 'There was a number of issues with the customer service
   ↪  of this company. I will take my business somewhere else. It
   ↪  was a bad experience.';
5  $doc4 = 'I will never return. I was treated badly by the man on
   ↪  the front desk.';
```

```
6   $doc5 = 'This is a great company, I will never go elsewhere.';
7
8   $documents = array();
9   array_push($documents, $doc1);
10  array_push($documents, $doc2);
11  array_push($documents, $doc3);
12  array_push($documents, $doc4);
13  array_push($documents, $doc5);
14  $allWords = array();
15  foreach($documents as $doc){
16      echo '----------docment----------<br>';
17      $cleaned = strtr($doc, array('.' => '', ',' => ''));
18      $terms = explode(' ', $cleaned);
19      foreach($terms as $term){
20          array_push($allWords, $term);
21
22      }
23  }
24  print_r(array_count_values($allWords));
```

SAMPLE CODE 16: tf.php — Sample term frequency calculation with PHP

Output

In this example, the term *badly* was seen once in record 1 and once in record 4. The term frequency for the term *badly*, therefore, would be set to two.

When processing these records, if the word *I* was counted, a value of 9 would be assigned. The issue with this can easily be seen, as very little insight can be gathered from this word. The raw term frequency can be considered naive for the purpose of calculating importance. In Table 5.4, a list of all the term frequency scores for words greater than one can be seen. Excluding the stop words that can be seen at the top of this table, interesting terms such as *badly*, *never*, and *happy* can be seen.

Example 10: Term frequency — Inverse Document Frequency

A modification of the raw term frequency is the Term Frequency — Inverse Document Frequency (TF-IDF). This term weighting scheme is focused on the assumption that terms that frequently appear across all documents should be given a lower score, and terms that are unique and

TABLE 5.4: Sample Term Frequency Scores

Count	Term
9	i
8	the
5	was
4	will
3	with
3	a
2	very
2	this
2	that
2	product
2	of
2	never
2	in
2	happy
2	got
2	company
2	badly

not seen as often should be given a higher score. This weighting scheme could be considered a direct solution to the issue of stop words that was seen with traditional term frequency calculations in the previous section. Table 5.5 describes two sample records for analysis.

TABLE 5.5: Sample Records for Term Frequency—Inverse Document Frequency

ID	Feedback
1	I was very happy with the product that I got in the mail. However, the package was handled badly.
2	I am very happy with the product that I got. I will come back again in the future.

The TF-IDF score for the term *mail* is calculated by first calculating the term frequency (tf) followed by the inverse document frequency (idf). *Mail* occurred once out of the 19 terms in document 1. The first piece of the equation is shown in Equation 5.1.

$$tf(mail, d1) = \frac{1}{19} = 0.05 \tag{5.1}$$

In document 2, the term frequency for *mail* is 0 out of the 18 words in the document as shown in Equation 5.2.

$$tf(mail, d2) = \frac{0}{18} = 0.0 \tag{5.2}$$

The inverse document frequency for the term *mail* is then calculated that takes into consideration the number of times the word appeared across all documents, *D*. In this example, out of the two documents, one document contained the term *mail*. The result is converted to logarithm base 10 as shown in Equation 5.3.

$$idf(mail, D) = log(\frac{2}{1}) = 0.301 \tag{5.3}$$

Once the term frequency has been calculated, and the inverse document frequency is calculated, both components of the equation can be brought together to form the TF-IDF score. For document 1, the TF-IDF is be calculated by multiplying the *tf* score by the *idf* score for the term *mail* as shown in Equation 5.4.

$$tfidf(mail, d1, d) = 0.05 \times 0.301 = 0.0158 \tag{5.4}$$

The TF-IDF for document 2 can then be calculated as shown in Equation 5.5.

$$tfidf(mail, d2, d) = 0.0 \times 0.301 = 0 \tag{5.5}$$

The resulting TF-IDF score is higher for less common words, providing a deeper insight into the terms that have been used. This approach naturally removes common stop words from the results as they often appear in the documents.

Example code: tfidf.php

Example 17 outlines a sample PHP TF-IDF algorithm. At the top of this example on lines 2 and 3, two simple feedback records are added with their original punctuation. On line 5, an array is created titled *documents* that is used to hold all documents that will be under consideration during the TF-IDF calculation process. On lines 6 and 7, the *array_push()* function is used to add the two documents onto the array.

To begin the process, a simple *foreach* statement is added on line 9 that is used to iterate over each document. On line 10, a simple line is added with a *br* tag appended to identify the document we are currently processing in the web browser. On line 11, the *strtr()* function is used to replace any occurrences of a full stop or comma with a space and place the result into the *cleaned* variable. On line 12, the *cleaned* is passed into the *explode()* function that takes the delimiter to break the string on. In this case, a space is passed, followed by a reference to the *cleaned* variable. This will leave a collection of individual terms inside the *terms* array.

On line 13, a simple call to the *count()* function is performed to find out how long the array is, e.g., how many terms we are working with. A second internal *foreach* statement is started to iterate over each individual term in the document. The *substr_count()* function is used to identify how many times the term appears in the document. The term under consideration, the *length* and the *count* are printed to the browser to aid debugging. The *tf* is calculated by taking the *count* and dividing it by the *length*.

On line 21, the *idf* is calculated by taking the log of the number of documents divided by the number of documents that contain the term under analysis. 10 is passed to the log function to return the answer in logarithm base 10. Finally, on line 23 the final TF-IDF score is generated by taking the *tf* value and multiplying it by the *idf* value. On line 24, a simple *echo* is used to print the score to the browser.

To aid the algorithm, on line 27, the body of the *countInDocs()* function can be seen. This function takes a single term and counts the number of documents that contain the term. At the end of this function, a *return* statement is added on line 35 to return the count.

```php
<?php
$doc1 = 'I was very happy with the product that I got in the
↪   mail. However, the package was handled badly.';
$doc2 = 'I am very happy with the product that I got. I will
↪   come back again in the future.';

$documents = array();
array_push($documents, $doc1);
array_push($documents, $doc2);

foreach($documents as $doc){
    echo '----------docment----------<br>';
    $cleaned = strtr($doc, array('.' => '', ',' => ''));
    $terms = explode(' ', $cleaned);
    $len = count($terms);
```

```
14    foreach($terms as $term){
15        $count  =substr_count($doc,$term);
16        echo ' term: ' .$term;
17        echo ' count: ' . $count;
18        echo ' length: ' . $len;
19        $tf = $count / $len;
20        echo ' - TF: ' . $tf;
21        $idf = log((count($documents) / countInDocs($term)),
          ↪  10);
22        echo ' IDF: ' . $idf;
23        $score = $tf * $idf;
24        echo ' - TF-IDF: ' . $score . '<br>';
25    }
26 }
27 function countInDocs($term){
28    global $documents;
29    $count = 0;
30    foreach($documents as $doc){
31        if(substr_count($doc,$term) > 0){
32            $count = $count + 1;
33        }
34    }
35    return $count;
36 }
```

SAMPLE CODE 17: tfidf.php — Sample PHP TF-IDF algorithm.

Output

Figure 5.14 shows the output for the first document during analysis by
the TF-IDF algorithm. For debugging, echo statements were added to
all calculations. In this output, we can see that the common terms that
were in both documents provided a lower TF-IDF score. Unique terms
have higher TF-IDF scores.

5.10   SENTIMENT ANALYSIS

When working with text, an additional opportunity is provided to gather
the overall *sentiment* of the text. The sentiment of a piece of text is the
categorization of a record into a defined category of *positive*, *negative*, or
neutral sentiment. Traditional statistic metrics such as ranges between
1–10 easily allow us to see if a user was satisfied or not with a service.
Working with text, however, is a little bit more difficult as the terms in a

```
----------docment----------
term: I count: 2 length: 19 - TF: 0.10526315789474 IDF 0 - TF-IDF: 0
term: was count: 2 length: 19 - TF: 0.10526315789474 IDF 0.30102999566398 - TF-IDF: 0.03168736796463
term: very count: 1 length: 19 - TF: 0.052631578947368 IDF 0 - TF-IDF: 0
term: happy count: 1 length: 19 - TF: 0.052631578947368 IDF 0 - TF-IDF: 0
term: with count: 1 length: 19 - TF: 0.052631578947368 IDF 0 - TF-IDF: 0
term: the count: 3 length: 19 - TF: 0.15789473684211 IDF 0 - TF-IDF: 0
term: product count: 1 length: 19 - TF: 0.052631578947368 IDF 0 - TF-IDF: 0
term: that count: 1 length: 19 - TF: 0.052631578947368 IDF 0 - TF-IDF: 0
term: I count: 2 length: 19 - TF: 0.10526315789474 IDF 0 - TF-IDF: 0
term: got count: 1 length: 19 - TF: 0.052631578947368 IDF 0 - TF-IDF: 0
term: in count: 1 length: 19 - TF: 0.052631578947368 IDF 0 - TF-IDF: 0
term: the count: 3 length: 19 - TF: 0.15789473684211 IDF 0 - TF-IDF: 0
term: mail count: 1 length: 19 - TF: 0.052631578947368 IDF 0.30102999566398 - TF-IDF: 0.015843683982315
term: However count: 1 length: 19 - TF: 0.052631578947368 IDF 0.30102999566398 - TF-IDF: 0.015843683982315
term: the count: 3 length: 19 - TF: 0.15789473684211 IDF 0 - TF-IDF: 0
term: package count: 1 length: 19 - TF: 0.052631578947368 IDF 0.30102999566398 - TF-IDF: 0.015843683982315
term: was count: 2 length: 19 - TF: 0.10526315789474 IDF 0.30102999566398 - TF-IDF: 0.03168736796463
term: handled count: 1 length: 19 - TF: 0.052631578947368 IDF 0.30102999566398 - TF-IDF: 0.015843683982315
term: badly count: 1 length: 19 - TF: 0.052631578947368 IDF 0.30102999566398 - TF-IDF: 0.015843683982315
```

FIGURE 5.14: Example TF-IDF output for each term in a single document.

sentence can easily be considered positive if specific keywords are used. These words may, however, be associated to a negative response.

Example 11: Sentiment analysis

Synonyms are words that represent the same meaning as other words. An example of this is the word *happy*, synonyms include *cheerful, content, delighted, elated,* and *joyful*. If a feedback record contained the text *delighted* we would want to make this record as having a positive sentiment. Instead of using manual synonym detection, a sentiment analysis tool can be used.

This example contains one file and one library:

1. sentiment.php — This page shows an example of the sentiment analysis tool being used.

2. PHPinsight — This library provides us with the ability to run the sentiment analysis process.

Example code: sentiment.php
To perform sentiment analysis in PHP we will use the *PHPinsight* package. This package is available from *https://packagist.org/packages/jwhennessey/phpinsight*. Instead of manually downloading files and then attempting to integrate them into the project, we will use *composer*.

From the command prompt in the root directory of our project, we will issue the following command:

composer require jwhennessey/phpinsight

SAMPLE CODE 18: Example composer require for PHPinsight.

In Sample Code 19, on line 2, a *pre* tag is used to format the generated output. On line 3, an array is added that contains the sentences that the sentiment analysis process will be run on. Additional sentences can be added into this array for analysis. On line 8, a reference to the *vendor* folder is added that contains PHPinsight. The *autoload.php* is used to pull in the required functionality from the library for the sentiment analysis process. A simple *foreach* statement is used on line 10 to loop over each individual string that has been added to the array. The *score()* function is used on line 12 to retrieve the sentiment scores. On line 13, the *categorise()* function is used to output the dominant result, e.g., *positive, negative* or *neutral* for the individual sentences.

```php
1  <?php
2  echo "<pre>";
3  $strings = array(
4      1 => 'I am very happy with the staff',
5      2 => 'I did not like the staff they are unhelpful',
6      3 => 'The food was bad',
7  );
8  require_once('vendor/autoload.php');
9  $sentiment = new \PHPInsight\Sentiment();
10 foreach ($strings as $string) {
11     // calculations:
12     $scores = $sentiment->score($string);
13     $class = $sentiment->categorise($string);
14     // output:
15     echo "String: $string\n";
16     echo "Dominant: $class, scores: ";
17     print_r($scores);
18     echo "\n";
19 }
```

SAMPLE CODE 19: sentiment.php — Gathering the sentiment of text using the PHPInsight library.

```
String: I am very happy with the staff
Dominant: pos, scores: Array
(
    [pos] => 0.5
    [neg] => 0.25
    [neu] => 0.25
)

String: I did not like the staff they are unhelpful
Dominant: neg, scores: Array
(
    [neg] => 0.5
    [pos] => 0.25
    [neu] => 0.25
)

String: The food was bad
Dominant: neg, scores: Array
(
    [neg] => 0.5
    [pos] => 0.25
    [neu] => 0.25
)
```

FIGURE 5.15: Result of the sentiment-analysis process.

Output

Figure 5.15 shows an example of the output of the sentiment analysis process. Three different scores ranges between 0.0 and 1.0 are shown. These show the positive, negative, and neutral score for each sentence. The dominant score can also be seen, indicating the overall highest out of all three categories.

5.11 SUMMARY

This chapter described the issues that can be seen when working with text. Unlike numeric values, text requires additional processing to remove irrelevant terms and regain focus on terms of relevance. The practical components of text processing were described, including stop word removal, red flag term identification, n-gram generation, stemming, and synonym detection.

As text can come in any size, retaining the focus on relevant terms can be difficult. To aid this process metrics such as term frequency (TF) and term frequency—inverse document frequency (TF-IDF) were discussed. To further analyze text, sentiment analysis was described allowing the positive, negative, and neutral scores of text to be identified.

Chapter 6, outlines the libraries available for creating dynamic interactive visualizations for text.

Text Visualization

6.1 INTRODUCTION

When working with small amounts of text, it can be easy to identify patterns and records of interest in a data set. However, the larger the data set becomes, the more difficult the analysis process becomes. This chapter describes various text visualization approaches that can easily be included in a project to enhance the data exploration process. For these visualizations, JavaScript-based libraries will be used such as D3.js[1], Charts.js[2] and HiCharts.[3]

6.2 WORD CLOUD

Example 1: Word cloud

One of the most simplistic but insightful visualizations possible is the word cloud. This allows a user to quickly view the key terms in a large body of text. A sentence is tokenized into individual terms where the frequency is used to dictate the size an individual word will be in the final visualisation. In this example, we will be working with the *wordcloud2.js* plug-in that is available from https://github.com/timdream/wordcloud2.js. Although the steps outlined in the documentation describe the process installing the library using node's npm, we will look at the manual installation and setup process as very little setup is required.

---

[1] https://d3js.org
[2] https://www.chartjs.org
[3] https://www.highcharts.com

This example requires two files:

1. wordcloud.html — This contains the main HTML and JavaScript to run the example.

2. wordcloud2.js — This is the core JavaScript library required to generate the visualization.

Example code: wordcloud.html

The first step in this process is downloading the *wordcloud2.js* file that can be found at https://github.com/timdream/wordcloud2.js. This single folder contains all the needed tools to create the word cloud. After this has been downloaded, we will create a new HTML file that will be used for holding the word cloud. In Sample Code 1, on line 1, a reference to the JavaScript file is first added, followed by a single *canvas* HTML tag on line 3 that is used to hold the generated word cloud. This tag is given a unique *ID*, which will be used in the next step.

On line 6, a simple JavaScript array is created that takes in a list of the terms to be represented in the cloud, along with the size each term should be in the cloud. In this example, no stop words have been removed. On line 8, an instance of the *WordCloud* is created. A reference to the *canvas* element that was created earlier is selected, and the list of terms is passed into the cloud.

```
1   <script src="wordcloud2.js">
2   </script>
3   <canvas id="my_canvas">
4   </canvas>
5   <script>
6   var list = [['this', 40], ['is', 20], ['my', 60], ['sample', 20],
7   ['chart', 60]];
8   WordCloud(document.getElementById('my_canvas'), { list: list } );
9   </script>
```

SAMPLE CODE 1: wordcloud.html — Sample code to generate a custom word cloud.

Output

After the file has been saved and opened using a web browser, Figure 6.1 shows the sample output that is generated. Each different term that is added to the cloud is represented in a different color. The size of the terms is dictated by the variables set in the array. Although this provides a working example of using a word cloud it does not dynamically take in a string of text or perform any calculation on the text to determine the number of occurrences of each term.

FIGURE 6.1: Sample word cloud without stop words removed.

Example 2: Dynamic word cloud

This example word cloud builds on the previous example. Instead of having hard-coded terms and sizes, they are dynamically generated based on an input string. This example requires two files:

1. wordcloud2.html — This contains the main HTML and JavaScript to run the example.

2. wordcloud2.js — This is the core JavaScript library required by the application.

Example code: wordcloud2.html

Sample Code 2 begins on line 1 with a reference to the *wordcloud2.js* file that is the driving force behind this visualization. A *canvas* tag is added on line 3 that will be the location for the visualization. The important element to retain here is the *ID* that is set to *my_canvas*. A *height* and *width* is set for the canvas.

On line 6, a variable titled *text_string* is added that contains the data that will be added to the visualization. A second string titled *common* is added on line 7 that is used to hold a collection of common terms, e.g., stop words that are separated by commas. This will act as a filter that will be applied to the visualization before it is rendered. As text may come in a number of different formats with different punctuation for separating terms, a Regular Expression pattern is used for the *split()* function on line 8 that is applied to the *text_string*. In this case, if a space, full stop or comma is encountered, it will then break on this token.

Two arrays are created on lines 9 and 10. The first of these is used to hold the terms, and the second is used to hold the count of the terms. The next process is to count the number of occurrences for each term in the *tokens* array that was generated after the *split()* function runs.

On line 11, a *for loop* is used to iterate over each element in the *tokens* array from 0 to the length of the *tokens* array. When this loop is running, one individual token will be taken from the *tokens* array and then forced into lower case to reduce duplication. The *trim()* function is called on each term to remove white space.

In the body of the *for loop*,on line 14, for each individual term, the *words* array is checked to see if the current term under analysis exists in it by using the *indexOf()* function. If the term does exist, on line 16, the term is pushed into the *words* array. On line 17, the value 1 is pushed on to the *wordsCount* array.

If the term does exist in the array, then the *else* statement on line 19 is run. To find where the word is stored, the *indexOf()* function for the individual term is used that will return the position of the term in the array that is stored in the *index* variable. This is passed directly into the *wordsCount* array on line 21 to retrieve the current value. On line 22, the current value is incremented by one and set into the *wordsCount* array at position *index*.

On lines 25–31, a simple *for loop* is used to iterate over the terms and the associated values and print them to the browser console to aid debugging. On line 33, a new array titled *list* is created that will be passed to the visualization. To populate this, a *for loop* iterates over each of the individual terms gathered in the *words* array. For each iteration, the value from *words* at position *i* is gathered on line 35, and on line 36, the *wordsCount* at position *i* is gathered. Both values are placed in local variables.

On line 38, the S pattern is used to specify that for anything but white space, the individual term will be pushed onto the *list* array. A check is also performed to ensure the term does not appear in the *common* string, which would indicate it is a stop word. On line 39, the term and value, e.g., the size of the term in the visualization, is the *count* of the term multiplied by 20.

Finally, on line 42, the canvas with the *ID* set to *my_canvas* is selected, and the *list* array is passed to it for rendering.

```
1  <script src="wordcloud2.js">
2  </script>
3  <canvas id="my_canvas" style="width:400px; height;300px">
4  </canvas>
5  <script>
6  var text_string = "I was very happy with the product that I got
↪    in the mail. However, the package was handled badly. I am
↪    very happy with the product that I got. I will come back
↪    again in the future. There was a number of issues with the
↪    customer service of this company. I will take my business
↪    somewhere else. It was a bad experience. I will never
↪    return. I was treated badly by the man on the front desk.
↪    This is a great company, I will never go elsewhere.";
7  var common = "i, you, me, is, was, of, a, with, that, in";
8  var tokens = text_string.split(/[ .,]/);
9  var words = new Array();
10  var wordsCount = new Array()
11  for (var i = 0; i < tokens.length; i++) {
12     var term = tokens[i].toLowerCase().trim();
13     console.log(term);
14     if(words.indexOf(term) == -1){
15        console.log("does not exist");
16        words.push(term);
17        wordsCount.push(1);
18     }
19     else {
20          var index = words.indexOf(term);
21          var currentValue = wordsCount[index];
22          wordsCount[index] = currentValue + 1;
23     }
24  }
25  for (var i = 0; i < words.length; i++) {
26     var term = words[i];
27     var count = wordsCount[i];
28     if(/\S/.test(term) != false){
29        console.log("term: " + term + " count" +count);
30     }
31  }
32  // viewing the resuls
33  var list = new Array();
34  for (var i = 0; i < words.length; i++) {
35     var term = words[i];
36     var count = wordsCount[i];
37
38     if(/\S/.test(term) != false && common.indexOf(term) == -1){
```

```
39        list.push([term,count*20]);
40    }
41  }
42  WordCloud(document.getElementById('my_canvas'), { list: list }
    ↪  );
43  </script>
```

SAMPLE CODE 2: wordcloud2.html — Sample word cloud with a
dynamic data source.

Output

Figure 6.2 shows the output of the dynamically created word cloud
based on term frequency.

FIGURE 6.2: Output from the dynamic generation of a word cloud
using term frequency.

Although this visualization provides great insights into the data at
a glance, the larger the data set becomes the more difficult the visualization process becomes. Considerations should be made to remove stop
words before the visualization process is started as these can easily build
up the bulk of the content. The second consideration needed is to use a
metric to assign a weight to individual terms of interest.

6.3 COLLAPSIBLE TREE LAYOUT

Example 3: Tree Layout

When working with text-based feedback, often there are times when a number of different feedback records will contain similar sentences but end differently. An example of this can be seen in the following feedback records:

- The food was good but I did not like the service.

- I did not like how the chairs were dirty.

- Why was their no chicken today? I did not like how the table was not cleaned.

- The food was great but I did not like the attitude of the server.

Each of the sentences contains similar terms *did not like*. Although this is a short example, if we sorted through a large collection of records that contained these three terms, we can gain additional insight into the context of the terms. The collapsible tree layout allows us to create a tree-based structure horizontally across the page. At the root of the tree we can place a common piece of text, and each branch can contain N different child nodes, which in turn can have N children. The advantage of using a collapsible tree is that we can easily hide away different branches on the tree, allowing us to focus on the areas of interest.

This example consists of three files:

1. create.sql — SQL to create the required *feedback_tree* table.

2. tree.html — Core visualization example.

3. generateJSON.php — A simple PHP script to retrieve records from the database table and convert them into JSON format.

4. D3.js — This is used as the main library to render the graph.

5. jQuery — This is used to perform a JavaScript *GET* request.

Example code: create.sql

For this example, as shown in Sample Code 3, a simple database table is used that contains a unique *ID* column, time stamp column that is automatically inserted when the record is created, and a comment column, which is where the text-based feedback will be stored.

```
1  CREATE TABLE IF NOT EXISTS `feedback_tree` (
2      `id` int NOT NULL AUTO_INCREMENT,
3      `mytime` timestamp NULL DEFAULT CURRENT_TIMESTAMP,
4      `comments` text,
5      PRIMARY KEY (`id`)
6  );
```

SAMPLE CODE 3: Feedback_tree database table.

The collapsible tree-based visualization is built from a single JSON document. Each individual node is defined with a *name* attribute, followed by the piece of text to be shown. In the JSON in the following example, the root of the tree is *did not like*. This node has four child nodes.

```
1  {
2    "name": "did not like",
3    "children": [
4      {
5        "name": "the service"
6      },
7      {
8        "name": "how the chairs were dirty"
9      },
10     {
11       "name": "how the table was not cleaned"
12     },
13     {
14       "name": "the attitude of the server"
15     }
16   ]
17 }
```

JSON documents need to be fully valid to be rendered. This can be a difficult process during development. The JSON, however, does not need to be spaced apart, as shown in the example above. To aid the process of editing JSON during development, online JSON formatting tools can structure or compress JSON as needed. An example of this can be found at *https://jsonformatter.org/json-editor*.

Example code: tree.html

In Sample Code 4, a reference is made to the CSS style on lines 4–18 that is used by the visualization. A reference is made to include D3.js on line 21. On line 22, jQuery is included. jQuery will allow us to dynamically call the PHP page that will generate the JSON content for the visualization. To aid us in identifying how far we have progressed during the loading of the code, a simple *console.log()* is added on line 28 to state we are about to call the server-side to generates the JSON content.

On line 29, a jQuery *GET* request is made that is responsible for calling the *generateJSON.php* page. The result of this call will be available in the *data* variable. However, the content that is returned to us although it is valid JSON, it is not stored in JSON format. On line 31, to convert the string into JSON format, we can use the *JSON.parse()* function that takes in a variable containing a string and converts it into objects. These JSON objects are stored in the *treeData* variable that is passed to the *generateTree()* function on line 32 that is responsible for rendering the tree. For brevity, the code for this function is excluded but can be found in the online examples that accompany this book.

```
1   <!DOCTYPE html>
2   <meta charset="UTF-8">
3   <style>
4   .node circle {
5     fill: #fff;
6     stroke: steelblue;
7     stroke-width: 3px;
8   }
9
10  .node text {
11    font: 12px sans-serif;
12  }
13
14  .link {
15    fill: none;
16    stroke: #ccc;
17    stroke-width: 2px;
18  }
```

```
19  </style>
20  <!-- load the d3.js library -->
21  <script src="https://d3js.org/d3.v4.min.js"></script>
22  <script
23    src="https://code.jquery.com/jquery-3.5.1.js"
24    integrity="sha256-WpOohJOqMqqyKL9FccASB9O0KwACQJpFTUBLTYOVvVU="
25    crossorigin="anonymous"></script>
26  <body>
27  <script>
28  console.log("Calling the genreateJSON.php page");
29  $.get( "generateJSON.php", function( data ) {
30      console.log(data);
31      treeData = JSON.parse(data);
32      generateTree(treeData);
33  });
```

SAMPLE CODE 4: tree.html — Retrieving data to be graphed with D3.

Example code: generateJSON.php

The *generateJSON.php* page is responsible for connecting to a MySQL database, collecting records that are relevant to the query that was executed, and then formatting them in a JSON structure. The core behind the process of gathering records from the database is the loose-fitting SQL query. In this example, the *LIKE* statement is used, with % surrounding the text of interest. This indicates that the terms may appear at the beginning, the middle or the end of a feedback record. Additional processing however, will be required to remove the text at the beginning of the records as it is not required.

In Sample Code 5 a variable titled *rawtext is* is added on line 7. This variable contains the text that is treated as the stem for all the text we are interested in finding. On line 8, a connection is made to the database. On line 10, a new array titled *params* is created that takes in the single *rawtext* variable with the percentage signs at the start and end of the variable. On line 11, the SQL query is created.

On line 15, the beginning of the JSON content is first created in the variable titled *header*. A *footer* variable is created that contains the JSON to append to the end of the content. A variable titled *body* is added on line 22 that will be used as the main holder for the generated JSON.

On line 23, a simple *foreach* is used to iterate over the database results. For each individual result, the data is first placed into the *record* variable on line 24. On line 24, the starting point for the text of interest is found by using the *strpos()* function that takes in two parameters. The first of these is the raw *record* variable, and the second is the text of interest in the form of the *rawtext* variable. This function will return an integer of where to start the extraction process from.

On line 27, the *body* variable is built up. This begins with JSON content and enters in a substring that is received by calling the *substr()* function and passing the complete *record* variable followed by the *start* position added to the length of the *record* variable. This will strip off any additional text before the terms of interest. To finish on line 32, the *header* is first printed, followed by the body on line 33 and finally by the footer JSON content on line 34. Together these three components make a single valid JSON document.

```
1   <?php
2   try {
3       $host = 'localhost:3306';
4       $dbname = 'bookexamples';
5       $user = 'sampleuser';
6       $pass = '3C9038A509BE6145AAD6827B4568AD918BC3DAC0';
7       $rawtext = 'did not like';
8       $DBH = new PDO("mysql:host=$host;dbname=$dbname", $user,
9         $pass);
10      $params = array("%$rawtext%");
11      $sql = " SELECT * FROM feedback_tree WHERE comments LIKE ?";
12      $sth = $DBH->prepare($sql);
13      $sth->execute($params);
14      $res = $sth->fetchAll();
15      $header = '
16        {
17        "name": "did not like",
18        "children": [';
19      $footer = '
20           ]
21        }';
22      $body = '';
23      foreach ($res as $row){
24          $record = $row[2];
25          $start = strpos($record, $rawtext);
26
27          $body .= '
```

```
28          {
29              "name":"'. substr($record, $start+strlen($rawtext)).'"
30          },';
31      }
32      echo $header;
33      echo substr_replace($body ,"", -1); // strip the last comma.
34      echo $footer;
35  } catch(PDOException $e) {echo $e;}
```

SAMPLE CODE 5: generateJSON.php — Dynamically building a JSON document.

Output

Figure 6.3 shows the completed tree-based structure running in a web browser. On the left, we have the stem of the sentence, and on the right, we have all the comments that contained the original stem.

6.4   TERMS OF INTEREST NODE GRAPH

Example 4: Term node graph

When reviewing text-based feedback from users, often there are connections between the feedback records that may not see when looking at individual records. An example of this could be seen in the following five different records that may have been left by different users:

- The staff are horrible here, I am really not happy.

- The staff have been great, I am really not happy about the pool.

- I was five minutes late and they said I cannot have breakfast.

- The breakfast was great.

- More coffee is needed at breakfast time. How can I work without it?

- Breakfast was good but the staff are great.

Although a very simplistic example, we can see that there are two

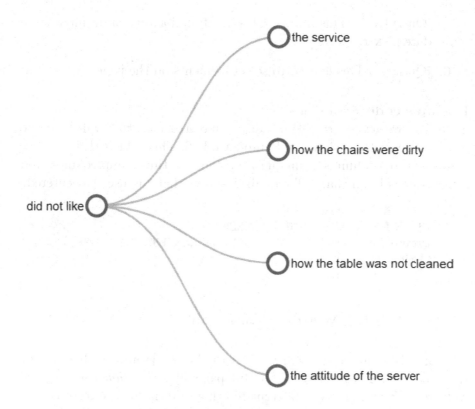

FIGURE 6.3: Completed tree-based structure with the root of the sentence as the parent node.

references to the *staff*, and there are three different references to *breakfast*. In this section, we will outline the process of identifying terms that are of interest to us that we may have seen in a record such as *breakfast* and *staff* and use this as the terms to connect different feedback records together in a node and edge-based graph.

This example consists of three files:

1. create.sql — Create SQL for the *nodetree* table.

2. graph.php — This is the main script that allows the user to enter terms of interest along with a date.

3. getRecords.php — The file retrieves the records from the database.

4. Viz.js — This library is used to add nodes to the graph.

5. jQueryUI — This library adds the functionality of an interactive date picker.

6. jQuery — This is used to select elements on the page.

Example code: create.sql

To begin, we will start with a basic table structure that will hold the feedback records, as shown in Sample Code 6. This table titled *nodetree* contains three columns, a unique *ID* column, a timestamp column, and a feedback column that will contain the text that the user has entered.

```
1   CREATE TABLE `nodetree` (
2       `id` INT NOT NULL AUTO_INCREMENT,
3       `mytime` DATETIME NOT NULL DEFAULT CURRENT_TIMESTAMP,
4       `feedback` TEXT,
5       PRIMARY KEY (`id`)
6   );
```

SAMPLE CODE 6: Node tree database table.

For this example, we will work with the Vis.js library that can be downloaded from the following GitHub page: *https://github.com/visjs/vis-network*. We will use two different filtering criteria for the records that will be plotted. The first of these is the date that is stored in *YYYY-MM-DD* format, and a collection of comma-separated terms that we are searching for on that particular date. The two terms we will be searching for are *breakfast* and *staff*.

Example code: getRecords.php

The first step in this process is to create a PHP page that will allow us to select records from the database for visualization. In Sample Code 7, the *date* and *terms* variables are received on lines 2 and 3. A connection to the database is made on line 9. On line 10, the *explode()* function is used to break the terms apart based on the comma between the terms. On line 11, a variable titled *whereClause* is created that will be used as the placeholder for the SQL *WHERE* clause that will be built up.

For each of the terms, on line 13, additional *WHERE* clauses are added to search for terms that are like the term entered by the user. An *OR* operator is added at the end of the statement allowing additional *WHERE* clauses to be appended. When the foreach statement has finished, on line 15 the *substr()* function is used to remove the last *OR* statement from the *whereClause* variable as SQL cannot have an *OR* as the ending of a valid SQL statement.

On line 16, the *date* is entered into a new array that is stored in a local variable titled *params*. The main body of the SQL statement is added to line 17, which searches the *notetree* table for records where the time stamp is greater than the date provided. The *WHERE* clause is appended to this SQL query. On line 19, the query is finally executed. On line 21, for each record returned, the column at position 2 of the row is gathered and placed in the *record* variable. This is the feedback text that is output to the page.

```php
1   <?php
2   $date = $_GET['date'];
3   $terms = $_GET['terms'];
4   try {
5       $host = 'localhost:3306';
6       $dbname = 'bookexamples';
7       $user = 'sampleuser';
8       $pass = '3C9038A509BE6145AAD6827B4568AD918BC3DAC0';
9       $DBH = new PDO("mysql:host=$host;dbname=$dbname", $user,
        ↪ $pass);
10      $words = explode(',',$terms);
11      $whereClause = '';
12      foreach( $words as $word) {
13          $whereClause .= ' feedback LIKE "%' . $word . '%" OR';
14      }
15      $whereClause = substr($whereClause, 0, -2);
16      $params = array($date);
17      $sql = "SELECT * FROM nodetree WHERE timestamp > ? AND " .
        ↪ $whereClause;
18      $sth = $DBH->prepare($sql);
19      $sth->execute($params);
20      $res = $sth->fetchAll();
21      foreach ($res as $row){
22          $record = $row[2];
23          echo $record . '<br>';
24      }
25  } catch(PDOException $e) {echo $e;}
```

SAMPLE CODE 7: getRecords.php — Retrieving records using a *WHERE* clause.

Example code: graph.php

A second page is created titled *graph.php*. This is the main interface that will be presented to the user allowing them to select a date and enter terms of interest.

In Sample Code 8, at the top of this file, a reference to the jQueryUI CSS is included that will be used to aid the pop-up date picker. On line 3, a reference to jQuery is included. On line 4, the JavaScript required by jQueryUI is included. On lines 6 and 7, the *vis-network.min.js* file and the *vis-network-min.css* file are included. These two files can be found inside of the *dist* folder, which is in the root of the Vis.js source code. On line 10–15, CSS is used to define the *height, width, border*, and *background* of the *div* tag titled *mynetwork* that will be used to hold the visualization.

The body of the document page contains two input boxes. The first of these on line 22, with the *ID* set to *datepicker* will allow the user to select the date of interest from a jQueryUI date picker tool. The second input box is added on line 24, with an *ID* set to *terms* that will allow the user to enter in terms of interest. The user can enter a single term or multiple terms that have been separated using commas. A button is added on line 25 with the *ID* set to *generate*, which, when clicked, will generate the graph. On line 26, a *div* tag with the *ID* set to *mynetwork* is added that is the main placeholder for the visualization.

```
1   <link rel="stylesheet"
     ↪  href="http://code.jquery.com/ui/1.12.1/themes/base/
2   jquery-ui.css">
3   <script src="https://code.jquery.com/jquery-1.12.4.js"></script>
4   <script src="https://code.jquery.com/ui/1.12.1/jquery-ui.js">
5   </script>
6   <script type="text/javascript"
     ↪  src="vis-network.min.js"></script>
7   <link href="vis-network.min.css" rel="stylesheet"
     ↪  type="text/css" />
8   <head>
9   <style type="text/css">
10  #mynetwork {
11      width: 1000px;
12      height: 1000px;
13      border: 1px solid lightgray;
14      background:#d1d1d1;
15  }
16  p {
```

```
17      max-width:600px;
18  }
19  </style>
20  </head>
21  <body>
22      <p>Date of interest: <input type="text" id="datepicker"
        ↪  value="2019-08-05"></p>
23      Please enter terms of interest
24      <input type="text" value= "breakfast" size="30" id="terms">
25      <button id="generate"> Generate graph </button>
26      <div id="mynetwork"></div>
27  </body>
```

SAMPLE CODE 8: graph.php — Providing a date and terms of interest — part 1.

After the HTML component has been created, the next step is to implement the JavaScript that will be used to generate the graph.

In Sample Code 9, inside a *script* tag, two data sets are created on lines 29 and 30. The first is used to hold the nodes for the graph, and the second is used to hold the edges for the graph. The edges are the connections that will be created between each different node. A variable titled *nodeId* is created on line 31 that is used as a reference point for storing a unique *ID* for each node. Whenever a new node is added to the graph, this variable will be incremented.

To begin the graph generation process, a *click()* handler is added on to the *generate* button on line 32. The graph generation will be added inside of this click handler. The jQuery selector is used to select the terms and the date input boxes on lines 33 and 34. The *val()* function will extract the values from the input fields. On line 35, a *GET* request is made to the *getRecords.php* page that was created earlier. Two variables are passed to this page, *terms* and *date* on lines 36 and 37. The values *t* and *d* are retrieved from the variables that were used temporarily to store the values.

This *GET* request has a *done()* function on line 39 that returns the variable *data*. This will return the selected rows from the database. To view these records before any processing is performed a *console.log(data)* can be added to aid debugging.

Using this *data* variable, on line 40, each individual record is split apart based on the *br* tags that were appended to the end of each line in the *getRecords.php* page. This *br* tag serves as a marker to identify one row from the next. After the *split()* function has been called, the *feedbackRecords* variable will then contain an array, with each row being one individual position in the array.

To identify the number of terms that have been entered by the user, the *t* variable is split on line 42 based on the comma between each term. These terms are placed into the *termsSplit* array variable. On line 44, A *for loop* is added to iterate over each of the terms entered by the user. For each individual term, the *trim()* function is called on line 45 to remove any additional white space around the term. A call then is made to the *generateGraphForTerm()* function on line 47. This function takes a single term as a parameter. This is the core of the graphing process for each term.

On line 51, the function *generateGraphForTerm()* can be seen. On line 52, a new array is created titled *connections*, which will be used to store the edges between the nodes. A parent node with the current *nodeId* is created. This will serve as a reference point for all nodes that are generated. In the case of the term *staff*, any records that contain this term will be linked back to this parent node.

To create the parent node, the *nodes* data set is called on line 54 and the *add()* function is called. This takes in the unique *ID* for the node and the *label*, which contains the text the node will hold. In this case, for the parent node, on line 56, the text will come from the *singleT* variable, which is one individual term entered by the user. The font size and color are then added. A crucial element in this process is to increment the *nodeId* variable when a new node is created, as shown on line 63. This will allow each node to have a unique *ID* in the graph.

After the generation process of the root nodes for each individual term, nodes for each record that has been returned need to be created. To do this a *for loop* is added on line 65 to iterate over the *feedbackRecords* array that contains the individual feedback records. To aid the debugging process a *console.log()* function is added on line 66 to print out the *nodeId* that we are currently working with.

Two variables are created to monitor the processing of the individual record. The first variable is the *termCount* record on line 67, which is used to store the number of terms the user has entered that have appeared inside the record we are currently processing.

On line 69, while processing each record, an internal *for loop* is used to loop over each of the terms that the user has entered. These terms were stored inside of the *termsSplit* array. The *indexOf()* function is called on line 71 inside an *if statement* and passed one term the user has entered. If the feedback record contains the term, then the function will return a number greater than -1. When we have found the term, the *termCount* is incremented on line 72.

For each of the individual records that are added to the graph, if one term entered by the user is found in the record, it is treated as a normal record. In this case, the default font color *black* will be used. In the case where all the terms are found, then the color of the record is changed to *red*. After the internal for loop has run, a check is performed on line 77 to see if the *termCount* is less than the number of terms entered by the user. If this is the case, then the record is identified as a normal record by setting the *normalRecord* boolean variable to true on line 78.

```
28  <script>
29  var nodes = new vis.DataSet();
30  var edges = new vis.DataSet();
31  var nodeId = 1; // unique Node ID for each.
32  $("#generate").click(function() {
33      var t = $('#terms').val();
34      var d = $('#datepicker').val();
35      $.get("getRecords.php", {
36              terms: t,
37              date: d
38          })
39      .done(function(data) {
40      var feedbackRecords = data.split('<br>');
41      // count number of terms entered by the user
42      var termsSplit = t.split(',');
43      // for each indivudal term entered by the user
44      for (var i = 0; i < termsSplit.length; i++) {
45          var singleTerm = termsSplit[i].trim();
46          console.log("running graph for " + singleTerm);
47          generateGraphForTerm(singleTerm);
48      }
49      // main function for generating a graph for
50      // a specific term
51      function generateGraphForTerm(singleT) {
52          var connections = new Array();
53          var parentNode = nodeId;
54          nodes.add({
55              id: nodeId,
56              label: singleT,
57              font: {
58                  size: 16,
59                  color: 'black',
```

```
60          face: 'arial'
61        }
62      });
63      nodeId++;
64      // for each row in the data set we are working with.
65      for (var i = 0; i < feedbackRecords.length; i++) {
66          console.log("NodeiD " + nodeId);
67          var termCount = 0;
68          var normalRecord = false;
69          for (var y = 0; y < termsSplit.length; y++) {
70              console.log("looking in" + feedbackRecords[i]);
71              if (feedbackRecords[i].indexOf(termsSplit[y]) >
                ↪   -1) {
72                  termCount++;
73                  console.log("found occurrence for " +
                    ↪   termsSplit[y]);
74              }
75          }
76          console.log("term count " + termCount);
77          if (termCount < termsSplit.length) {
78              normalRecord = true;
79          }
```

SAMPLE CODE 9: graph.php — Identifying terms of interest — part 2

In Sample Code 10, on line 80, if the *normalRecord* is set to true, and the record we are working with does contain the term of interest, then a new node is added to the nodes data set. Similar to how the record was added for the parent record, the *add()* function is called on line 82. The unique *nodeId* and *label* is added. To visualize the complete record on line 84, the *label* for the node is set to be the *feedbackRecords[i]* where *i* is the current position of the array we are iterating over. As this is a normal record, the font color is set to *black* on line 87.

On line 92, the final step in this process is to push the node that has just been created to the *connections* array for the later attaching of edges. On line 95, again, it is essential to increment the *nodeId* after the new node has been created to prevent any duplicate node IDs on the graph.

On line 97, in the case of a record where all of the terms entered by the user appear in the feedback record, the same process is used to add the node to the graph. The only modification that is made is that instead of adding an *if statement*, an *else* is used as this will only run if the *normalRecord* variable is equal to *false*. The color of the font in this case is changed to *red* on line 102 to make a distinction to other records.

After the parent nodes have been created for each individual term and the child nodes, e.g., the individual feedback record nodes have been created the process of making the edges must be performed. The edges are the connections that appear between the nodes. On line 112, a *for loop* is used to iterate over all of the connections that have been stored. This connections array contained a list of all the IDs of the nodes, which have been added in the previous step.

On line 113, for each individual connection, the node counter variable is used to select the node *ID* from the *connections* array. This will begin at 0 and iterate up to the length of the *connections* array. For each node *ID* that is stored in the *connection* array, they are first placed into a temporary variable title *leftNode*. On line 115, the *edges* data set is used and the *add()* function is called on the data set to make a connection between the *leftNode* which we currently have and the *parentNode* which was created earlier. This parent node will only contain one term, e.g., *staff* where the *leftNode* will contain the complete text feedback record that contained the term *staff*.

```
80   if (normalRecord == true) {
81       if (feedbackRecords[i].indexOf(singleT) > -1) {
82           nodes.add({
83               id: nodeId,
84               label: feedbackRecords[i],
85               font: {
86                   size: 11,
87                   color: 'black',
88                   face: 'arial'
89               }
90           });
91           console.log(nodeId + feedbackRecords[i]);
92           connections.push(nodeId);
93       }
94
95       nodeId++;
96   } else {
97       nodes.add({
98           id: nodeId,
99           label: feedbackRecords[i],
100          font: {
101              size: 11,
102              color: 'red',
```

```
103            face: 'arial'
104          }
105       });
106       console.log(nodeId + feedbackRecords[i]);
107       connections.push(nodeId);
108       nodeId++;
109     }
110   }
111   // make edges
112   for (var node = 0; node < connections.length; node++) {
113     var leftNode = connections[node];
114     console.log("connected nodes" + leftNode + " to " +
        ↪  parentNode);
115     edges.add({
116         from: leftNode,
117         to: parentNode
118     });
119   }
120 } // function
```

SAMPLE CODE 10: graph.php — Creating the edges — part 3.

In Sample Code 11, the final step in the process is to initialize the graph on the web page. This is done by using the *getElementById()* selector on line 122 to select the *div* tag with the *ID mynetwork* that was created earlier. This reference is placed into a variable titled *container*. The *data* is created which contains references to the *nodes* and the *edges* data sets on lines 124 and 125 that has been built up.

After this, the options for the graph are specified. On lines 129 and 130, the dot shape of size 10 is specified. The three references *container*, *data*, and *options* are passed to the *vis.Network()* constructor on line 133. This will create a graph based on the data we have provided. The click handler function that was originally used to generate the graph process is closed.

To initialize the jQueryUI date picker, a the jQuery selector is used to select the *datepicker* input box on line 137. The *datepicker()* function is called. As the dates in the database are stored in *YYYY-MM-DD* format, an additional option can be set on the date picker to use this format, as shown on line 138. If this step is not performed, the days and months will become reversed.

```
te a network
tainer = document.getElementById('mynetwork');
a = {
es: nodes,
es: edges

ions = {
es: {
 shape: 'dot',
 size: 10


work = new vis.Network(container, data, options);


) {
epicker").datepicker();
epicker").datepicker("option", "dateFormat",
-mm-dd');
```

ODE 11: graph.php — Creating the jQueryUI datepicker

ovides an example of the output for the selected date, *2019-*
ie keywords *breakfast* and *staff*. In this example, we can see
s entered by the user become the parent nodes for all records
the term. Whenever a record contains all the terms the
ered, the color of the record is changed to red for additional

SERIES ANALYSIS WITH POSITIVE AND NEGATIVE
EW CHART

n, we will outline the process of creating a time-series graph.
s are focused on the temporal element, allowing data to be
a series of days or weeks. This approach to data analysis
view the impact of a marketing campaign or feature imple-

est: 2019-08-05

terms of interest breakfast, staff   [Generate graph]

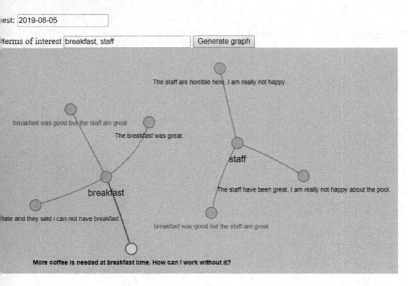

Ξ 6.4: Vis.js graph output for two keywords and a single date.

on has on our users. To do this, we will plot the positive and
feedback that has occurred on the days across a week.
example contains three components:

eate.sql — This contains the create SQL for the *pastime* table
at contains the review scores.

ne.php — This is used to retrieve records from the database and
the main visualization page.

nart.js — This is the main library used to generate the graph.

oment.js — A JavaScript-based library used for working with
ne stamps.

ple 5: Positive and negative reviews

graph generation process is broken into two components. The
mponent that is used for gathering the relevant records from the
e and the HTML/JavaScript component that is used for creating
alization. In this example, a file titled *time.php* is created. The
de will be placed at the top of the file, followed by JavaScript
MI.

ode: create.sql

egin the process of building the graph, a database table is
his example, we will create a table titled *pastime*. This table
unique *ID* column, that is a primary key and is also auto-
when a new record is entered. The *mytime* column will
current time stamp from the system when a new record is
eedbacktext is of type text, which will allow the user to enter
back. The most important column in this example is the
1 that we will use to store a rating score between 1 and 10.
e is small, a *TINYINT* data type can be used.

```
E `pastime` (
`  INT NOT NULL AUTO_INCREMENT,
time` TIMESTAMP NULL DEFAULT CURRENT_TIMESTAMP,
edbacktext` TEXT,
ore` TINYINT,
MARY KEY (`id`)
```

ode: time.php

e Code 12, The PHP component to generate the records for
broken into four distinct components. The first of these is a
o the MySQL database on line 7. This database will be used
g the positive feedback records and the negative feedback
line 10, a new function is defined titled *getNumberOfPos-*
takes in a single parameter in the form of a date. On line
ce to the database object is made. On line 12, The date is
the PHP *explode()* function that will break the date apart
e spaces between the day, month, and year. Each of these
d as an array element in the *date* array.
: is accessed by referencing the *date* object at position 0
1 the *justYear* variable. On line 14, a SQL query is created.
the number of records that are returned using the SQL
tion on the *score* column. A *WHERE* clause is added to
1e SQL statement to specify where the year is like the year
ear variable. In addition to this, to classify the records as
additional *AND* operator is added to ensure the scores must
1an 5. On line 18, the result record that contains the total
tive records is returned

process is repeated again for the *getNumberOfNegative()* func-
line 20. The only modification that is made is on line 24, the
1st be less or equal to 5.

etrieve a list of dates to visualize, a new SQL query is adde to on
The *distinct* keyword is used to remove duplicate dates. On line
each individual date, the *row* at position 0 that stores the date
1 in the *labels* variable. The positive scores for that date are re-
by calling the *getNumberOfPositive()* function on line 42 followed
nma to separate the result from the next to be generated. The
repeated for the negative scores by calling the *getNumberOfNeg-*
function on lines 45—47 the PHP *substr()* function is used to
the trailing colon from the *labels*, *positive* and *negative* variables
ng -1 to the *substr()* PHP function.

```
st = 'localhost:3306';
name = 'bookexamples';
er = 'sampleuser';
ss = '3C9038A509BE6145AAD6827B4568AD918BC3DAC0';
H = new PDO("mysql:host=$host;dbname=$dbname", $user,
  $pass);
(PDOException $e) {echo $e;}

n getNumberOfPositive($date){
bal $DBH;
te = explode(' ', $date);
stYear = $date[0];
l = "SELECT COUNT(score) as score FROM pastime WHERE
  TIMESTAMP LIKE '$justYear%' AND score > 5 LIMIT 7;";
h = $DBH->prepare($sql);
h->execute();
s = $sth->fetchAll();
urn $res[0][0];

n getNumberOfNegative($date){
bal $DBH;
te = explode(' ', $date);
stYear = $date[0];
l = "SELECT COUNT(score) as score FROM pastime WHERE
  TIMESTAMP LIKE '$justYear%' AND score <= 5 LIMIT 7;";
h = $DBH->prepare($sql);
h->execute();
 = $sth->fetchAll();
```

```
$res[0][0];
```

```
st of unique dates from the
ECT DISTINCT timestamp FROM pastime';
->prepare($sql);
te();
->fetchAll();
';
  '';
  '';
es as $row){
   = $labels . "'" .$row[0]. "',";
ve = $positive . getNumberOfPositive($row[0]) . ',';
ve = $negative . getNumberOfNegative($row[0]) . ',';

ubstr($labels, 0, -1); // remove the final colon from
  of the string
  substr($positive, 0, -1);
  substr($negative, 0, -1);
```

ODE 12: time.php — Retrieving labels, positive and
es — part 1.

e Code 13, the graph generation process will be performed
js. To avoid the need to download additional files on our
itent delivery network (CDN) for Chart.js and moment.js
The second library, moment.js, is a JavaScript-based library
king with time stamps. On lines 54–56 these CDN references
. On line 59, the *canvas* tag CSS is modified to prevent
of elements for moz (Firefox), ms (Internet Explorer), and
ri) browsers.

e body of the document, on line 67, a *div* tag is created with
ɔ be 75 percent of the available space. Inside of this *div* tag,
single *canvas* tag is added with an *ID* set to *canvas*. This
graph will be generated. On line 74, a *script* tag is added
ɔ the exact RGB values for seven different colors. Additional
s can be added if required.

```
pe html>                                                                    30
                                                                            31
                                                                            32
Positive and Negative Feedback</title>                                      33
                                                                            34
="https://cdnjs.cloudflare.com/ajax/libs/moment.js/2.18.1/                  35
min.js"></script>                                                           36
                                                                            37
="https://www.chartjs.org/dist/2.8.0/Chart.min.js"></script>               38
 src="https://code.jquery.com/jquery-1.12.4.js"></script>                   39
                                                                            40
{                                                                           41
z-user-select: none;                                                        42
bkit-user-select: none;                                                     43
-user-select: none;                                                         44
                                                                            45
>                                                                           46
                                                                            47
                                                                            48
v style="width:75%;">                                                       49
 <canvas id="canvas"></canvas>                                              50
iv>                                                                         51
                                                                            52
                                                                            53
                                                                            54
                                                                            55
>                                                                           56
chartColors = {                                                             57
 red: 'rgb(255, 99, 132)',                                                  58
 orange: 'rgb(255, 159, 64)',                                               59
 yellow: 'rgb(255, 205, 86)',                                               60
 green: 'rgb(75, 192, 192)',
 blue: 'rgb(54, 162, 235)',
 purple: 'rgb(153, 102, 255)',
 grey: 'rgb(201, 203, 207)'
```

.E CODE 13: time.php — Initial page setup — part 2.

ample Code 14, the *config* object that stores all the configuration
graph is added on line 85. On line 86, the type of graph that will
rated is specified. In this case, we will be generating a line graph.
87, the *data* for the graph is defined. This will contain the labels
a for the graph. On line 88, the labels in this case, are the

individual dates that feedback has been gathered for. To aid the graph generation process, the labels are generated using PHP. These labels are stored inside the *labels* PHP variables and are separated by commas.

The data set that will be represented consists of individual days in a month, with the count for positive and negative feedback records for each day. On line 92, to facilitate this, the *datasets* variable contains the label, which will be used to show the first data set, in this case, the positive feedback. The background color for this data is set to *red* on line 94. This color red is gathered from the *chartColors* defined earlier. The data for the graph is defined on line 98. The values will be dynamically added using PHP on line 99.

A second data set is added. This is done by first specifying the label on line 102 that we wish to appear, followed by the color we wish to use to represent the data set. On line 103, *blue* is set. The *fill* attribute allows us to define if we would like the area under the line to be filled with color or not. To keep this graph clear, we will set this to *false* on line 106. Similar to the positive feedback, the data for this data set is gathered from the *negative* variable that is output from the PHP variable on line 108.

On line 113, additional options for the graph can be specified. The title is set followed by the scales which will be present on the data graph. On line 119, the *xAxes* is defined as *time*. The display is set to *true* and the *label* is set to the value *Date* on line 123. The *yAxes* for the graph is defined on line 126.

The final step in the process is to generate the graph. On line 135, the *window.onload()* function is used to trigger this process. When the window loads the *canvas* is selected using the *getElementById()* selector on line 136. The *getContext()* function is called and *2d* is set. Finally, on line 137, the *window.myLine* is set to a new Chart with the *ctx* variable being passed as the context and the *config* variable containing the configuration for the graph.

```
84   var color = Chart.helpers.color;
85   var config = {
86       type: 'line',
87       data: {
88           labels: [ // Date Objects
89               //'2019-08-06 21:04:11',
90               <?php echo $labels; ?>
91           ],
92           datasets: [{
```

```
 93          label: 'Positive Feedback',
 94          backgroundColor:
            ↪ color(window.chartColors.red).alpha(0.5).
 95          rgbString(),
 96          borderColor: window.chartColors.red,
 97          fill: false,
 98          data: [
 99              <?php echo $positive; ?>
100          ],
101      }, {
102          label: 'Negative Feedback',
103          backgroundColor:
            ↪ color(window.chartColors.blue).alpha(0.5).
104          rgbString(),
105          borderColor: window.chartColors.blue,
106          fill: false,
107          data: [
108              <?php echo $negative; ?>
109          ],
110
111      }]
112    },
113    options: {
114        title: {
115            text: 'Time Feedback Analysis'
116        },
117        scales: {
118            xAxes: [{
119                type: 'time',
120
121                scaleLabel: {
122                    display: true,
123                    labelString: 'Date'
124                }
125            }],
126            yAxes: [{
127                scaleLabel: {
128                    display: true,
129                    labelString: 'Feedback Count'
130                }
131            }]
132        },
133    }
134 };
135 window.onload = function() {
```

```
136    var ctx =
       ↪ document.getElementById('canvas').getContext('2d');
137    window.myLine = new Chart(ctx, config);
138  };
139  </script>
```

SAMPLE CODE 14: time.php — Generating the graph object — part
3.

Output

Figure 6.5 shows the final output of the graph generation process.
Two lines are added to the graph, one for the positive feedback count and
one for the negative feedback count. The days which are being shown
are outlined across the bottom of the graph.

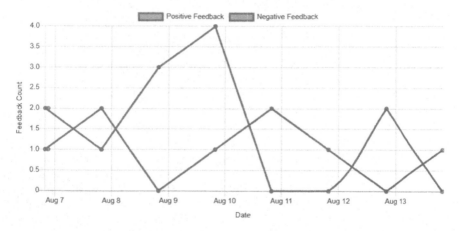

FIGURE 6.5: Time graph showing seven days of positive and negative
feedback for a week.

6.6 SUMMARY

This chapter outlined the visualizations that are possible when working
with text. Word clouds were introduced as a quick method of viewing the
most popular terms in a collection of text. As text comes in a structured
format such as sentences and paragraphs, tree-based structures were then
explored, outlining how the root of a single term can be used to connect
to other sentences.

An important element of any feedback record is the time when it was left. A line graph based on the number of positive and negative feedback records for a given day was then explored, providing quick glance statistics for numeric data.

Chapter 7, next, explores the temporal component of data in detail.

Time-Based Feedback Analysis

7.1 INTRODUCTION

When feedback data is gathered, time stamps are often added. These time stamps can be used to leverage additional insights from the data. Feedback records in a specific time range can indicate an issue with the current operation of a business or an issue that appeared at a specific time in the past. These insights may have otherwise been lost if a collection of records was viewed without a temporal component.

In this chapter, the temporal aspect of data is explored.

7.2 GATHERING TIMELINES AND DATABASE DATA TYPES

When gathering feedback from users, MySQL offers a range of different date and time-based data types. Table 7.1 provides an outline of these data types. A dividing line can be placed between where the time/date is created, either programmatically during the data collection process or automatically during the process of submitting the data to the database.

Example 1: Date and time

In PHP we can use the *date()* function to return the current date stamp. Different parameters can be passed to this function to return the date in different formats.[1] Sample Code 1 outlines the process of retrieving the year, month and day. The Y parameter returns the year in four digits, e.g., 2021, the m parameter returns a two digit representation of the

---

[1]http://php.net/manual/en/function.date.php

TABLE 7.1: MySQL Database Data Types for Time and Dates

Data type	Description
DATE	The date is stored in *YYYY-MM-DD* format with a range from *1000-01-01* to *9999-12-31*.
TIME	*HH:MM:SS* format with a range from *-838:59:59* to *838:59:59*. A trailing fraction in microseconds with 6 digit precision is available.
YEAR	Year from *1901* to *2155*. This can be assigned in integer or string format. Integers between 1 and 99 can be used, which are converted to a four-character representation.
DATETIME	Auto-generated field with a *YYYY-MM-DD HH:MM:SS* format.
TIMESTAMP	Auto-generated field with a range of *1970-01-01 00:00:01* UTC to *2038-01-19 03:14:07* UTC. MySQL converts the current time zone into UTC format for storage and back to the current time during the retrieval process.

month, e.g., 08, and finally the *d* parameter returns the day in two digit format, e.g., 12.

```
1  <?php
2  echo "Today is " . date("Y-m-d") . "<br>";
3  ?>
```

SAMPLE CODE 1: Retrieving the date using PHP.

An alternative method of storing the time is in epoch format. This format is the number of seconds that have elapsed since the Unix Epoch, which is January 1 1970 00:00:00 GMT. When storing this format, a standard date/time data type is not required. Sample Code 2 outlines the process of retrieving the time in Epoch format.

```
1  <?php
2  $date = new DateTime();
3  echo $date->getTimestamp();
4  ?>
```

SAMPLE CODE 2: Returning the current Epoch time.

The advantage of using an epoch based format is that calculations can easily be performed on the time stamp. An example of this is the epoch time stamp 1540470653. We can add three hours onto this by simply converting three hours into seconds as shown in Equation 7.1

$$60 \, seconds \times 60 \, minutes \times 3 \, hours = 10800 \qquad (7.1)$$

A simple addition can be performed on the original epoch time to give the new epoch time, as shown in Equation 7.2.

$$1540470653 + 10800 = 1540481453 \qquad (7.2)$$

7.3 TIME-SEGMENT ANALYSIS AND VISUALIZATION

When viewing feedback, many different options are available to us, depending on how close or how far away from the data we wish to be. In this example, we will describe the process of generating a graph for positive and negative feedback for a given time segment. In this example, we will use one day as the largest amount of time to view. For this day, we will focus on each different hour to view the number of positive and negative feedback records. This approach allows us to look closer at the positive or negative feedback that may have been received and review the exact time the feedback was recorded.

Example 2: Time-segment analysis

This example consists of three files and five libraries:

1. create.sql — This file outlines the create SQL for the *exampleexample* table.

2. timesegment.php — This contains the controls allowing the user to select the date and time of interest along with the time segment size.

3. getTimeRecords.php — This file retrieves the records of interest from the database.

4. Chart.js — This is used to plot the positive and negative feedback graph.

5. Moment.js — This library is used for working with time stamps in JavaScript.

6. jQuery — Used to perform JavaScript *POST* requests.

7. jQueryUI — Provides an interactive date picking utility.

8. timepicker.co — Provides an interactive time picking utility.

Example code: create.sql

Sample Code 3 outlines the structure of the database table. The time stamp is recorded in the *mytime* column when a new record is created. The feedback score is stored in the *score* column.

```
1  CREATE TABLE `timeanalysis` (
2      `id` INT NOT NULL AUTO_INCREMENT,
3      `mytime` TIMESTAMP NOT NULL DEFAULT CURRENT_TIMESTAMP,
4      `score` INT,
5      PRIMARY KEY (`id`)
6  );
```

SAMPLE CODE 3: SQL to create the *timeanalysis* database table.

Example code: timesegment.php

The first step in this process is to create a new PHP page titled *timesegment.php* that will be used to hold the HTML options for the user to choose from and the JavaScript for the visualization. For each JavaScript library that will be utilized, content delivery networks (CDNs) will be used to remove the need to downloaded and place each individual library into the project folder.

In Sample Code 4, on lines 5–15, the CDN references are included. These include Moment.js, which is used for the manipulation of time stamps in JavaScript. This library is available from *https://momentjs.com/*. Chart.js is used for the main graphing process. In this example, we will be using a line chart with two axes. To manipulate the HTML document and avail of the DOM object selector jQuery will be used. To provide the user with an interactive calendar, the jQueryUI library is utilized along with the jQueryUI CSS file. The calendar widget is available from *https://jqueryui.com/datepicker/*. To select a time window, a jQuery based timepicker is used which is available from *https://timepicker.co/*. The timepicker also utilizes a CSS file for styling that is also included.

Similar to previous examples, on lines 17–21, the *canvas* tag is manipulated to prevent a user from making selections in Firefox, Chrome, and Internet Explorer.

On lines 25 and 26, two input fields are added. The first of these is used to present the date value to the user, and the second is used to show the time selected to the user. By default, the widgets will not be present until the user has clicked on the input field. To convert these regular *input* fields into widgets, additional JavaScript is used that is shown later in this section. The two important elements here is the IDs for each field. *datepicker* for the first *input* field and *timepicker* for the second.

As the main objective of this visualization is to utilize time, a HTML *select* field is added on line 28. The *ID* for this field is set to *minutes*. The initial increments that are used are 15 minutes until the hour mark. Then the increments are performed in hours. The hour is denoted by the additional *h* that is appended to the number. This will be used during the collection of the data to convert the hour selected into minutes. After the time window has been specified, on line 57, a *button* is added that will be used to trigger the visualization process. The *ID* of this button is set to *loadData*.

On line 58, a *div* tag is added with a width of 75% of the available space. Inside of this *div* tag, a single *canvas* tag is added that is the core of the visualization. The *ID* for this is set to *canvas*.

```
1  <!doctype html>
2  <html>
3  <head>
4  <title>Time Segment Analysis</title>
5  <script
    ↪  src="https://cdnjs.cloudflare.com/ajax/libs/moment.js/2.18.1/
6  moment.min.js"></script>
7  <script src="https://www.chartjs.org/dist/2.8.0/Chart.min.js">
8  </script>
9  <script src="https://code.jquery.com/jquery-1.12.4.js"></script>
10 <link rel="stylesheet"
    ↪  href="//code.jquery.com/ui/1.12.1/themes/base/jquery-ui.css">
11 <script
    ↪  src="https://code.jquery.com/ui/1.12.1/jquery-ui.js"></script>
```

```
12    <link rel="stylesheet"
   ↪    href="https://cdnjs.cloudflare.com/ajax/libs/timepicker/
13    1.3.5/jquery.timepicker.min.css">
14    <script src="https://cdnjs.cloudflare.com/ajax/libs/timepicker/
15    1.3.5/jquery.timepicker.min.js"/>
16    <style>
17        canvas {
18            -moz-user-select: none;
19            -webkit-user-select: none;
20            -ms-user-select: none;
21        }
22    </style>
23    </head>
24    <body>
25    Date: <input type="text" id="datepicker">
26    Time From: <input type="text" id="timepicker">
27    Time Window
28    <select id="minutes">
29        <option value="15">15 Minutes</option>
30        <option value="30">30 Minutes</option>
31        <option value="45">45 Minutes</option>
32        <option value="1h">1 Hour</option>
33        <option value="2h">2 Hour</option>
34        <option value="3h">3 Hour</option>
35        <option value="4h">4 Hour</option>
36        <option value="5h">5 Hour</option>
37        <option value="6h">6 Hour</option>
38        <option value="7h">7 Hour</option>
39        <option value="8h">8 Hour</option>
40        <option value="9h">9 Hour</option>
41        <option value="10h">10 Hour</option>
42        <option value="11h">11 Hour</option>
43        <option value="12h">12 Hour</option>
44        <option value="13h">13 Hour</option>
45        <option value="14h">14 Hour</option>
46        <option value="15h">15 Hour</option>
47        <option value="16h">16 Hour</option>
48        <option value="17h">17 Hour</option>
49        <option value="18h">18 Hour</option>
50        <option value="19h">19 Hour</option>
51        <option value="20h">20 Hour</option>
52        <option value="21h">21 Day</option>
53        <option value="22h">22 Day</option>
54        <option value="23h">23 Day</option>
55        <option value="24h">All Day</option>
```

```
56  </select>
57  <button id="loadData"> Load Data </button>
58  <div style="width:75%;">
59      <canvas id="canvas"></canvas>
60  </div>
61  </body>
62  </html>
```

SAMPLE CODE 4: timesegment.php - part 1.

Output

Figure 7.1 shows the final output of the HTML.

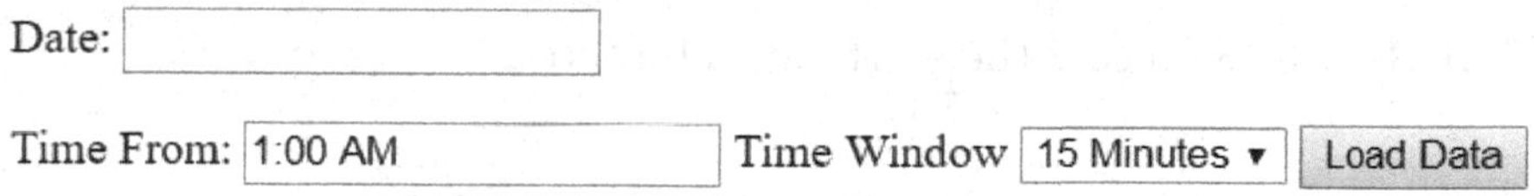

Date: [   ]

Time From: [1:00 AM   ]   Time Window [15 Minutes ▼] [Load Data]

FIGURE 7.1: Time-segment analysis controls.

Figure 7.2 shows the jQueryUI calendar widget after the date input field has been clicked.

Date: [   ]

| ❶ | August 2019 | ❶ | ow [15 Minutes ▼] [Load Data] |

Su	Mo	Tu	We	Th	Fr	Sa
				1	2	3
4	5	6	7	8	9	10
11	12	13	14	15	16	17
18	19	20	21	22	23	24
25	26	27	28	29	30	31

FIGURE 7.2: Selecting the start time for the analysis process.

Figure 7.3 shows an example of the timepicker widget in use to select the start time of interest.

Date: [   ]

Time From: [1:00 AM|]   Time Window [15 Minutes ▾] [Load Data]

| 1:00 AM ▲ |
| 1:15 AM |
| 1:30 AM |
| 1:45 AM |
| 2:00 AM |
| 2:15 AM |
| 2:30 AM ▾ |

FIGURE 7.3: Selecting the start time of interest.

In Sample Code 5, on line 63, a *window.chartColors* is created. This specifies the RGB values for a range of colors. In this graph, red and green will be used. When the page is loaded the *function()* is called on line 72. Inside of this, the jQuery selector is used to select the *datepicker* input field on line 73. The format that we are using for the date is specified as a parameter. In this example, we will pass *yy-mm-dd*, which will provide a date such as *2020-08-28*. The selector is used again to select the *timepicker input* field on line 74. The time format is passed as *h:mm p*. This will provide us with output such as 10:00am. On line 76, the interval specifies the gap between the times that are added. In this example, we are using 15 minutes intervals between each time present. The default time is specified as 1:00am on line 77. On line 79, the dropdown is set to *true*, providing a dropdown menu to allow the user to select the date. On line 80, the scrollbar is set to *true*, providing a visual scroll bar.

On line 83, a *click()* handler is appended on to the button created earlier by using the jQuery selector to select the *loadData* button. When the button is clicked, a call is made to the *generateNewGraph()* function that is responsible for the complete graph generation process. On line 86, this new function is created. Both the positive and the negative feedback will be retrieved from the database when this function is called and plotted on separate lines.

Inside of this function a reference to the *Chart.helpers.color* is stored inside of a variable titled *color* on line 87. The configuration for the graph is created and stored in the *config* variable on line 88. In this configuration the first parameter is the type of graph that will be generated which in this case the value is set to *line*. The *data* variable on line 91, contains the *datasets* array.

This array contains two distinct data sets. The first of these is stored at position 0 of the array, which is the negative feedback score. The *chartColours* that was defined earlier is used to select the colour *red* on line 93. This colour is converted into an RGB string using the *rgbtoString()* function. The *border* color is also defined as *red*. On line 96, the *fill* attribute allows us to color in below the line on the chart. As there may be a large number of feedback records, to avoid overfilling the graph, this is set to *false*. The *data* variable on line 87 is an array that is left blank when first initialized. This will be input in a later step.

Beginning on line 100, the second data set is defined. This data set is stored at position 1 of the array. This data set is used to store the positive feedback. This process is the same as the previous step, with the only alteration being the color of the line being set to *green* on line 103.

```
63   window.chartColors = {
64          red: 'rgb(255, 99, 132)',
65          orange: 'rgb(255, 159, 64)',
66          yellow: 'rgb(255, 205, 86)',
67          green: 'rgb(75, 192, 192)',
68          blue: 'rgb(54, 162, 235)',
69          purple: 'rgb(153, 102, 255)',
70          grey: 'rgb(201, 203, 207)'
71   };
72   $( function() {
73          $( "#datepicker" ).datepicker({dateFormat: "yy-mm-dd"});
74          $('#timepicker').timepicker({
75          timeFormat: 'h:mm p',
76          interval: 15,
77          defaultTime: '1:00am',
78          startTime: '1:00am',
79          dropdown: true,
80          scrollbar: true
81          });
82   });
83   $( "#loadData" ).click(function() {
84          generateNewChart();
```

```
85  });
86  function generateNewChart(){
87      var color = Chart.helpers.color;
88      var config = {
89          type: 'line',
90          data: {
91              datasets: [{
92                  label: 'Negative Feedback Score',
93                  backgroundColor:
                    ↪ color(window.chartColors.red).alpha(0.5).
94                  rgbString(),
95                  borderColor: window.chartColors.red,
96                  fill: false,
97                  data: []
98              },
99              {
100                 label: 'Positive Feedback Score',
101                 backgroundColor:
                    ↪ color(window.chartColors.green).alpha(0.5).
102                 rgbString(),
103                 borderColor: window.chartColors.green,
104                 fill: false,
105                 data: []
106             }
107
108             ]
109         },
```

SAMPLE CODE 5: timesegment.php — Basic graph configuration — part 2.

In Sample Code 6, the options for the graph are defined. In this example, we have set the graph to be responsive on line 111. This allows the graph to move when the user interacts with a mouse when there is more data than available space on the graph. The *title* is set to *true* to be visible, and the text for the *title* is set on line 114

On line 116, the *scales* for the graph is used to define the X and Y axes of the graph. The X is shown horizontally on the graph. On line 122, the *labelString* is set to *Time stamp* to show the user we are working with time. The ticks for the graph, e.g., the individual markings for each record, has the *fontColor* set to #000000, which is black on line 127. On line 131, the Y axes for the graph is used to display the text *Feedback Score* which is visible vertically on the left-hand side of the graph.

```
110        options: {
111            responsive: true,
112            title: {
113                display: true,
114                text: 'Time Segment Analysis'
115            },
116            scales: {
117                xAxes: [{
118                    type: 'time',
119                    display: true,
120                    scaleLabel: {
121                        display: true,
122                        labelString: 'Time stamp'
123                    },
124                    ticks: {
125                        major: {
126
127                            fontColor: '#000000'
128                        }
129                    }
130                }],
131                yAxes: [{
132                    display: true,
133                    scaleLabel: {
134                        display: true,
135                        labelString: 'Feedback Score'
136                    }
137                }]
138            }
139        }
140    };
```

SAMPLE CODE 6: timesegment.php — Adding X and Y axes — part 3.

In Sample Code 7, once the configuration has been created, the main graph can be defined. A single variable titled *ctx* is created on line 141 that serves as a reference point to the *canvas* tag that was defined earlier in the graph. The context for the graph is set to *2d*, which is two dimensional. On line 142, the *window.myLine* variable is set to be a new instance of the *Chart()* object that takes in two parameters, the *context* in the form of the *ctx* reference and the *config* variable that was defined in the previous step.

As the user interface provides the user the ability to select the date, time, and time window they want to see, each of these values must be retrieved. The first of these is the *date* variable. As the data is stored inside a simple HTML *input* field, the jQuery selector can be used to select the element by the *ID* that was set to *datepicker* earlier, as shown on line 145. The *val()* function then extracts the value present from the selected field.

The time entered by the user is also stored in a simple text *input* field, but as the time format of times can vary, the JavaScript library *moment* is used to process the time.

On line 147, the first step in this process is to create a new call to the moment library. Inside of this call, two parameters are passed. The first of these is the raw time format that was entered. This is retrieved by using the jQuery selector to select the input field and the *.val()* function is used to extract the raw value. The second parameter that is passed is the original format of the time stamp. In this case, *h:mm A*, which takes in the raw date format, e.g., *1:00 AM*. This is formatted into *HH:mm* which is the 24 hour clock variant of the time, e.g., *01:00*.

Further information about these patterns can be found on the *moment.js* website.[2] The final variable that is extracted is the *minutes* input field on line 150. This contains the time window selected by the user. On line 152, a simple *if statement* is used to check if the minutes entered by the user contains the letter *h*. If this is present, it identifies to us that we are looking at an hour rather than 15, 30 or 45 minutes. In the case where the *h* is present, on line 153, the *replace()* function is called on the string to remove the *h* and replace it with nothing. The remaining value is the hour that can be multiplied by 60 to get the total desired time window in minutes.

To gather the feedback records for the chart, two *GET* requests are made. One for the positive feedback and one for the negative feedback. On line 157, a *GET* request is made to the *getTimeRecords.php* page. The *type* parameter is passed to identify that we wish to receive only negative records. These negative records are feedback records that have been rated below 5. The *dstart* variable is passed, which is the date we are interested in. The *date* variable that was previously selected is passed as the value. Similar to this, the *tstart* is passed to indicate the time of interest, and the *time* value is passed that was selected earlier. The final variable that is passed is titled *minutes* that outlines how large a window we are interested in seeing from the defined start time.

---

[2]https://momentjs.com/docs/#/manipulating/

The results that are returned will be in the format of a date followed by a feedback score. Each individual record that is returned is separated using a comma. For this reason, to process each individual record, on line 159, the *split()* function is called passing a comma as the delimiter to break on. The result of this process is an array of records that is stored in the *result* variable. On line 160, a simple iteration is done using the *forEach()* function that provides us access to each individual *record* in the set. This is a variable name that we are assigning to the single record.

The record that is returned must be split into four parts: at position 0 of the array is the *year*, *day* and *month*, position 1 is the *time*, and position 3 is the *feedback score*. To perform this action, the *split()* function is called passing a single space as the delimiter on line 161.

To add the data to the chart data set, on line 162, the *config.data.datasets[0]* is referenced. This points to the original array that was created in the *config* variable. Position 0 of the dataset is only used for negative feedback records. To add the new data to the charts data set arrays, the *push()* function is called. This takes two parameters, the *x* value, and the *y* value. The first of these is the single *date[0]*, which is the date followed by position 1, which is the time the record was logged. The Y-axes value is the feedback score between 1 and 10 that is stored at position 2 of the array.

After the loop has finished iterating, a call is made to the *window.myLine.update()* function on line 167 to render the changes that have been made to the graph.

```
141   var ctx = document.getElementById('canvas').getContext('2d');
142   window.myLine = new Chart(ctx, config);
143
144   // get values entered by the user
145   var date = $('#datepicker').val();
146   console.log($('#timepicker').val())
147   var time = moment($('#timepicker').val(), ["h:mm
      ↪   A"]).format("HH:mm");
148   console.log("time new" + time);
149
150   var minutes = $('#minutes').val();
151
152   if(minutes.indexOf('h') > -1){
153       minutes = minutes.replace('h', '');
154       minutes = minutes * 60;
155   }
156   // get negative records
```

```
157  $.get( "getTimeRecords.php", { type: "negative", dstart: date,
     ↪  tstart: time, minutes:minutes} )
158    .done(function( data ) {
159      var result = data.split(',');
160      result.forEach((record) => {
161          var single = record.split(' ');
162          config.data.datasets[0].data.push({
163                  x: newDate(single[0]+single[1]),
164                  y: single[2],
165              });
166      });
167      window.myLine.update();
168  }); // end of get
```

SAMPLE CODE 7: timesegment.php — Appending records to the data set — part 4.

In Sample Code 8, to gather the positive feedback records, the code is identical, with the only changes being the the *type* parameter on line 170 is set to *positive* and the reference to the positive dataset records on line 175, which is at position 1 of the data set array. Again, the graph is updated by making a call to the *window.myLine.update()* function on line 180.

After the main function has been added to render the graph, a second function is added titled *newDate()* on line 183. This takes in a time stamp from the database and formats it with the year, month, and day format followed by the hours, minutes, and seconds. This would return a time stamp stored in the database as *2020-08-26 10:22:01*.

```
169  // get positive records
170  $.get( "getTimeRecords.php", { type: "positive", dstart: date,
     ↪  tstart: time, minutes:minutes} )
171    .done(function( data ) {
172      var result = data.split(',');
173      result.forEach((record) => {
174          var single = record.split(' ');
175          config.data.datasets[1].data.push({
176                  x: newDate(single[0]+single[1]),
177                  y: single[2],
178              });
179      });
180      window.myLine.update();
181  }); // end of GET
182  }
```

```
183   function newDate(stamp) {
184      return moment(stamp, "YYYY-MM-DD HH:mm:ss");
185   }
186   </script>
```

SAMPLE CODE 8: timesegment.php — Performing the *GET* request — part 5.

Example code: getTimeRecords.php

To retrieve the records from the database for the graph generation process, a second PHP page is created titled *getTimeRecords.php*. In Sample Code 9, on line 2, the *GET* function is used to retrieve the *type* of feedback that is requested, e.g., *positive* or *negative*. This is stored inside the *type* variable. On lines 3–9, a connection to the database is established.

On line 10, a simple *if statement* is used to check if the *type* variable was set to *positive* or *negative*. Based on the value, a call is made to the *getRecords()* function on line 11 or 14 that takes in the *type*. This allows us to reuse the same body of code for both positive and negative records. On line 16, the *getRecords()* function is declared that takes in a single parameter *sort* which will contain the value *positive* or *negative*.

Inside of this function on lines 18, 19, and 20, each parameter that was passed via the JavaScript *GET* is retrieved. These include the date of interest, the time of interest, and the size of the time window required in minutes. A new variable titled *start* is created that concatenates the date and time together with a single space in between. On line 22, This date is passed to a new instance of the *DateTime* PHP object. This DateTime allows us to create an offset to the time, e.g., the number of minutes after our time of interest. This process is done to derive the end time of interest, which will be used in our SQL query. On line 24, the *modify()* function takes in the offset, which is the number of minutes we want to alter the original time stamp by. This end-time is stored in the *end* variable on line 25. The *format()* function is called to format the date and time in the desired format for retrieval from the database.

As this function is used for both positive and negative feedback, a simple *if statement* is used to generate a piece of SQL that will be added to the SQL query. This begins by creating an array titled *params* on line 26 that contains the start and end time of interest. If the *sort* variable that was passed to the function was positive then the *scoreSort* variable is set to *score* $>=5$ on line 29. When the variable is set to negative, then the *scoreSort* is set to *score* < 5 on line 32.

On line 34, the SQL query is built up to select the *mytime* and the *score* columns from the *timeanalysis* table. The filtering is done by adding a *WHERE* clause defining that we are interested in records where the time stamp is greater or equal to ?, which is the first value in the *params* array and the time stamp is less or equal to ?, which is the second parameter in the array, e.g., the end time. Another *AND* is appended. The SQL for the *scoreSort* is appended. The final step in the process is the *ORDER BY*, which outlines that we want to order the records by the time stamp.

On line 36, the *execute()* function is called, passing the parameters followed by a call to the *fetchAll()* function to return all the records.

The final step in the process is to generate the *output* variable. This variable is built up based on the content retrieved from the database. For each row in the database, on line 40, the output is appended to include the row[0], which contains the time stamp followed by a space followed by row[1], which contains the score. Each row is completed by adding a colon, which is used as the separator between the records that are returned to the JavaScript *GET* request defined earlier.

The output that generated is processed on line 42 by making a call to the *substr()* function that takes two parameters: the starting index, which is set to 0, and the end index, which is set to -1 to remove the final semicolon from the *output* variable.

All the data is output to the page, which is returned back to the original JavaScript *GET* request on the *timesegment.php* page for graphing.

```php
<?php
$type = $_GET['type'];
try {
    $host = 'localhost:3306';
    $dbname = 'bookexamples';
    $user = 'sampleuser';
    $pass = '3C9038A509BE6145AAD6827B4568AD918BC3DAC0';
    $DBH = new PDO("mysql:host=$host;dbname=$dbname", $user,
      ↪ $pass);
} catch(PDOException $e) {echo $e;}
if($type=='positive'){
    getRecords('positive');
}
else if($type=='negative'){
    getRecords('negative');
}
function getRecords($sort){
```

```
17    global $DBH;
18    $dateStart = $_GET['dstart'];
19    $timeStart = $_GET['tstart'];
20    $minutes = $_GET['minutes'];
21    $start = $dateStart . ' ' . $timeStart;
22    $dt = new DateTime($start);
23    $offSet = $minutes;
24    $dt->modify("+{$offSet} minutes");
25    $end= $dt->format('Y-m-d H:m');
26    $params = array($start, $end);
27    $scoreSort = '';
28    if($sort == 'positive'){
29        $scoreSort = 'score >= 5';
30    }
31    else if($sort == 'negative'){
32        $scoreSort = 'score < 5';
33    }
34    $sql = "SELECT timestamp, score FROM timeanalysis  where
      ↪  TIMESTAMP >= ? AND TIMESTAMP <= ? AND $scoreSort ORDER
      ↪  BY timestamp";
35    $sth = $DBH->prepare($sql);
36    $sth->execute($params);
37    $res = $sth->fetchAll();
38    $output = '';
39    foreach ($res as $row){
40        $output .= $row[0] . ' ' . $row[1] . ',';
41    }
42    echo substr($output, 0, -1);
43 }
```

SAMPLE CODE 9: Retrieving positive and negative feedback based on a time stamp and score.

Output

Figure 7.4 shows an example time segment analysis for a two-hour window starting at 10 a.m. The positive records can be seen in green, and the negative feedback records can be seen in red.

7.4   REAL-TIME FEEDBACK ANALYSIS

When working with feedback from customers, often the time the feedback has been left may be important. Consider a collection of users who

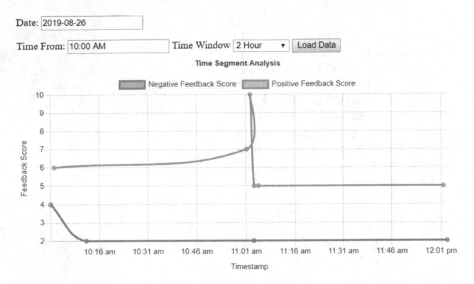

FIGURE 7.4: Time-segment analysis for positive and negative feedback for a two-hour window.

are interacting with a web application attempting to place orders, and the site begins to malfunction. This can quickly cause an issue for a business. In this case, the time when the feedback has been placed may be of great importance. A focus on the negative feedback instead of the positive feedback would be the primary area of interest.

In this section, we will outline the process of viewing feedback from customers in a real-time environment. An example of this is when a user leaves feedback below a specific threshold, e.g., below 5 on a scale of 1 to 10. The Smoothie charts JavaScript library will be used for the graph generation process. This graph, unlike previous graphs, will continue to move from right to left across the screen as feedback is placed by users in real-time. It can be considered a moving line graph. This library is available from http://smoothiecharts.org/.

Example 3: Real-time graph analysis
This example consists of three files and two libraries:

1. create.sql — This contains the SQL to create the *realtime* table to hold feedback records.

2. realtime.php — This file is used to render the chart.

3. recordFetch.php — This file is used to retrieve feedback records from the database.

4. Smoothie Charts — This is the main JavaScript library used for rendering the graph.

5. jQuery — This library is used to perform a JavaScript *GET* request.

Example code: create.sql

In Sample Code 10, the database table contains a unique *ID* column that is a primary key and auto-incremented. A *datetime* column is added that will automatically set the current time stamp when the record is created. Finally and a *score* column is added that will hold the score entered by the user. In this example, we will be working with scores between 1 and 10.

```
1   CREATE TABLE `realtime` (
2       `id` INT NOT NULL AUTO_INCREMENT,
3       `datetime` DATETIME NOT NULL DEFAULT CURRENT_TIMESTAMP,
4       `score` TINYINT,
5       PRIMARY KEY (`id`)
6   );
```

SAMPLE CODE 10: Sample realtime database table.

Example code: realtime.php

In Sample Code 11, a new file titled *realtime.php* is shown. At the top of this file, we will include two JavaScript libraries. The first of these is a reference to the *smoothie.js* file on line 5, which is placed in the same folder as the PHP page. On line 6, a reference is made to the jQuery CDN, which will allow us to use the JavaScript *GET* function.

After the header has been completed, the body of the document can be added. A simple *h1* tag is used on line 9 to add text to the top of the page. This is followed by a *canvas* tag on line 10. The *ID* for this tag is set to *mycanvas*. The *height* and *width* attributes for the *canvas* are set to 500 and 500, respectively. This is the main container for holding the graph.

The core of the graph generation process is based on the additional JavaScript libraries that are added. To begin this process, a *script* tag is first added on line 13. This is followed by a reference to the current date that can be retrieved using the *new Date()* function on line 15. This function by its self will return a complete string with reference to the time zone the user is in. As this may not correlate with the data that is stored in our database, the variable containing the date will need further processing.

On lines 16 and 17, two variables titled *date* and *time* are created. Calls are made to the *getFullYear()*, *getMonth()*, and *getDate()* functions on the *now* variable retrieved earlier. After these have been extracted. Additional calls can be made to extract the hours minutes and seconds. The benefit of this approach is that we can add in the desired separator between the dates and times. In this case, a dash is used between the date components, and a colon is used between the time. On line 18, both of the *date* and *time* variables are appended together and placed inside the *currentTime* variable.

Once the time has been gathered, a new line needs to be added onto the graph. This is done by making a call to the *TimeSeries()* object on line 19. A reference to this is placed inside the *line1* variable. As there is a number of different records in the database table, each of which has its own *ID*, a variable is created titled *currentIdProcessed* on line 20. This will be used as a storage facility for the *ID* of the record that has been added to the graph, ensuring that no records with this *ID* or less will be added on to the graph. Only new records will be visualized, keeping to the theme of real-time.

On line 22, the *setInterval()* function is used to create a loop that will cause the graph to move as new records are added. At the very end of this code, 2000 is added as the number of milliseconds to be added between the iterations. This can be changed to make the updates more or less frequent. In this case, 2000 will give us a two-second delay between the updates.

For each call of the function of the *setInterval()*, a call is made to the jQuery *GET* function on line 23 to call the *recordFetch.php* page that is the primary source of information for the graph. Two pieces of data are passed with this call: the *time* variable, which is set to be the current time of the system and the *currentRecord* variable, which is set to be the value of the *currentIdProcessed* variable that stores the *ID* of the most recent record that has been retrieved from the database. When the *recordFetch.php* page is called, the data will be returned in the *data* variable on line 24 as a single string. When records are returned the *done()* function will be triggered on line 24.

Inside this function, the *data* variable is available. This variable contains a string that contains the *ID* of the record retrieved and the score that has been left by the user. This value is separated using a single dash. On line 25, a simple *if statement* is used to check if the *data* variable contains data or not. If it does, then the processing of the *data* variable is started. To process this on line 26, the *split()* function is called on the *data* variable. The dash is used as a separator to split the records. The result of this process is an array that is titled *result*.

After the splitting process has been completed, on line 27, a new time stamp is generated using *new Date().getTime()* which returns the time in epoch format. This is followed by *result[1]* that contains the feedback score that has been entered by the user. This data is appended to the *line1* object.

On line 28, a simple *console.log()* is used to print out to the console the *ID* and the score that have been appended to the graph for the debugging process. On line 29, the *ID* of the current record that is stored in the *result[0]* of the array is set to be the current value of the *currentIdProcessed* variable. This will be used in future iterations of the loop, preventing the same record from being called again.

A new SmoothieChart is created on line 33 with a reference stored inside the *smoothie* variable. The color and style of the graph can be set. In this example, the *strokeStyle* is set using RBG numbers, followed by the *fillStyle* and *lineWith*. The *millisPerLine* is set to 250 which is the gap between the grid shown in the background. The number of vertical sections shown is set to 6. On line 34, the *addTimesSeries()* function is called that takes in a reference to the *line1* object. The *strokeStyle*, *fillStyle*, and *lineWidth* are set. On line 35, the final step in this process is to set smoothie graph to stream to the *canvas* tag that was created earlier with the *ID* set to *mycanvas*. We set 2000 as the interval for this process.

```
1   <!DOCTYPE html>
2   <html>
3   <head>
4       <title>Negative Feedback Real-time view</title>
5       <script type="text/javascript" src="smoothie.js"></script>
6       <script
        ↪ src="https://code.jquery.com/jquery-1.12.4.js"></script>
7   </head>
8   <body>
9       <h1>Negative Feedback Real-time view</h1>
10      <canvas id="mycanvas" width="500" height="400"></canvas>
11  </body>
12  </html>
```

```
13   <script type="text/javascript">
14   // get the current date and time
15   var now = new Date();
16   var date =
     ↪   now.getFullYear()+'-'+(now.getMonth()+1)+'-'+now.getDate();
17   var time = now.getHours() + ":" + now.getMinutes() + ":" +
     ↪   now.getSeconds();
18   var currentTime = date+' '+time;
19   var line1 = new TimeSeries();
20   var currentIdProcessed = '';
21   // start the updating loop
22   setInterval(function() {
23       $.get( "recordFetch.php", { time: currentTime,
         ↪   currentRecord: currentIdProcessed} )
24           .done(function( data ) {
25               if(!(data.length == 1)){
26                   var result = data.split('-');
27                   line1.append(new Date().getTime(), result[1]);
28                   console.log("adding new record" + result[0] + " "
                     ↪   + result[1]);
29                   currentIdProcessed = result[0];
30               }
31       });
32   }, 2000);
33   var smoothie = new SmoothieChart({ grid: { strokeStyle:
     ↪   'rgb(125, 0, 0)', fillStyle: 'rgb(60, 0, 0)', lineWidth: 1,
     ↪   millisPerLine: 250, verticalSections: 6 },
     ↪   labels:{fontSize:16} });
34   smoothie.addTimeSeries(line1, { strokeStyle: 'rgb(255, 0, 0)',
     ↪   fillStyle: '', lineWidth: 3 });
35   smoothie.streamTo(document.getElementById("mycanvas"), 2000);
36   </script>
```

SAMPLE CODE 11: realtime.php — Graph that updates in real-time as records are added to the database.

Example code: recordFetch.php

A second page is created that is responsible for retrieving records from the database titled *recordFetch.php*. In Sample Code 12, the *currentRecord* variable is fetched from the *GET* on line 2. This is followed by the *date* variable that contains the time stamp of the records of interest on line 3. To allow this example to be used for a static record collection during testing, the *date* record can be replaced with a static date that contains a collection of feedback records. On line 9, a connection to the MySQL database is created.

To retrieve the records from the database, on line 11, an array titled *params* is created that contains the *ID* of the last record retrieved and the date of interest. On line 12, the *SELECT* statement is created. This statement contains a *WHERE* clause that only returns IDs that are greater than the one provided. These results are ordered by the date which is greater or equal to the date provided. Question marks are used to replace the variables in the string as unnamed placeholders. A second Ordering is set as the *ID* column in ascending order. A *LIMIT 1* is added to only return a single record. The statement and the parameters are placed together using the *prepare()* function on line 13 which is followed by the *execute()* function on line 14.

On line 15, the records are fetched and placed into a local variable titled *res*. On line 16, the final output is generated in a format that will be processed by the graph. This format is the column 0 of the database row stored in the *res* variable, which is the *ID* of the row followed by a dash, followed by the score, which is stored in position 2 of the *res* database row.

```php
1  <?php
2  $id = $_GET['currentRecord'];
3  $date = '2019-8-18 20:36:18'; // only used for static example
4  try {
5      $host = 'localhost:3306';
6      $dbname = 'bookexamples';
7      $user = 'sampleuser';
8      $pass = '3C9038A509BE6145AAD6827B4568AD918BC3DAC0';
9      $DBH = new PDO("mysql:host=$host;dbname=$dbname", $user,
            ↪ $pass);
10 } catch(PDOException $e) {echo $e;}
11 $params = array($id, $date);
12 $sql = "SELECT * FROM realtime  WHERE id > ? ORDER BY datetime
       ↪ >= ?, id asc LIMIT 1";
13 $sth = $DBH->prepare($sql);
14 $sth->execute($params);
15 $res = $sth->fetch();
16 echo $res[0] . '-' . $res[2];
```

SAMPLE CODE 12: recordFetch.php — Retrieving the records from the *realtime* database table.

Negative Feedback Real-Time View

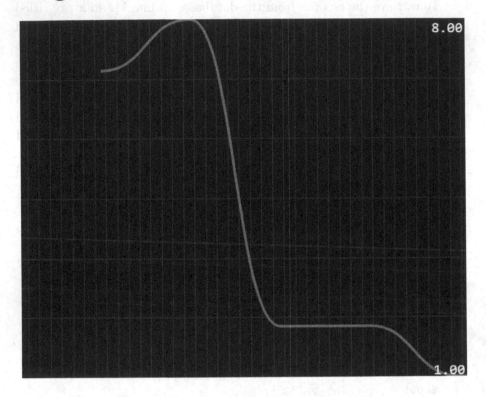

FIGURE 7.5: Real-time feedback score-report line graph.

Output

Figure 7.5 shows the final graph. In this graph, the maximum and the minimum scores will be stored on the right hand-side of the graph. For every 2 seconds, the graph will update with more data.

7.5 POSITIVE VS. NEGATIVE FEEDBACK CALENDARS

When viewing feedback scores, viewing an entire year can be a beneficial process as context is given for when the feedback was recorded day by day. In this section, we will outline the process of using Google Charts to generate JavaScript-based graphs. These charts provide a simplistic minimal implementation for graphing with little overhead required. The complete API for the calendar can be found at *https://developers.google.com/chart/interactive/docs/gallery/calendar.* As these are calendar-based charts, two different charts will be added to the same page, one chart for the positive feedback for a year, and the second chart showing the negative feedback for the same year.

Example 4: feedback calendars

This example consists of three files and two libraries:

1. create.sql — This contains the SQL to create the *calendar* database table.

2. calendar.php — This contains the main JavaScript for the visualization.

3. calendarGetRecords.php — This retrieves records to plot on the calendar.

4. Google Charts — This library contains the main calendar that is used during the visualization process.

5. jQuery — This is used to perform a JavaScript *GET* request to the *calendarGetRecords.php* page.

Example code: create.sql
Before we begin with the process of visualizing records, a number of positive and negative feedback records are needed for a selection of calendar dates. A MySQL table will be created that will contain the *ID* of the record, the *time stamp, feedback text* entered by the user, and the *score* given by the user between 1 and 10.

```
1  CREATE TABLE `calendar` (
2      `id` INT NOT NULL AUTO_INCREMENT,
3      `timestamp` TIMESTAMP NULL DEFAULT CURRENT_TIMESTAMP,
4      `feedbacktext` TEXT,
5      `score` TINYINT,
6      PRIMARY KEY (`id`)
7  );
```

Example code: calendar.php

We will create a new PHP page titled *calendar.php*. In Sample Code 13, a content delivery network is added on line 3 to include jQuery. On line 4, the Google Charts JavaScript loader is included. On line 6, a call is made to the Google Chart *load()* function. This function takes two parameters *current*, which specifies that we would like to use the current release of the API. The *packages* then makes a reference to the different types of charts that can be used. In this case, we are loading the *calendar* package.

When the chart is ready, the *setOnLoadCallback()* function is called on lines 7 and 8, which takes a reference to the function we want to use to generate the graphs. In this example, the function we are calling is the *drawPositiveChart()* function and the *drawNegativeChart()* function. On line 9, the *drawPositiveChart()* function is added that will be used for the graph generation process. Inside this function, we will create a new *DataTable* object on line 10 that will contain all the positive and negative reviews. A call is made to the *dataTable.addColumn()* function on line 11 that allows us to add the columns required for the visualization. In this example, we are adding one for the date and one for the feedback count that will be present when a mouse hovers over the chart.

On line 13, a sample structure of a record is commented out for future reference. No data is added here when the chart is first loaded. On line 17, a new *chart* object is created with a reference to the *calendar_positive* that will be added later. On line 19, a *options* object is created that allows us to specify the *title* and the *height* for the graph.

After the columns have been added, the process of adding the data to the chart can begin. Each row that is added to the chart is a new *Date* object which contains the year, month, and day that we would like to plot the information for. This is followed by a single number that can be positive or negative, which will be shown when a mouse cursor is placed over the cell. The number will be colored from white to a shade of dark blue, depending on the number added. The higher the number, the darker shade of blue the cell will receive.

On line 23, a jQuery *GET* request is made to the *calendarGetRecords.php* page to fetch the data to plot. A *type* parameter is passed that indicates we want to retrieve *positive* feedback records. On line 24, when the result is returned the *data* variable becomes available. This contains the records that will be plotted to the graph.

Inside of the *done()* on line 24, a simple *console.log()* is added on line 25 to view the data that is returned to aid debugging. The *data* variable is split based on a comma that was used to separate each date on line 26 that is placed inside the *singleDates* array.

The results that are returned in the *data* variable contain a date and score separated by dashes for individual values, and a comma between the records, e.g., 2019-02-11-3 would be the date 2019-02-11 followed by a score of 3. The next records are separated by commas as the unique delimiter e.g., *2019-02-11-3,2019-02-24-11,2019-03-24-9,2019-06-19-25*. On line 27, a *for loop* is used to iterate over each of the dates. For each individual date on line 28, the *split()* function is called to separate the date based on the dash that exists between the year, month, day, and feedback score total. To aid debugging, another *console.log()* is added on line 29. Each component of the *singleDate* being viewed can be accessed using the array index 0 to 3.

Finally, to add the new data on to the chart, on line 30, a call is made to the *dataTable.addRow()* function. This function takes in a *date* object followed by a number that will represent the total count of records for that day. A new *date* is created and the *oneDate[0]* for the year, *oneDate[1]* for the month, and *oneDate[2]* for the day are added. The *date* object is closed, and a comma is used to separate the *score* that is appended from the *oneDate* array at position 3.

As the original returned representation of this number is a string, the *Number()* function is used to cast it into a number. After the row has been added to the chart and the *for loop* has completed the final iteration, a call is made to the *chart.draw()* function on line 32 that takes in the *dataTable* that has just been populated, followed by the *options* array.

```
1   <html>
2   <head>
3   <script
    ↪   src="https://code.jquery.com/jquery-3.4.1.min.js"></script>
4   <script type="text/javascript"
    ↪   src="https://www.gstatic.com/charts/loader.js"></script>
5   <script type="text/javascript">
6   google.charts.load("current", {packages:["calendar"]});
7   google.charts.setOnLoadCallback(drawPositiveChart);
8   google.charts.setOnLoadCallback(drawNegativeChart);
9   function drawPositiveChart() {
10      var dataTable = new google.visualization.DataTable();
11      dataTable.addColumn({ type: 'date', id: 'Date' });
12      dataTable.addColumn({ type: 'number', id: 'Feedback Count'
        ↪   });
```

```
13    dataTable.addRows([
14        // Sample records that can be added to the chart.
15        //[ new Date(2019, 3, 13), 2 ],
16    ]);
17    var chart = new
      ↪   google.visualization.Calendar(document.getElementById
18    ('calendar_positive'));
19    var options = {
20        title: "Positive Feedback Analysis",
21        height: 350,
22    };
23    $.get( "calendarGetRecords.php", { type: "positive"} )
24        .done(function( data ) {
25            console.log(data);
26            var singleDates = data.split(',');
27            for(var i=0; i< singleDates.length; i++){
28                var oneDate = singleDates[i].split('-');
29                console.log(oneDate[0], oneDate[1], oneDate[2],
                  ↪   oneDate[3]);
30                dataTable.addRow( [ new Date(oneDate[0],
                  ↪   oneDate[1], oneDate[2]), Number(oneDate[3])
                  ↪   ] );
31            }
32        chart.draw(dataTable, options);
33    });
34 }
```

SAMPLE CODE 13: calendar.php — Initital chart setup and *GET* request — part 1.

In Sample Code 14, for the negative feedback chart, the same process is completed, with minor changes. The *GET* request that is made to the *calendarGetRecords.php* page is passed the *type* variable with the value set to *negative* on line 50.

The final step in the process is to create the body of the HTML page. A *body* tag is added on line 64 and inside of this, a *div* tag is created with the unique *ID calendar_positive* on line 65. The style attribute is used to set the *height* and *width* of the visualization. The same process is repeated for a second *div* with the *ID* set to *calendar_negative* on line 67.

```
35 function drawNegativeChart() {
36     var dataTable = new google.visualization.DataTable();
37     dataTable.addColumn({ type: 'date', id: 'Date' });
```

```
38    dataTable.addColumn({ type: 'number', id: 'Feedback Count'
      ↪  });
39    dataTable.addRows([
40        // first sample records that can be hardcoded.
41        //[ new Date(2019, 3, 13), 2 ],
42    ]);
43
44    var chart = new
      ↪  google.visualization.Calendar(document.getElementById
45    ('calendar_negative'));
46    var options = {
47        title: "Negative Feedback Analysis",
48        height: 350,
49    };
50    $.get( "calendarGetRecords.php", { type: "negative"} )
51        .done(function( data ) {
52            console.log(data);
53            var singleDates = data.split(',');
54            for(var i=0; i< singleDates.length; i++){
55                var oneDate = singleDates[i].split('-');
56                console.log(oneDate[0], oneDate[1], oneDate[2],
                  ↪  oneDate[3]);
57                dataTable.addRow( [ new Date(oneDate[0],
                  ↪  oneDate[1], oneDate[2]), Number(oneDate[3])
                  ↪  ] );
58            }
59    chart.draw(dataTable, options);
60 });
61 }
62 </script>
63 </head>
64 <body>
65    <div id="calendar_positive" style="width: 700px; height:
      ↪  200px;"></div>
66    <hr>
67    <div id="calendar_negative" style="width: 700px; height:
      ↪  200px;"></div>
68 </body>
69 </html>
```

SAMPLE CODE 14: calendar.php — Gathering data for negative
chart — part 2.

Example code: calendarGetRecords.php

For the *GET* request to get the data from the database, a second PHP page is created titled *calendarGetRecords.php*. In Sample Code 15, this page begins with a *type* variable on line 2 that is used to get the type of request that was sent to the page. In this chart, the two types of available data are *positive* and *negative* feedback scores. On lines 10–15, depending on the value of the *type* variable, a function is called for either to get the positive feedback using the *getPositiveRecords()* function or the negative feedback using the *getNegativeRecords()* function.

Inside of the *getPositiveRecords()* function, the keyword *global* is added on line 17 to reference the database connection *DBH*. On line 18, the SQL query is built up to retrieve all the positive feedback records from the database. This query selects the time stamp from the database and casts it into a date and then references the column as *date*. A *count(score)* is performed to count the number of score records that is referenced as the *score* column. These actions are performed on the *calendar* database table *WHERE* the score is greater than 5. A *GROUP BY* statement is added to the group the records together based on the time stamp column. This approach allows the database to return the total score for each unique date that feedback has been stored for.

On line 19, the *prepare()* function is called followed by the *execute()* function. The *fetchAll()* function is called on line 21 that will return all relevant records from the database. A variable titled *output* on line 22 is used as the place holder for records that are being built up every time the loop iterates.

In this example, the *row[0]* indicates the date in *YYYY-MM-DD* format followed by a single dash followed by *row[1]* which contains the total count of records for that given date. For each individual record, a comma is added to separate them. This is important as the *GET* function in the JavaScript described earlier uses this separator to break apart the dates during processing. The final step in the process is to use the *substr()* function on line 26 that takes in the *output* variable, the starting position, e.g., 0 and the ending position, e.g., -1, which will strip the final comma of the complete *output*. This output is printed using an echo statement, which will return the contents back to the *GET* JavaScript function when called.

The process for the negative feedback records is very similar to the positive feedback records. The only modification that is needed is in the

WHERE clause. The scores of interest are those that are less or equal to 5.

```php
1   <?php
2   $type = $_GET['type'];
3   try {
4       $host = 'localhost:3306';
5       $dbname = 'bookexamples';
6       $user = 'sampleuser';
7       $pass = '3C9038A509BE6145AAD6827B4568AD918BC3DAC0';
8       $DBH = new PDO("mysql:host=$host;dbname=$dbname", $user,
        ↪ $pass);
9   } catch(PDOException $e) {echo $e;}
10  if($type=='positive'){
11      getPositiveRecords();
12  }
13  else if($type=='negative'){
14      getNegativeRecords();
15  }
16  function getPositiveRecords(){
17      global $DBH;
18      $sql = "SELECT  DATE(TIMESTAMP) AS date,COUNT(score) AS
        ↪ score FROM calendar WHERE score > 5 GROUP BY
        ↪ date(TIMESTAMP)";
19      $sth = $DBH->prepare($sql);
20      $sth->execute();
21      $res = $sth->fetchAll();
22      $output = '';
23      foreach ($res as $row){
24          $output .= $row[0] . '-' . $row[1] . ',';
25      }
26      echo substr($output, 0, -1);
27  }
28  function getNegativeRecords(){
29      global $DBH;
30      $sql = "SELECT  DATE(TIMESTAMP) AS date,COUNT(score) AS
        ↪ score FROM calendar WHERE score <= 5 GROUP BY
        ↪ date(TIMESTAMP)";
31      $sth = $DBH->prepare($sql);
32      $sth->execute();
33      $res = $sth->fetchAll();
34      $output = '';
35      foreach ($res as $row){
36          $output .= $row[0] . '-' . $row[1] . ',';
37      }
```

```
38      echo substr($output, 0, -1);
39  }
```

SAMPLE CODE 15: calendarGetRecords.php — Retrieving records from the database.

Output

Figure 7.6 shows the final output of the graphing process. Two charts are shown with the positive feedback records in the top graph and the negative feedback records in the bottom graph. In the top right corner of the screen, we can see the color shading index. The lighter the color, the fewer records are present. The darker the color, the more feedback records are present.

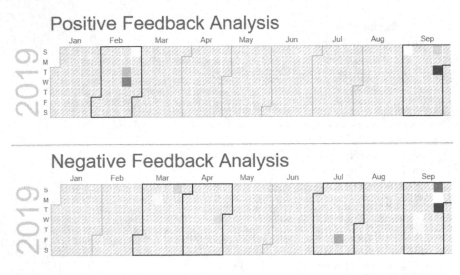

FIGURE 7.6: Calendar view of positive and negative feedback. The shading of the cells indicates the number of records.

In Figure 7.7, we can see that when a mouse is placed over the calendar, the total number of feedback records for that date are provided.

7.6 FEEDBACK HEAT MAP

During the analysis of feedback, patterns often occur in the time of day the feedback was left. When feedback is viewed in a linear format, these patterns can be easily lost. In this section, we will describe the process of creating a heat map of feedback for a given day. The heat map will

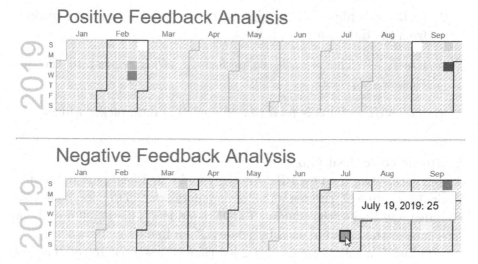

FIGURE 7.7: Mouse hovering shows the number of records for a given day.

represent a single calendar day that the user can select. For the selected day, each hour will be represented as an individual block. Within each hour block, it is further broken down into five-minute time windows.

For each of the individual time windows, the total number of feedback records collected will be counted. These blocks will be colored depending on the number of records found. A lighter color will be used to identify low numbers of records, and a darker color will be used to identify the higher count of records.

This color-based approach provides detailed feedback on the time periods when feedback was left at a glance. For each different time segment, the cursor can be used to dynamically show the total count for that segment. By using this cursor-based approach, the overall quantity of data added to the chart is minimal by default with additional data available when required.

Example 5: Heat map

This example consists of two files and two libraries:

1. heat.php — This is the main PHP page used to show the visualization.

2. getRecords.php — This page is responsible for gathering records from the database.

3. jQuery — This is used to perform a *GET* request to the *getRecords.php* page.

4. jQueryUI — This is used to add a custom date picker widget.

Example code: heat.php

To begin this graph a new PHP file is created titled *heat.php*. In Sample Code 16, on line 3, the content delivery network (CDN) for jQuery is included. On line 4, the jQueryUI CDN is added. This is followed by a reference to the CSS file used by jQueryUI on line 5.

On line 7, a new *style* tag is added that is first used to set the *font* of the page. In this example, we are using the *arial* font. On line 11, the CSS class *colorRow* is created. This class is used to alter the layout of each individual time segment that will be shown. The *height* is first set, followed by the *width*. The margin from the *left* is set to *35px* to provide a space between the time that will be first printed, and the colored row that will be shown beside it. The background color of the individual row is set to *red* by default. This will be changed later to lighter shades depending on the volume of feedback that was found for the given time.

On line 19, a new *variable* tag is created titled *step*. This variable is used as the core of the color-coding process. For a given collection of feedback records, e.g., 20 individual records, for a given five minute time window between 09:00 a.m. and 09:05 a.m., there may be only 12 feedback records. For a later time, e.g., 10:30 a.m. to 10:35 a.m., there may have been two records collected. Each of the other times that feedback records were collected may fall outside of these times, e.g., the other six records. In this case, the max possible count for a given time slot on that day is 12 records. To color code this from a light color to a dark color, red would be used to indicate the 12, and a lighter shade of red would be used to indicate the 2. The minimum amount of record possible is zero, which would be the lightest color desired for the chart.

To calculate this, the *step* variable is equated by taking the maximum records for a given day divided by 10. This allows ten different shades to be represented on the chart. Instead of changing the color directly the *opacity* of the color red will be changed. This allows for easy manipulation of any base color, allowing it to range from 0.0 as the lightest to 1.0 being the darkest shade.

On line 22, a simple *span* tag is used to add a title to the chart. This is followed by a single *input* box on line 23 with the *ID* set to *datepicker*. This *input* box will be modified to allow the jQueryUI calendar to be used as the date selection mechanism later. On line 24, a *button* is added that will be used to trigger the graph generation process. The *ID* of this button is set to *viewChart* to which a *click()* handler will later be appended.

On line 26, a script tag is created, and a call to the *on load* function is made. When the page loads, the HTML *input* box is converted into a jQuery UI date picker on line 27. The desired date format can be added. In this example, we are formatting the date to *yy-mm-dd*, which allows us to represent the date in a format such as *2020-09-02*. On line 30, one *div* tag is added with the *ID* set to *chart*. This is used to hold the main graph that will be generated.

```
1   <html>
2   <head>
3   <script
    ↪  src="https://code.jquery.com/jquery-3.4.1.min.js"></script>
4   <script src="http://code.jquery.com/ui/1.12.1/jquery-ui.min.js">
    ↪  </script>
5   <link rel="stylesheet" type="text/css"
    ↪  href="http://code.jquery.com/ui/1.12.1/themes/base/
6   jquery-ui.css">
7   <style>
8   *{
9       font-family: arial;
10  }
11  .colorRow {
12      height:13px;
13      width:50px;
14      margin-left: 35px;
15      background-color:red;
16  }
17  </style>
18  </head>
19  <script>
20  var step = 0;
21  </script>
22  <span style="font-size:16pt">Feedback Heat Map </span>
23  <p>Date: <input type="text" id="datepicker">
24  <button id="viewChart">View Chart</button></p>
25  <script>
26    $( function() {
```

```
27      $( "#datepicker" ).datepicker({dateFormat: "yy-mm-dd"});
28    } );
29  </script>
30  <div id="chart">
31  </div>
32  </html>
```

SAMPLE CODE 16: heat.php — Initial page setup — part 1.

In Sample Code 17, on line 34 the jQuery selector is used to select the *viewChart* button. A *click()* handler is appended to this button. Inside of this click handler, the graph generation process is started. On line 35, the jQuery selector is used to select the *datepicker* input field and extract the value using the *val()* function. This is placed inside of a variable titled *date*. For this process to work correctly, it is essential that the date entered by the users matches the date stamps that are stored in the database.

On line 36, a single *GET* request is made to a second page titled *getData.php* to retrieve the records from the database. This page takes a single parameter titled *selectedDate* with the value set to the value entered by the user that was stored in the *date* variable. When the *GET* call is completed on line 37, the *done()* function is called. The result of this is a single variable titled *data* that contains the HTML and records for each time slot that will be shown. On line 38, The *data* is set into the *chart div* tag using the jQuery selector to select the *div* tag with the ID set to *chart*. The *html()* function takes the HTML content as input to set into the *div*. After the HTML has been added onto the chart, it still does not have the correct color coding. To complete this, a second process is started to add additional CSS styling to each *div* tag added.

Each hour has twelve individual slots. To color code these records correctly, three variables are used. The first variable is the *start* on line 40 that is used to store the starting number for the color coding and the *end* variable on line 41 that stores the value for the end of the color-coding range.

An example of this is time slots that have counts between 1 and 10. The first search will be for records that are between 0 and 1, e.g., the lowest counts in the set. The next search will be between 1 and 2, etc. This allows us to process the records in an incremental ascending method. The text *op* variable on line 42 is used for storing the current opacity of the *div* that that is being processed. The lowest possible we are using is 0.1 that will be used to represent time slots with a low number of records.

The data record that was returned during the *GET* request to the PHP page contains 24 different *div* tags representing a day, each of which contains 12 time slots. Each individual time slot has the CSS *class* set to *colorRow*, which allows us to perform a filter on the entire document to select all *div* tags with this class.

For each individual time slot in a 1-hour time block, a simple debugging output is added with the *console.log()* function. The starting point to color the individual time slot begins with the *start* variable set to 0 as there may be time slots with zero records. The *end* position is set to be the value of *step*, which as described earlier, is the maximum count of records in the collection divided by 10. The *op* is set to 0.1 and the *score*, e.g., the number of records counted for a given time slot is extracted from the *div* tag attribute titled *score* on line 48 that was added during the generation of the HTML when the *GET* request was performed.

On line 49, a *for loop* is added to iterate over the available ranges, e.g., 0 to 1, 1 to 2, 2 to 3, etc. To aid this process, a *console.log()* is added on line 50 that prints out the score we are currently processing and the *start* and *end* variable values at that moment. On line 51, during the iteration process, if the score we find is greater or equal to the *start* variable or less and equal to the *end* variable, then the color coding is added.

On line 52, a simple *console.log()* is added to print out the word *found* to the console to aid debugging. On line 53 and 54, the *css()* function is called on the *div* tag being processed to update the colour to be *red* and the *opacity* is set to the current value of the variable *op*. After the *div* has been updated, the *break;* is called to exit the *for loop*.

On lines 57 and 58, if the record is not in the first *start* and *end* range then the start variable is updated to be the value of *end* and the *end* variable is updated to be *end+step*. The *op* variable is also updated to add an additional 0.1 making the opacity of the *div* darker the longer the for loop iterates. On line 65, to aid the user during the analysis of records, the jQueryUI tooltip is added to the entire document.

When the attribute *track* is set to *true* on line 66, the tooltip is updated based on where the mouse is currently located. This tooltip gets the value from the *title* attribute of an individual *div* tag that is generated by the PHP.

```
33  <script>
34  $("#viewChart").click(function() {
35      var date = $('#datepicker').val();
36      $.get( "getData.php", { selectedDate: date } )
37      .done(function( data ) {
38      $("#chart").html(data);
39      // ------- add color style
40      var start = 0;
41      var end = 0;
42      var op = 0.1;
43      $(".colorRow").filter(function() {
44          console.log("processing new record.......");
45          start = 0;
46          end = step;
47          op = 0.1;
48          var score = $(this).attr("score");
49          for(var i=0; i < 10; i++){
50              console.log("checking if "+score+" is between" +
                ↪   start + " and " + (end) + " op is..." + op);
51              if(score >= start && score <= end  ){
52                  console.log("found");
53                  $(this).css('background-color', 'red') ;
54                  $(this).css( "opacity", op );
55                  break;
56              }
57              start = end;
58              end = end + step;
59              op = op + 0.1;
60          }
61      })
62      }); // end .done()
63  }); // end .click()
64  $( function() {
65      $( document ).tooltip({
66      track: true
67      });
68  } );
69  </script>
```

SAMPLE CODE 17: heat.php — Modifying the cell colors dynamically — part 2.

Example code: getData.php

To drive this chart, a PHP page is created titled *getData.php*. In Sample Code 18, on line 7, a connection to the database is first made. On line 9, a variable titled *totalRecords* is created that is used to store the total number of records we are working with at a given time. On line 10, a *div* tag is started with the *style* set to *overflow: hidden* which allows us to put *div* tags side by side. The *width* of this is set to *900px*, which can be changed depending on the required layout.

On line 11, the core of the generation process is started by running a for loop from 0 to 24. Each number represents one hour in the given calendar day. While looping, a call is made to the *getBlockForHour()* function on line 12 that generates a single hour with 12-time slots (5 minutes in each slot). No color coding is performed during this process as this is done on the client-side. This component is purely to gather the records for a given day and count the total for each time slot in the day. On line 16, a JavaScript variable titled *step* is created that will be returned to the client-side. This has the value set to *max* which is set later, divided by 10, indicating there will be 10 color ranges. On line 17, the *getBlockForHour()* function is defined. This is responsible for generating the 24-hour blocks for a given day. On line 18, a variable titled *output* is added. This acts as the placeholder for all content that will be returned.

On line 20, the *output* begins with a single *div* tag with the *class* set to *oneRow*. Inside of the *style* attribute is set to *float:left* and a width is defined as *100px*. This single row will contain a time stamp e.g., 0:00, followed by a coloured bar. The time is added in a *span* tag which allows us to set the *font-size* to *11pt*. The content of the *span* tag is the *hour* variable that was passed to the function followed by :00. On line 23, a *hourStamp* variable is created. On lines 24–28, if the hour we are currently process is less then 10 for example if hour only has one digit, then a 0 is added before the hour. On line 30, a *for loop* is started to get each of the 12 time slots for the given hour. Each of these time slots represents five minute time windows.

For each hour, a call is first made to the *getScore()* function on line 31 that will calculate the total number of records left for the given time window. This function is passed the *hourStamp* variable followed by the *minutes* variable we are viewing. This function would return a single integer that is 0 if no records were found for that time slot, or greater than 0 if records were found.

This result is stored inside of the *score* variable on line 31. On line 32, the main body of HTML for the time slot is generated. A new *div* tag is created with a *width* of *500* and the *overflow* set to *hidden*. This allows the content inside this *div* tag to float to the left. On line 33, the *div* inside this contains a small *50px div* that that contains a *span* tag on line 34 with the *font size* set to 10pt to represent the time that will be printed for the user. The *hourStamp* is added followed by a colon which is followed by the *minutes* stamp. The *span* tag and the *div* tag are then closed.

After this, on line 36, a new *div* is created with the *class* set to *colorRow*. This is the main color-coded bar the user will see for the time slot. The *title* attribute of the *div* tag is set to be the *score* that was returned. This *title* attribute is used by the jQueryUI tooltip to gather the score for the given timeslot when the mouse hovers. The *score* attribute is set to be the *score* that was returned. This *score* attribute is used during the color-coding process on the client-side. On line 39, the *minutes* variable is incremented by five minutes to move onto the next time slot before the *for loop* iterates again. On line 40, if the *minutes* variable is less than 10, then a single 0 is added to the start of the variable to aid the appearance of the time stamp. After all 24 of the hours have been added, each of which contains 12 five minute time windows, then a final closing *div* tag is appended to the *output* variable. The *output* variable is returned on line 45.

```php
1   <?php
2   try {
3       $host = 'localhost:3306';
4       $dbname = 'bookexamples';
5       $user = 'sampleuser';
6       $pass = '3C9038A509BE6145AAD6827B4568AD918BC3DAC0';
7       $DBH = new PDO("mysql:host=$host;dbname=$dbname", $user,
        ↪ $pass);
8   } catch(PDOException $e) {echo $e;}
9   $totalRecords = 0;
10  echo '<div style="overflow: hidden; width:900px">';
11  for($h=0; $h<24; $h++){
12      echo getBlockForhour($h);
13  }
14  echo '</div>';
15  // update the step variable before chart generation
16  echo '<script> step = ' . ($max / 10) .'; </script>';
17  function getBlockForhour($hour){
18      $output = '';
19      $minutes = '00';
```

```
20    $output .='<div class="oneRow" style="float:left;
      ↪ width:100px">';
21    $output .= '<span style="font-size:11pt;">' . $hour .
      ↪ ':00</span>';

22
23    $hourStamp = '';
24    if($hour < 10){
25        $hourStamp = '0' . $hour ;
26    } else{
27        $hourStamp = $hour;
28    }

29
30    for($i=1; $i<13; $i++){
31        $score = getScore($hourStamp, $minutes);
32        $output .= '<div style="width:300px; overflow: hidden;">
33                <div style="width:40px; float: left">
34                <span style="font-size:10pt"> '. $hourStamp.':'
↪ . $minutes . ' </span>
35                </div>
36                <div class="colorRow" id="colorRow"
↪ title="'.$score.' Feeback records" score="'.$score.'">
37                </div>
38                </div>';
39        $minutes += 5;
40        if($minutes < 10){
41            $minutes = '0' . $minutes;
42        }
43    }
44    $output .= '</div>';
45    return $output;
46 }
```

SAMPLE CODE 18: getData.php — Generating an hour block of
HTML — part 1.

To calculate the score for a given time slot, the *getScore()* function is
used as shown in Sample Code 19. This function takes in two parameters,
the *hourStamp* followed by the *minuteStamp*. On line 48, references to
the *max* and *min* variables are made as these may change during the
score gathering process. On line 49, the *endTime* provided is set to be the
current minute's stamp + 4 minutes, creating a 5 minute time window.
An example of this would be for the time stamp 17:30, the time slot we

are interested in retrieving records for is between 17:30 and 17:35. On line 50, the *date* of interest is stored in a local variable.

The SQL query is defined on line 51. Inside this query, the *SELECT* statement is used to count all the *score* records and handle them as *score*. This removes the need to work with a column titled *count(score)*. The *feedbackheat* table is selected, and a *WHERE* clause is added to state that the records of interest are between ? and ?, which are unnamed placeholders for the current *start* and *end* time stamps of interest.

On lines 52–54, the *stDate* and *finish* variables are created. The *stDate* is the current calendar date entered by the user, followed by a space, followed by the hour stamp, a colon, the minute stamp, a colon, and 00 seconds. This is to match the format the records are stored in the database. The *finish* stamp is the current calendar date followed by the same *hourStamp*, followed by a colon, followed by the *endTime* variable followed by a colon and 59 seconds. As shown earlier, we increment the minutes variable by 4 minutes, the seconds are used to identify we want all the records from between 0:00 and 4:59 seconds.

To gather the results, a call is made to the *fetch()* function on line 57. The results are stored inside of the *res* variable. On lines 58 and 59, a reference to the *totalRecords* is made as it stores a reference to the overall count of records found. This variable is updated to include *res[0]*, which contains the total count of records in the current time slot.

On lines 62–67, a reference to the *max* and *min* variables are made. If the result returned is greater then the *max*, then the new score is stored. If the result is less than the current *min*, then it is also stored. At the end of this process, the final *result* variable is returned back to the caller of the *getScore()* function as described earlier.

```
47   function getScore($hourStamp, $minuteStamp){
48       global $DBH, $max, $min;
49       $endTime = $minuteStamp+4;
50       $date = $_GET['selectedDate'];
51       $sql = "SELECT COUNT(score) AS score  FROM feedbackheat
         ↪  WHERE TIMESTAMP BETWEEN ? AND ?";
52       $stDate = $date . " ". "$hourStamp:$minuteStamp:00";
53       $finish = "$date $hourStamp:$endTime".":59";
54       $params = array($stDate, $finish);
55       $sth = $DBH->prepare($sql);
56       $sth->execute($params);
57       $res = $sth->fetch();
58       global $totalRecords;
59       $totalRecords = $totalRecords + $res[0];
```

```
60      $result = $res[0];
61      global $max, $min;
62      if($result > $max){
63          $max = $result;
64      }
65      if($result < $min){
66          $min = $result;
67      }
68      return $result;
69  }
70  ?>
```

SAMPLE CODE 19: getData.php — Finding the scores — part 2.

Output

Figure 7.8 shows an example of the date input box being clicked and the jQueryUI date picker becoming visible. When a date is selected, the *View Chart* button must be clicked.

FIGURE 7.8: Calendar day picking using the jQueryUI date picker.

Figure 7.9 shows the final generated graph. For each hour of the day from 0:00 to 23:59 five-minute time windows are shown. For each of the five-minute time windows, the *opacity* of the color *red* is lighter or darker, depending on the number of records that have been added. This provides a simple method of viewing the most popular feedback times for a given day.

Feedback Heat Map

Date: 2019-09-02   [View Chart]

0:00	1:00	2:00	3:00	4:00	5:00	6:00	7:00	8:00
00:00	01:00	02:00	03:00	04:00	05:00	06:00	07:00	08:00
00:05	01:05	02:05	03:05	04:05	05:05	06:05	07:05	08:05
00:10	01:10	02:10	03:10	04:10	05:10	06:10	07:10	08:10
00:15	01:15	02:15	03:15	04:15	05:15	06:15	07:15	08:15
00:20	01:20	02:20	03:20	04:20	05:20	06:20	07:20	08:20
00:25	01:25	02:25	03:25	04:25	05:25	06:25	07:25	08:25
00:30	01:30	02:30	03:30	04:30	05:30	06:30	07:30	08:30
00:35	01:35	02:35	03:35	04:35	05:35	06:35	07:35	08:35
00:40	01:40	02:40	03:40	04:40	05:40	06:40	07:40	08:40
00:45	01:45	02:45	03:45	04:45	05:45	06:45	07:45	08:45
00:50	01:50	02:50	03:50	04:50	05:50	06:50	07:50	08:50
00:55	01:55	02:55	03:55	04:55	05:55	06:55	07:55	08:55

9:00	10:00	11:00	12:00	13:00	14:00	15:00	16:00	17:00
09:00	10:00	11:00	12:00	13:00	14:00	15:00	16:00	17:00
09:05	10:05	11:05	12:05	13:05	14:05	15:05	16:05	17:05
09:10	10:10	11:10	12:10	13:10	14:10	15:10	16:10	17:10
09:15	10:15	11:15	12:15	13:15	14:15	15:15	16:15	17:15
09:20	10:20	11:20	12:20	13:20	14:20	15:20	16:20	17:20
09:25	10:25	11:25	12:25	13:25	14:25	15:25	16:25	17:25
09:30	10:30	11:30	12:30	13:30	14:30	15:30	16:30	17:30
09:35	10:35	11:35	12:35	13:35	14:35	15:35	16:35	17:35
09:40	10:40	11:40	12:40	13:40	14:40	15:40	16:40	17:40
09:45	10:45	11:45	12:45	13:45	14:45	15:45	16:45	17:45
09:50	10:50	11:50	12:50	13:50	14:50	15:50	16:50	17:50
09:55	10:55	11:55	12:55	13:55	14:55	15:55	16:55	17:55

18:00	19:00	20:00	21:00	22:00	23:00
18:00	19:00	20:00	21:00	22:00	23:00
18:05	19:05	20:05	21:05	22:05	23:05
18:10	19:10	20:10	21:10	22:10	23:10
18:15	19:15	20:15	21:15	22:15	23:15
18:20	19:20	20:20	21:20	22:20	23:20
18:25	19:25	20:25	21:25	22:25	23:25
18:30	19:30	20:30	21:30	22:30	23:30
18:35	19:35	20:35	21:35	22:35	23:35
18:40	19:40	20:40	21:40	22:40	23:40
18:45	19:45	20:45	21:45	22:45	23:45
18:50	19:50	20:50	21:50	22:50	23:50
18:55	19:55	20:55	21:55	22:55	23:55

FIGURE 7.9: Heat map showing 24 hours in a single calendar day.

Figure 7.10 shows the tooltip being presented when the cursor is placed over a single time slot. The value for the time slot is extracted from the *score* attribute of the time slot *div* tag.

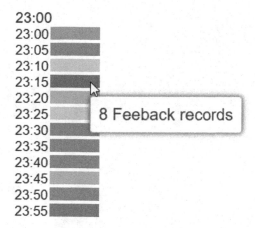

FIGURE 7.10: Tooltip showing the number of feedback records for a given time slot.

7.7 SUMMARY

This chapter described the temporal aspect of working with data. First, a time-segment analysis approach was described. This approach allows the user to select an individual segment of time they are interested in to graph a smaller quantity of data. The area of real-time feedback analysis was then described as often, as feedback occurs, it needs to be monitored. This approach focused on charting the positive and negative feedback on a graph.

To provide a more comprehensive view of data, a positive versus negative feedback calendar approach was described. This charted an entire year of positive feedback and negative feedback. Each was given their own charts, with color-coding outlining the number of records that were received for each day. Finally, a 24-hour custom heat map was described, which breaks an entire day down into smaller hours, and they are broken down again further into five-minute slots. This approach allows the analyst to view the trending times of a day when feedback records were left.

Chapter 8, outlines statistics that can be gathered from both numeric and text-based data.

Feedback Statistics and Overviews

8.1   INTRODUCTION

When working with large collections of data, statistics can play a vital role in understanding the data and provide key insights that would otherwise be lost.

This chapter describes the different tasks that can be performed on large data collections to provide insights at a glance to a data analyst. Many of these methods can be integrated with charts to further aid the delivery of the statistics for quick and efficient analysis.

8.2   BASIC STATISTICS

To work with basic statistics, one database table will be used titled *statistics*. For the *score1*, *score2*, and *score3* columns, values between 1 and 5 can be entered.

Example code: create.sql
This table contains a unique *ID* column, three separate score fields, and a *mytime* that is set to be the current time when the record was created.

```
1  CREATE TABLE `statistics` (
2         `id` INT NOT NULL AUTO_INCREMENT,
3         `score1` TINYINT,
4         `score2` TINYINT,
5         `score3` TINYINT,
6         `mytime` DATETIME NULL DEFAULT CURRENT_TIMESTAMP,
7         PRIMARY KEY (`id`)
8  )
```

Example 1: Calculating the mode

When working with a large collection of feedback records, often we are interested to see what the most frequent feedback score was. This is referred to as the *mode*. A simple example of the mode can be seen with the following 10 feedback scores In Sample Code 1.

```
1, 2, 2, 5, 6, 7, 7, 7, 7, 10
```

SAMPLE CODE 1: Sample values for mode calculation.

In this, we can see that the most frequent feedback score that was entered by users is 7. The *mode* would be defined as 7 for this data set.

Example code: getMode.php

To get the mode of a larger data set, e.g., 1000 records, a new PHP page will be created titled *getMode.php*. In Sample Code 2, at the top of this file, a connection to the database is made on line 7. On line 9, a new PHP function is created titled *getMode()*. On line 10, a reference to the database connection is made. Although it is possible to calculate the mode using PHP, to remove the burden from the PHP server, the database is used for this calculation. On line 11, the SQL query to calculate the mode is added. The *score1* column is first selected, followed by the *count* of the *score 1* column. This is represented as the *scoreCount* variable for future reference.

A *GROUP BY* is performed on the *score1* column to bring all similar values together. An *ORDER BY* is added to order the results by the *scoreCount* column, as this will place the score with the highest number of occurrences as the first record in the result set. As we are not interested in any other records apart from the mode, a *LIMIT 1* is appended to the end to only return a single record.

On lines 12 and 13, the *prepare()* and *execute()* functions are run. As only one record is required, on line 14 a single call to the *fetch()* function can be performed. The result of this call is placed in the *res* variable as an array. Position 0 of the array contains the mode, and position 1 contains the count for the *score1*. On line 17, a simple *return* is performed to send these values back to the caller.

On line 19, a simple *echo* is used to output text followed by a call to the *getMode()* function to retrieve the values.

```php
1   <?php
2   try {
3       $host = 'localhost:3306';
4       $dbname = 'bookexamples';
5       $user = 'sampleuser';
6       $pass = '3C9038A509BE6145AAD6827B4568AD918BC3DAC0';
7       $DBH = new PDO("mysql:host=$host;dbname=$dbname", $user,
    ↪ $pass);
8   } catch(PDOException $e) {echo $e;}
9   function getMode(){
10      global $DBH;
11      $sql = 'SELECT score1, COUNT(score1) AS scoreCount FROM
    ↪ statistics GROUP BY score1 ORDER BY scoreCount DESC
    ↪ LIMIT 1';
12      $sth = $DBH->prepare($sql);
13      $sth->execute();
14      $res = $sth->fetch();
15      $mode = $res[0];
16      $count = $res[1];
17      return $mode . ' with count ' . $count;
18  }
19  echo 'The mode is: ' . getMode();
```

SAMPLE CODE 2: getMode.php — Returning the mode.

Output

Figure 8.1 shows the final result that contains the two columns, one for the mode, e.g., 9 and one showing the count of the selected score e.g., 116.

The mode is: 9 with count 116

FIGURE 8.1: Output showing the mode and total count of records for the mode.

Example 2: Calculating the mean/average

The average score for a given column can easily be found by making a call to the SQL *AVG()* function that takes a single column name as a parameter. Like the previous example, the database is doing the processing removing the burden from the web server.

Example code: getAverage.php

In Sample Code 3, on line 7, a connection is first made to the database. On line 9, the *getAverageScore()* function is defined. This function takes a single parameter, the name of the column we wish to find the average for. On line 11, the SQL is defined. The SQL *avg()* function is called and the *column* parameter is passed in. To remove the text *avg()* from the result column title, the column is represented as *average*.

On lines 12 and 13, the *prepare()* and *execute()* functions are called. On line 14, as only one variable will be returned, the *fetch()* function can be used. On line 15, this is placed into a local variable titled *avg* which is returned to the function caller on line 16. To call this function, on line 18, an echo statement is used to print a small piece of proceeding text followed by a call to the *getAverageScore()* function that takes in the name of the column of interest.

```php
1  <?php
2  try {
3      $host = 'localhost:3306';
4      $dbname = 'bookexamples';
5      $user = 'sampleuser';
6      $pass = '3C9038A509BE6145AAD6827B4568AD918BC3DAC0';
7      $DBH = new PDO("mysql:host=$host;dbname=$dbname", $user,
         ↪ $pass);
8  } catch(PDOException $e) {echo $e;}
9  function getAverageScore($columnName){
10     global $DBH;
11     $sql = "SELECT AVG($columnName) AS average FROM statistics";
12     $sth = $DBH->prepare($sql);
13     $sth->execute();
14     $res = $sth->fetch();
15     $avg= $res[0];
16     return $avg;
17 }
18 echo 'The averages for score1 is ' . getAverageScore('score1');
```

SAMPLE CODE 3: getAvg.php — Calculating the average for a column.

Output

The result of calling this function for a given column can be seen in Figure 8.2.

The averages for score1 is 5.4410

FIGURE 8.2: Average result for a given column.

Example 3: Calculating the standard deviation

When reviewing a collection of feedback records, a useful statistic that can easily be derived is the standard deviation, often shown as σ (sigma). The standard deviation is a method of identifying how far away a given number is from the mean. An example of this is feedback scores 1, 2, 2, and 5. When looking at these four numbers, we can easily see that the number two has been represented twice. The mean for this set is 2.5. This is calculated, as shown in Equation 8.1, by taking the four numbers and dividing them by four.

$$\frac{1+2+2+5}{4} = 2.5 \tag{8.1}$$

When looking at the last feedback score, 5, we can see that it is vastly higher from the other feedback scores. The standard deviation can be useful for identifying how far away from the mean the score we are looking at is. If we looked at the feedback score 5 by itself, it would seem to be positive on a scale of 1 to 5. However, when the standard deviation is also viewed, it would show us that 5 is actually quite distant from the true representation of the scores.

For each individual score, we subtract the value from the mean and the square the result. Each result is added together and divided by the number of scores in the data set as shown in Equation 8.2.

$$\frac{(1-2.5)^2 + (2-2.5)^2 + (2-2.5)^2 + (5-2.5)^2}{4-1} = \frac{9}{4} \tag{8.2}$$

We are then left with 2.25, as shown in Equation 8.3.

$$\frac{9}{3} = 2.25 \tag{8.3}$$

Finally, the square root of 2.25 is found as shown in Equation 8.4.

This provides the final result, 1.5 which is defined as the standard deviation for this set of scores.

$$\sqrt{2.25} = 1.5 \tag{8.4}$$

This example contains two files:

1. create.sql — This file is used to create the *smallset* database table.

2. getStdDev.php — This file retrieves the standard deviation from the database.

Example code: create.sql
This example uses a simple database table titled *smallset*. This table contains an *ID* column that is auto-incremented and a *score* column to hold the sample score values between 1 and 5.

```
1   CREATE TABLE `smallset` (
2           `id` INT NOT NULL AUTO_INCREMENT,
3           `score` INT,
4           PRIMARY KEY (`id`)
5   )
```

Example code: getStdDev.php
When working with a MySQL database, calculating the standard deviation can easily be performed using the *std()* function. This function takes in a single parameter in the form of the column that we wish to calculate the standard deviation for.

In Sample Code 4, on line 7, a new connection to the database is created. On line 9, the *calculateStdDev()* is defined. Inside this function on line 11, the SQL is added. The function titled *std()* is added after the *SELECT*, passing in the name of the column of interest. On line 14, as only a single record will be returned, a call to the database *fetch()* is performed. The result of this call is placed into the *res* variable. The *res* at position 0 is extracted and placed into a local variable titled *stdev* that is returned to the function caller on line 16.

On line 18, a simple *echo* is used to output the proceeding text, followed by a call to the *calculateStdDev()* function.

```php
1   <?php
2   try {
3       $host = 'localhost:3306';
4       $dbname = 'bookexamples';
5       $user = 'sampleuser';
6       $pass = '3C9038A509BE6145AAD6827B4568AD918BC3DAC0';
7       $DBH = new PDO("mysql:host=$host;dbname=$dbname", $user,
    ↪ $pass);
8   } catch(PDOException $e) {echo $e;}
9   function calculateStdDev(){
10      global $DBH;
11      $sql = 'SELECT STD(score) AS sd FROM smallset;';
12      $sth = $DBH->prepare($sql);
13      $sth->execute();
14      $res = $sth->fetch();
15      $stdev=$res[0];
16      return $stdev;
17  }
18  echo 'The standard deviation is ' . calculateStdDev();
```

SAMPLE CODE 4: getStdDev.php — Calculating the standard deviation.

Output

Figure 8.3 shows the result of the SQL query, printing the standard deviation to the browser.

The standard deviation is 1.5000

FIGURE 8.3: Example standard deviation result.

8.3 WORKING WITH SAMPLES

The larger a collection of feedback records becomes, the process of gathering insights from it becomes difficult. In each of the examples we have previously described, we have been working with relatively small samples, such as 100 records. When we are working with data sets above this, providing a quick glance at the overall direction the feedback is taking can no longer be performed. *Sampling* is the process of working with a smaller data set that is accurately representative of the larger set. In this section, we will review common sampling methods.

An example of this can be seen with a collection of 50,000 feedback records. There may be a pattern in the data such as 20,000 of the records contained a feedback score of less than 5 out of 10. Rather than processing all of the 50,000 records to identify this, if the correct sampling methods are used, we can find the same approximate answers with fewer records.

This approach removes the strain on the information retrieval and processing requirements for an application. The overall sample size collected does not need to have a set size, but the accuracy of your results will help dictate an appropriate value.

Simple random sampling is a very simple method of gathering a sample. In this method, for a sample set of 1000 records, n number of samples are randomly selected for the sample, e.g., 100 records. In this approach, there is an equal chance of any record being selected and included in the sample set drawn.

Stratified sampling is an approach that first begins by taking a collection of records, e.g., 1000 individual feedback records and dividing them by a characteristic such as a day the record was taken. The first *strata* of records will contain N records and the second *strata* will also contain N records. This approach continues to divide the collection into smaller sets. Then from these sets, simple random sampling is performed to gather N feedback records from each set. This approach is useful as it provides a logical way of separating each of the collections of feedback and ensuring that each collection, in this case, the day of the week, is accurately represented in the final sample set.

Systematic sampling is a sampling approach, whereby, rather than randomly selecting feedback scores to use in a sample, a more systematic approach is taken. In a collection of 100 individual feedback records, a variable titled K is used, with a value set to 1. As $K=1$, the first record in the data set is added to the sample. After this, the variable is incremented, and five is added to the variable K, were K is equal to 6. After this increment, the 6th row in the data set is added to the sample.

The downside to this approach is that if any order is used in the data set, e.g., 70/100 records were added on a Monday and 30/100 of the records were added on a Tuesday, it can easily be seen that the sample set would be biased toward Monday as it contains a larger collection of records.

8.4   PERCENTAGE DIFFERENCE

Gathering an overview from a collection of data is an important step in understanding users. Percentages are often used as a simple way of delivering information to users with very little additional effort on the users part. A statistic such as 25% can easily be communicated, regardless of the sample size being used or the number of feedback records available. In this section, we will review how to calculate the percentage difference between two calendar dates.

Example 4: Calculating the percentage difference

This example consists of three files and three libraries:

1. create.sql — This contains the create code for the sample table titled *diffcalc*.

2. diff.php — This is the main user interface provided to the user.

3. getDiff.php — This file gathers the records and calculates the difference.

4. jQuery — This library is added to perform a JavaScript *GET* request.

5. jQueryUI — This file provides an interactive date picker to the user to select a date.

6. popper.js — Provides a positioning engine for Bootstrap.

To calculate the percentage difference between the two scores, Equation 8.5 can be used. Where V_1 is the first value and V_2 is the second value.

$$\frac{\mid V_1 - V_2 \mid}{\left[\frac{v_1 + v_2}{2}\right]} \times 100 \tag{8.5}$$

Example code create.sql

Sample Code 5 shows a simple database table that will be used to store feedback scores, and the date the feedback was left. This table contains a unique *ID* column, three *score* fields, and a *datestamp*.

```
1   CREATE TABLE `diffcalc` (
2        `id` INT NOT NULL AUTO_INCREMENT,
3        `score1` TINYINT,
4        `score2` TINYINT,
5        `score3` TINYINT,
6        `datestamp` DATE,
7        PRIMARY KEY (`id`)
8   );
```

SAMPLE CODE 5: Sample diffcalc table.

Example code: diff.php

A new page titled *diff.php* is created. In Sample Code 6, on line 3, a reference is first made to the jQuery content delivery network (CDN). This is followed by a reference to the jQueryUI JavaScript file on line 4, and the associated CSS file on line 5. jQueryUI will be used to create an interactive date picker. For the styling of the table, Bootstrap will be used. The requirements for this include popper.js, which included on line 8. This is a dependency for Bootstrap. On line 10–13, Bootstrap.js is included along with a reference to the BootStrap CSS file. On line 15, a small CSS modification is made to the *thread tr* tag. This will set the background of the first row to be *black* with *white* text.

On line 22, a *div* tag with the *class* set to *container* is added. This is the container that will be used to hold our table. The parameter *sm* is added to identify that we want a small-sized container. Inside this container, on line 23, an input box is added with the *ID* set to *datepicker*. Just below this, on line 24, a single *button* is added with the *ID* set to *viewData*. This is the main button that is responsible for generating the table.

To aid the layout, a HTML *table* is added on line 25 with the *class* set to *table table-striped*. This will have a different shading for even and odd rows in the table. Inside of this, on line 27, a table *row* is added with four columns. The first of these is the date, followed by the count of records, the sum of the scores for all the feedback records added for that column, and the percentage difference. A new tag is created titled *tbody* with the *ID* set to *content* on line 34. This is the main placeholder for the HTML that will be generated after a date had been selected, and the *viewData* button has been clicked.

On line 40, to trigger the content generation process, the jQuery selector is used to attach a *click()* handler onto the *viewData* button. When the button is clicked, the jQuery click handler will then trigger. Inside of this, on line 41, the jQuery selector is used to select the *datepicker input* field where the date is held. The *val()* function is used to extract the value and place it into a temporary variable titled *dateSelected*.

After we have gathered the selected date, on line 42, a jQuery *GET* is performed on the *getDiff.php* page that is responsible for generating the content. A single parameter titled *date* is passed with the value set as the *dateSelected* variable. When the request is completed, the *done()* function is called on line 43. On line 44, the jQuery selector is used to select the *content div* tag and set the content to be blank using the *html('')* function without any additional parameters. If this step is not performed, subsequent requests to the *getDiff.php* page will have the content appended to the current table.

On line 45, a call is made to the *append()* function that takes in a single parameter *data* that contains the complete HTML that was received from the *getDiff.php* page.

At the end of the *diff.php* page, on line 49, the jQuery selector is used to select the *datepicker input* field and convert it into a jQueryUI interactive date picker. The dateFormat is passed as a parameter to the *datepicker()* function in the form of *yy-mm-dd*. This will format the date selected by the user into a form such as *2020-09-01*.

```
1   <html>
2   <head>
3   <script
    ↪   src="https://code.jquery.com/jquery-3.4.1.min.js"></script>
4   <script src="http://code.jquery.com/ui/1.12.1/jquery-ui.min.js">
5   </script>
6   <link rel="stylesheet" type="text/css"
    ↪   href="http://code.jquery.com/ui/1.12.1/themes/base/
7   jquery-ui.css">
8   <script
    ↪   src="https://cdnjs.cloudflare.com/ajax/libs/popper.js/1.14.7/
9   umd/popper.min.js"></script>
10  <link rel="stylesheet"
    ↪   href="https://stackpath.bootstrapcdn.com/bootstrap/4.3.1/css/
11  bootstrap.min.css">
12  <script
    ↪   src="https://stackpath.bootstrapcdn.com/bootstrap/4.3.1/js/
13  bootstrap.min.js"></script>
```

```
14  <style>
15  thead tr {
16      background-color: #000000;
17      color: #FFFFFF;
18  }
19  </style>
20  </head>
21  <body>
22  <div class="container sm">
23  <p>View Week starting from: <input type="text" id="datepicker">
24  <button id="viewData">View Data</button></p>
25  <table class="table table-striped">
26      <thead style="">
27          <tr>
28              <th scope="col">Date</th>
29              <th scope="col">Number of records</th>
30              <th scope="col">Sum of scores</th>
31              <th scope="col">% difference</th>
32          </tr>
33      </thead>
34      <tbody id="content">
35      </tbody>
36  </table>
37  </div>
38  </body>
39  <script>
40  $( "#viewData" ).click(function() {
41      var dateSelected = $( "#datepicker" ).val();
42      $.get( "getDiff.php", { date: dateSelected} )
43          .done(function( data ) {
44              $( "#content" ).html('');
45              $( "#content" ).append(data);
46          });
47  })
48  $( function() {
49      $( "#datepicker" ).datepicker({dateFormat: "yy-mm-dd"});
50  } );
51  </script>
```

SAMPLE CODE 6: diff.php — Main user interface allowing the user to select a week.

Example code: getDiff.php
A page titled *getDiff.php* is created. This page is the core of the data re-

trieval and calculation process. In Sample Code 7, a single *GET* variable titled *date* is retrieved on line 2. This date is the date that was selected by the user and passed to the page via the jQuery *GET* performed on the previous page. This date is stored in a variable titled *startDate*. This will be used as the starting point for all the calculations that will be performed. For any given date, the algorithm will look at the difference between the start date and the next seven calendar days. If the date rolls onto the next month, the month will automatically adjust. After the date is gathered, a connection is made to the database on line 8.

On line 10, the core *calculateDiffFromDate()* function is created that receives a single parameter titled *basedate* that the function will work from.

Inside the function a variable titled *output* is created on line 12. This will be used as the main place holder for all the HTML that will be generated. On line 14, a call is made to the *getDateRecords()* function which is passed the current date of interest, *baseDate*.

The result of calling the *getDateRecords()* function, is three values, the *count*, *sum* and *difference*. Each of these is separated by a colon. On line 15, a call is made to the *explode()* function, to break the *resBase* variable into an array based format, allowing each of the three values to be extracted.

On lines 16–22, the *output* variable is appended to include the first HTML row. This row will contain the *baseDate* followed by the string *Start*, which is used as a visual indicator to tell the user that it is the date that all other statistics will be derived from. The count of records is added by making a call to *r[0]*, and the sum is added by calling *r[1]*. On line 23, to calculate the differences for each of the seven days following the initial calendar date, a call is first made to the *strtotime()* function to convert the calendar date into an accessible format. A *for loop* on line 24 is used to iterate over the seven days.

To find the next calendar date, on line 25, a call is made to the *date()* function to format a date in *Y-m-d* format. The *strtotime()* function is called, which allows us to pass in the number of days we want to offset the original date stamp by. The first time this loop runs, the original calendar date will be offset by +1 day, followed by +2 days, etc. When the next calendar date is found, a call is made to the *getDataRecords()* function on line 26, which is responsible for gathering the records from the database. This function will return 0 if no data is available.

In the case where data is available for the date, on lines 28, and 29, the *explode()* function is called on the *resBase* variable and the *res2* variable and places the results the coreesponding local variable, e.g., *r1*, representing the first day, and *r2*, representing the second day. Each of these contain three pieces of data separated by a colon.

The three pieces of data include the total number of records, the sum of the feedback, and the calendar date, e.g., *100:301:2020-09-02*. For both *r1* and *r2* arrays on lines 30–35, each value is extracted and placed in local variables.

On line 36, the calculation process can begin. The calculation performed by taking the *count1* and dividing it by the *sum1* of the records to get *v1*. The same process is repeated to get the value for *v2*. The equation is broken down into the *top* on line 38 and *bottom* on like 39.

On line 40, the final result is calculated by taking the *top* result and dividing it by the *bottom*. This result is multiplied by 100 to get the percentage difference. A call is made to the round() function to *round()* the result to 2 decimal places on line 41. On lines 43–45, if no records are present in the database for a given date, then the *count*, *sum*, and *diff* variables are set to 0. On line 47, the *output* is appended to include the values for the three variables as a new table row. On line 55, the *output* is printed to the screen to be returned to the client.

```php
<?php
$startDate = $_GET['date'];
try {
    $host = 'localhost:3306';
    $dbname = 'bookexamples';
    $user = 'sampleuser';
    $pass = '3C9038A509BE6145AAD6827B4568AD918BC3DAC0';
    $DBH = new PDO("mysql:host=$host;dbname=$dbname", $user,
      ↪ $pass);
} catch(PDOException $e) {echo $e;}
function calculateDiffFromDate($baseDate){
    global $DBH;
    $output = '';
    // Get data for starting record
    $resBase = getDateRecords($baseDate);
    $r = explode(':', $resBase);
    $output .= '
    <tr>
        <th scope="row"> '.$baseDate.'[Start]</th>
        <td>'.$r[0].'</td>
        <td>'.$r[1].'</td>
        <td>0</td>
    </tr>';
```

```
23      $timestamp = strtotime($baseDate);
24      for($d = 1; $d < 8; $d++){
25          $nextDate =  date('Y-m-d', strtotime('+'.$d.' day',
        ↪  $timestamp));
26          $res2 = getDateRecords($nextDate);
27          if($res2 != 0){
28              $r1 = explode(':', $resBase);
29              $r2 = explode(':', $res2);
30              $count1 = $r1[0];
31              $sum1 = $r1[1];
32              $viewingDate1 = $r1[2];
33              $count2 = $r2[0];
34              $sum2 = $r2[1];
35              $viewingDate2 = $r2[2];
36              $v1 = $count1 / $sum1;
37              $v2 = $count2 / $sum2;
38              $top = $v1 - $v2;
39              $bottom = ($v1 + $v2) / 2;
40              $re = ($top / $bottom) * 100;
41              $diff = round($re,2);
42          } else {
43              $count2 = 0;
44              $sum2 = 0;
45              $diff = 0;
46          }
47          $output .= '
48          <tr>
49              <th scope="row">'.$nextDate.'</th>
50              <td>'.$count2.'</td>
51              <td>'.$sum2.'</td>
52              <td>'.$diff.'%</td>
53          </tr>';
54      }
55      echo $output;
56  }
```

SAMPLE CODE 7: getDiff.php — part 1.

The retrieval process of records from the database is performed by making a call to the *getDataRecords()* function, which takes a single calendar date. In Sample Code 8, on line 57, this function is defined.

On line 59, a SQL query is made to the *count()* function to count the number of records. This result is represented as *count* in the result set. The sum of all the records in the column titled *score1* is found and represented as *sum* in the final result. The *datestamp* is also included to aid traceability of where the data came from. A simple *WHERE* clause is used to narrow down the collection of results based on the date of interest. A question mark is used as a placeholder for the date.

On line 60, a new array titled *params* is created that takes the *date* variable as input. On line 62, the *execute()* function is called. On lines 64–66, the *count*, *sum*, and *date* are placed into local variables. On line 67, if no records are returned, then a 0 is returned back to the caller of the function. In the case where there is records, the *count*, *sum*, and *date* are appended together with a colon : between each of the records. On line 73, a call is made to the *calculateDiffFromDate()* function which is passed the starting date. This is done to trigger the retrieval process.

```
57   function getDateRecords($date){
58       global $DBH;
59       $sql = "SELECT COUNT(score1) AS COUNT, SUM(score1) AS SUM,
         ↪ datestamp FROM diffcalc WHERE datestamp = ?;";
60       $params = array($date);
61       $sth = $DBH->prepare($sql);
62       $sth->execute($params);
63       $res = $sth->fetch();
64       $count= $res[0];
65       $sum =  $res[1];
66       $date = $res[2];
67       if($count == '0'){
68           return 0;
69       } else {
70           return $count . ':' . $sum . ':' . $date;
71       }
72   }
73   calculateDiffFromDate($startDate);
74
75   ?>
```

SAMPLE CODE 8: getDiff.php — part 2.

Output

Figure 8.4 shows the result of selecting a day in the calendar and clicking the *View Data* button. All the content in the table is dynamically generated by the *getDiff.php* page and called via a jQuery *GET* request.

View Week starting from: 2019-09-01 [View Data]

Date	Number of records	Sum of scores	% difference
2019-09-01 [Start]	100	455	0
2019-09-02	100	541	17.27%
2019-09-03	100	493	8.02%
2019-09-04	100	511	11.59%
2019-09-05	100	516	12.56%
2019-09-06	100	436	-4.26%
2019-09-07	100	490	7.41%
2019-09-08	0	0	0%

FIGURE 8.4: Calculating the percentage difference.

8.5 SUMMARY

As the size of a data collection grows, it becomes difficult for manual analysis. This chapter provided an outline of the common statistical methods that can be used during the analysis of larger data collections. As many of the statistical methods can be achieved by using PHP or by using existing database functions, both options were explored.

Chapter 9, next, outlines the process of developing a bespoke hosting solution for the data collection and analysis process. An emphasis is placed on the reporting component of data analysis and the distribution of findings to the key stakeholders in a project.

8.   SUMMARY

Hosting, Reporting, and Distribution

9.1 INTRODUCTION

Acting on data acquired in a timely manner is the key to customer satisfaction. In this chapter, different methods of generating and distributing reports are described. The content and frequency of the report generation process is described, outlining the core components of scheduling, automatic report creation, and delivery.

In addition to this, the Amazon cloud platform is explored as a method of hosting the solutions that have been discussed in previous chapters.

9.2 REPORT GENERATION

A key component of any analysis is generating an output that is accessible by a number of different people. Although some users may have the ability to login to a web application and view the charts and statistics that have been generated, it is not the case for all users. Having a simple formatted document such as a PDF that can easily be distributed to co-workers is still a common practice. In this chapter, we will look at the process of generating a PDF file based upon any given content. All the processing power to generate the PDF files is performed on the server-side using PHP.

Many different PDF generation libraries are available to use with PHP, but one particular tool TCPDF has stood the test of time. TCPDF is available from https://tcpdf.org. TCPDF allows you to generate a

PDF-based upon HTML/CSS and also has the ability to include graphics. This allows us to convert any currently existing visualizations and statistical information quickly into a PDF-based format.

Example 1: Generating a PDF

This example consists of three files and one library:

1. create.sql — Contains the SQL to create the *smallset* and *statistics* tables.

2. custom.php — This is the main code for generating the PDF file.

3. figure1.png — This is a sample graph that will be included in the PDF.

4. TCPDF — This library is used to generate the PDF.

Example code: create.sql
The *smallet* table is first created. This contains an *ID* column and a *score* column that is used to hold various scores. The *statistics* table is then created that contains an *ID* column and three *score* columns.

```
CREATE TABLE `smallset` (
        `id` INT NOT NULL AUTO_INCREMENT,
        `score` INT,
        PRIMARY KEY (`id`)
);
CREATE TABLE `statistics` (
        `id` INT NOT NULL AUTO_INCREMENT,
        `score1` TINYINT,
        `score2` TINYINT,
        `score3` TINYINT,
        `mytime` DATETIME NULL DEFAULT CURRENT_TIMESTAMP,
        PRIMARY KEY (`id`)
);
```

SAMPLE CODE 1: create.sql — SQL to create the *smallset* and *statistics* database tables.

Example code: TCPDF

To use TCPDF, it first must be downloaded from the official repository.[1] You will be given an option to download the contents of the repository as a single zip file. Once this zip file has downloaded, extract the contents of the *TCPDF-master* folder into the root of your *htdocs* folder of your local web server. By default, no additional configuration is needed for the examples in the *examples* folder to run.

Example code: custom.php

This page consists of two core components: the first of these are the functions that will be used to gather statistics from the previous chapter and utilize them in the PDF. The second is focused on the overall layout and content that will be added to the PDF. In Sample Code 2, on lines 1–39 the PHP functions for calculating the mode, average, and standard deviation can be seen as described in Chapter 8. When each function is called, a single value will be returned from each.

```php
1   <?php
2   try {
3       $host = 'localhost:3306';
4       $dbname = 'bookexamples';
5       $user = 'sampleuser';
6       $pass = '3C9038A509BE6145AAD6827B4568AD918BC3DAC0';
7
8       $DBH = new PDO("mysql:host=$host;dbname=$dbname", $user,
        ↪ $pass);
9   } catch(PDOException $e) {echo $e;}
10  function getMode(){
11      global $DBH;
12      $sql = 'SELECT score1, COUNT(score1) AS COUNT FROM
        ↪ statistics GROUP BY score1 ORDER BY count DESC LIMIT 1';
13      $sth = $DBH->prepare($sql);
14      $sth->execute();
15      $res = $sth->fetch();
16      $mode=$res[0];
17      $count = $res[1];
18      return $mode . ' with count ' . $count;
19  }
20
```

---

[1]https://github.com/tecnickcom/tcpdf

```
21   function getAverageScore($columnName){
22       global $DBH;
23       $sql = "SELECT AVG($columnName) AS average FROM statistics";
24       $sth = $DBH->prepare($sql);
25       $params = array($columnName);
26       $sth->execute($params);
27       $res = $sth->fetch();
28       $avg= $res[0];
29       return $avg;
30   }
31   function calculateStdDev(){
32       global $DBH;
33       $sql = 'SELECT STD(score) AS sd FROM smallset;';
34       $sth = $DBH->prepare($sql);
35       $sth->execute();
36       $res = $sth->fetch();
37       $stdev=$res[0];
38       return $stdev;
39   }
```

SAMPLE CODE 2: custom.php — Gathering statistics — part 1.

In Sample Code 3, on line 41, a call is made to include the *tcpdf_include.php* page that is used to include the TCPDF library in our project. On line 43, a new *pdf* object is created. *PDF_PAGE_ORIENTATION* has a value set to *P* indicating we are using portrait mode. The PDF_UNIT of measure is *mm* by default. The *PDF_PAGE_FORMAT* by default is set to *A4*. The encoding for the page is then set to use UTF-8. On lines 45–49, basic author and title information is set into the PDF. On line 51, the *monospaced* font is set.

On line 53, the margins for the PDF file are set. These are currently set to their default but can be manually changed. On line 54, basic header information for the PDF is set. PDF_HEADER_LOGO contains a reference to the TCPDF logo. This is followed by PDF_HEADER_LOGO_WIDTH that indicates the width the logo should be. This is followed by two strings that can be modified. To add color, two arrays are added that contain the RGB values for both arrays.

On lines 55 and 56, the margin for the header and the footer are set. On line 58, the PDF is set to have auto page breaks. On line 60, the default PDF_IMAGE_SCALE_RATIO is set, which is 1.25. On lines 62 to 67, the default fonts are set.

The core of the PDF generation process starts on line 69, when the *AddPage()* function is called. This is the blank canvas where our content will be added. On lines 71–73, calls are made to the functions that were created earlier. The result for each function that is returned is placed into local variables. On line 77–83, a new variable titled *HTML* is added. Instead of directly adding a string to the variable, the *EOD* tag is added, allowing any text to be entered. The spacing will be removed before it is printed. The three variables that we gathered are placed into this block along with some additional text. To finish, another *EOD* tag is added. HTML can be added into this tag, without causing any issues with regards to quotation marks.

On line 84, an image of a graph is added. This file titled *graph.png* is added into a folder titled *stats*. 10 indicates the position from the *left*, and 80 indicates the position from the *top* of the page. 170 is the *width* for the picture, and 80 is the *height*. A link can be embedded into this, allowing the user to be taken to a page of interest.

On line 85, a call is made to the *writeHTMLCell()* function that takes in the *html* parameter that had the content we wish to display. The parameters taken by this include: *width, height, X* position, *Y* position, *HTML, border, line, fill, reset header, align,* and *autopadding*.

On line 87, the folder where the file will be placed, and the name that will be given to the file is specified. When using the page as an interface, the parameter I can be set, rendering the PDF in the browser. When the PDF is required as a file, this can be changed to F, and it will be output in the desired folder.

```
40  // Include the main TCPDF library (search for installation
     ↪  path).
41  require_once('tcpdf_include.php');
42  // create new PDF document
43  $pdf = new TCPDF(PDF_PAGE_ORIENTATION, PDF_UNIT,
     ↪  PDF_PAGE_FORMAT, true, 'UTF-8', false);
44  // set document information
45  $pdf->SetCreator(PDF_CREATOR);
46  $pdf->SetAuthor('Kyle Goslin');
47  $pdf->SetTitle('Sample PDF');
48  $pdf->SetSubject('How to use TCPDF');
49  $pdf->SetKeywords('TCPDF, PDF, example, test, guide');
50  // set default monospaced font
51  $pdf->SetDefaultMonospacedFont(PDF_FONT_MONOSPACED);
52  // set margins
53  $pdf->SetMargins(PDF_MARGIN_LEFT, PDF_MARGIN_TOP,
     ↪  PDF_MARGIN_RIGHT);
```

```
54  $pdf->SetHeaderData(PDF_HEADER_LOGO, PDF_HEADER_LOGO_WIDTH,
    ↪   'Custom Sample Statistics', '', array(000,000,000),
    ↪   array(000,000,000));
55  $pdf->SetHeaderMargin(PDF_MARGIN_HEADER);
56  $pdf->SetFooterMargin(PDF_MARGIN_FOOTER);
57  // set auto page breaks
58  $pdf->SetAutoPageBreak(TRUE, PDF_MARGIN_BOTTOM);
59  // set image scale factor
60  $pdf->setImageScale(PDF_IMAGE_SCALE_RATIO);
61  // set default font subsetting mode
62  $pdf->setFontSubsetting(true);
63  // Set font
64  // dejavusans is a UTF-8 Unicode font, if you only need to
65  // print standard ASCII chars, you can use core fonts like
66  // helvetica or times to reduce file size.
67  $pdf->SetFont('dejavusans', '', 14, '', true);
68  // Add a page
69  $pdf->AddPage();
70  // Gather the data
71  $mode = 'The mode is: ' . getMode();
72  $average = 'The averages for score1 is: ' .
    ↪   getAverageScore('score1');
73  $stdev = 'The standard deviation of the database table is: ' .
    ↪   calculateStdDev();
74
75
76  // Set some content to print
77  $html = <<<EOD
78              Welcome to the statistics page!
79              <p>
80              $mode <br>
81              $average <br>
82              $stdev<br>
83  EOD;
84  $pdf->Image('stats/graph1.png', 10, 80, 170, 80, 'PNG',
    ↪   'http://www.tcpdf.org', '', true, 150, '', false, false, 1,
    ↪   false, false, false);
85  $pdf->writeHTMLCell(0, 0, '', '', $html, 0, 1, 0, true, '',
    ↪   true);
86  // Close and output PDF document
87  $pdf->Output(__DIR__ . '/stats/report.pdf', 'I');
```

SAMPLE CODE 3: custom.php — PDF generation using PHP — part 2.

Output

Figure 9.1 shows the completed PDF file, which can be viewed in a web browser or by saving it to an external file.

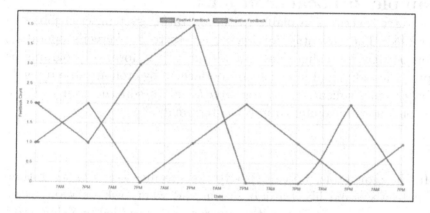

FIGURE 9.1: Statistics rendered in a PDF file.

9.3   CRON AND TASK SCHEDULING

An important aspect of reporting is passing the data to the stakeholders of a business at a consistent time. There may be times when reports are most useful, e.g., at 8 a.m. before a meeting on Friday morning, or at 9 a.m. on a Monday morning.

Cron, which is short for *chronological*, is an application that is designed to perform an action, e.g., run a program or call a URL, at a specific time, date, or as the result of an internal state change. It is a command-line utility in the Linux/Unix family of operating systems. This name, however, has been used as a generic name for any application that performs time or date based actions. In the Windows operating system, a similar application exists called *Task Schedular*. This application has a graphical user interface to aid the scheduling process.

In this chapter, PDF report generation was performed as a result of calling a PHP page in a web browser. Although the result was shown to the user directly, this does not need to be the case. A cron utility can be used to call the URL to generate the desired PDF.

For cron utilities to work correctly, the operating system where they are hosted must have a constant up-time. If the operating system is ever shut down, all of the cron jobs would not be able to execute. For this reason, there is a division in how cron jobs are created, either locally on the server or externally on someone else's server. A single task that is performed at a given time is called a *cron job*.

Example 2: Local cron jobs

When direct access is available to the operating system, cron jobs can be created. The advantage of having access to the server's operating system is that individual files can be run in the form of programs or scripts. The individual jobs that are performed by cron are stored inside of the *crontab*, which is short for *cron table*. To edit the cron jobs, we type the following command into the terminal:

```
crontab -e
```

In the cron table, we can specify the specific details of what time and date we would like the job to run and what task we want to be performed. In Sample Code 4, the order of options added to a single row in the cron table can be seen. A wild card in the form of an Astrix * can be used to specify all values. Intervals can be defined in the form of /15 to indicate every 15 minutes or /20 to indicate every 20th day.

```
MIN =  Minute 0-60
HOUR = Hour [24-hour clock] 0-23
MDAY = Day of Month 1-31
MON = Month 1-12
DOW =  Day of Week 0-6
COMMAND = Program or script to run
```

SAMPLE CODE 4: List of cron options

Sample Code 5 shows an example of a complete cron job that is designed to call *myscript.sh* every 15 minutes. Inside this script, the actual call to the PDF generator is performed. The script path, e.g., */home/user1/* can be replaced with the script we wish to run.

```
* /15 * * * /home/user1/myscript.sh
```

SAMPLE CODE 5: Sample cron job — every 15 minutes.

Sample Code 6 shows the pattern to call the *myscript.sh* file every sunday at 4 a.m.

```
0 4 * * sun /home/user1/myscript.sh
```

SAMPLE CODE 6: Sample cron job — every Sunday at 4 a.m.

Sample Code 7 outlines how to capture the output of a cron job. As the script we are calling will print out text, if successful, this text will be shown in the *output.log* file.

```
0 4 * * sun /home/user1/myscript.sh > /home/user1/output.log
```

SAMPLE CODE 7: Capturing cron output.

Sample Code 8 shows an example of the *myscript.sh* file. When this is run, on line 2, a piece of text will be output. On line 3, the *wget* tool is used to perform a HTTP *GET* request to the *custom.php* file, which was described in Section 9.2 to generate the PDF. The main consideration that is needed in *custom.php* is to have the output flag set to *F* to ensure a file is created and not just shown in the browser.

```
1  #!/bin/bash
2  echo "cron running.."
3  wget http://localhost/custom.php
```

SAMPLE CODE 8: myscript.sh — Example bash script performing a *GET* request.

When working with cron patterns, to aid the process, a number of online cron job pattern generator tools are available such as *https://crontab-generator.org*, *https://crontab.guru* and *http://www.cronmaker.com*.

Example 3: External cron jobs

Often on shared hosting solutions, the cron utility may not be accessible. In these cases, external cron services can be utilized. The disadvantage of using external cron utilities is that they only have access to pages that are public-facing on the web server. All scripts and files that are on the server but are not in the *htdocs* of the Apache server will not be available. The advantage, however, of using an external service is the up-time of the service is often high, and many come with easy to use interfaces instead of manually entering cron job patterns.

A number of different companies offer web cron utilities with additional features, such as when a cron fails to execute, an alert can be sent to the server administrator. On example of this is *cron-job.org* as shown in Figure 9.2.

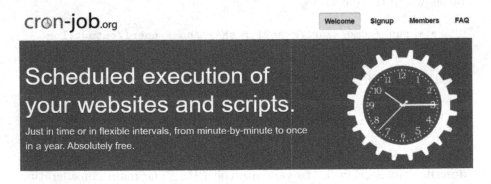

FIGURE 9.2: cron-job.org website.

Figure 9.3 shows the process of creating a new cron job. A title for the job is first specified. This is followed by the web-accessible URL that will be called. In this example, we are calling the *http://www.domain.com/scriptToCall.php* page. This PHP page can perform tasks for us, such as generating a PDF, deleting files or sending automated e-mails.

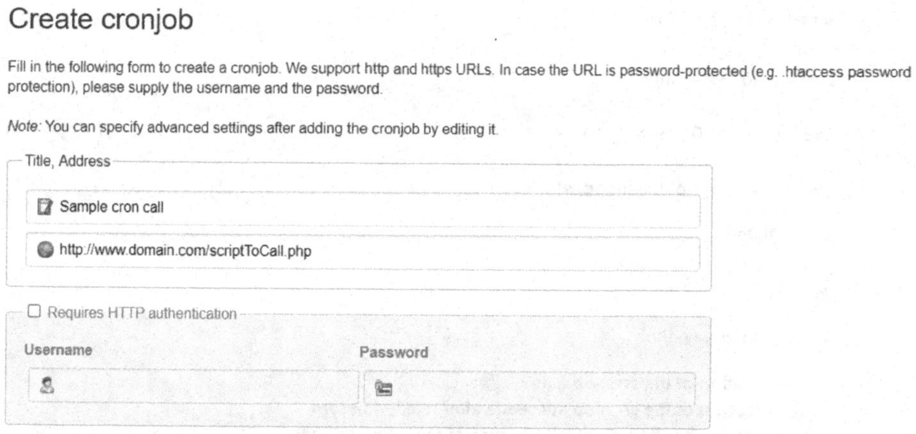

Create cronjob

Fill in the following form to create a cronjob. We support http and https URLs. In case the URL is password-protected (e.g. .htaccess password protection), please supply the username and the password.

Note: You can specify advanced settings after adding the cronjob by editing it.

Title, Address

☑ Sample cron call

🌐 http://www.domain.com/scriptToCall.php

☐ Requires HTTP authentication

Username

👤

Password

🔑

FIGURE 9.3: Creating a sample cron on cron-job.org.

In Sample Code 9.4, after these details are entered, the schedule for the cron can be specified. On this site, a simple user interface with intuitive options can be seen. Notification options are available to notify you if the cron fails to run. This can be useful as it often indicates that there is an issue with the server or task you are attempting to run.

9.4 CLOUD E-MAIL SERVICE INTEGRATION

As cron offers us the ability to perform an action at a specified interval, this can easily be used for everyday tasks such as report distribution. A simple method of distributing content is using e-mail. Although e-mail is used every day in a business environment, there is an ongoing issue with the process of successfully sending e-mail to users.

The issue with e-mail stems from the way in which it was originally designed. There are no restrictions on how e-mails are sent or the number of e-mails that are sent. As a result of this, many e-mail hosting providers mark e-mails as junk or spam quickly. This can be a result of the sender's IP address being previously used as spam or the quality of the e-mails that are being sent. Many departments that previously hosted inhouse e-mail solutions have begun to use e-mail hosting providers to deliver their mail. This can be seen as a robust approach as the e-mail provider will deal with the process of ensuring that sender's address is not marked as spam or junk.

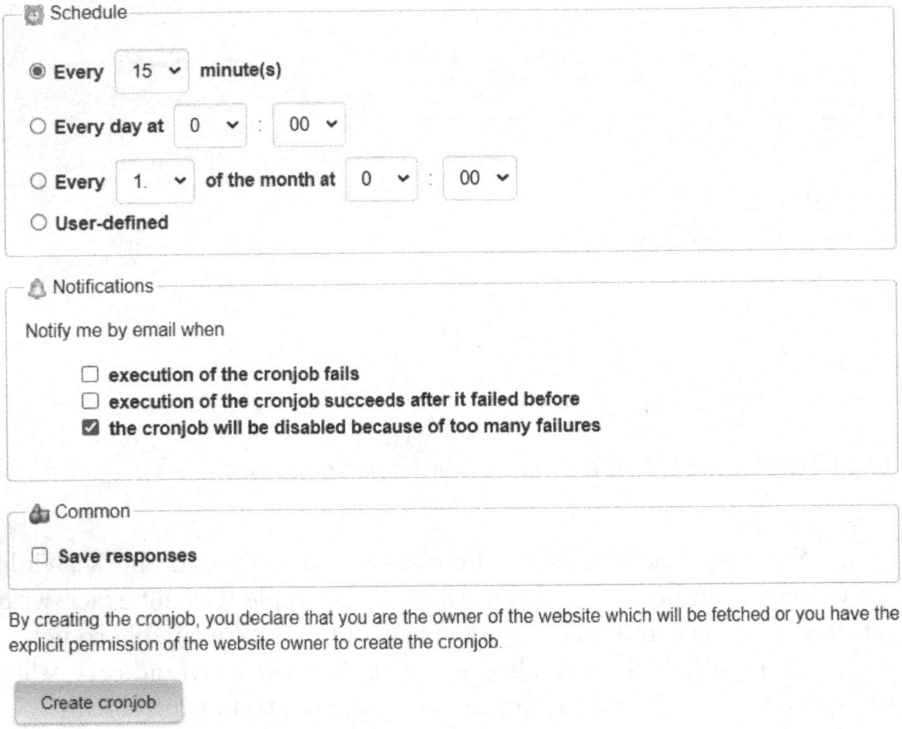

FIGURE 9.4: Creating a sample schedule for a cron job.

Example 4: Sending an e-mail

One successful e-mail hosting solution is SendGrid.[2] To use this API, two steps must be performed. The first of these is obtaining a unique API key from the SendGrid website. This key is used to differentiate one account from another for billing purposes. The second step is to validate an e-mail address that will be used. During this process, an e-mail is sent from the SendGrid.com website to the inbox of the desired sending address after the sign-up process is completed. This step ensures that the sender of the e-mails is, in fact, the owner. In cases where you own a domain name, SendGrid offers the ability to verify the domain name. This is done by adding key and value pairs into the DNS record of your domain proving authenticity.[3]

To integrate this solution into an existing web application, *composer* can be used to install the SendGrid library. In the *htdocs* folder of a web

---

[2]https://www.sendgrid.com
[3]https://app.sendgrid.com/settings/sender_auth/domain/create

server, a new file titled *composer.json* is created. In this file, the required JSON for the SendGrid API can be added, as shown in Sample Code 9.

```
1  {
2    "require": {
3      "sendgrid/sendgrid": "~7"
4    }
5  }
```

SAMPLE CODE 9: SendGrid composer.json content.

After this has been added, from a command prompt the following *install* command is run:

```
composer install
```

SAMPLE CODE 10: Installing the dependancy.

Output

In Figure 9.5, the automated installation of SendGrid using composer can be seen.

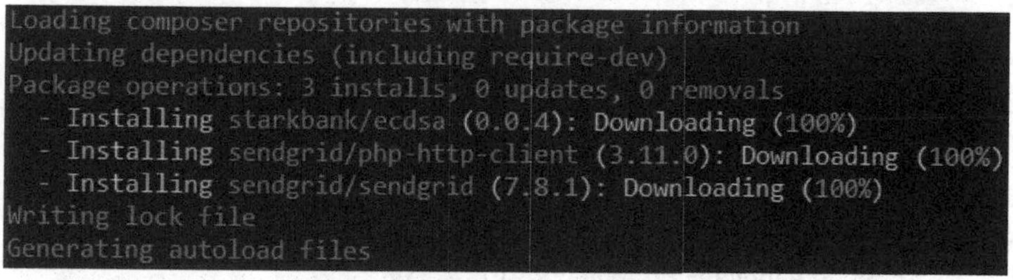

FIGURE 9.5: The SendGrid API being installed by composer.

Example code: sendmail.php

A new file can be created in the same folder where the SendGrid library was installed, titled *sendmail.php*. In Sample Code 11, on line 2, a reference is made to the *autoload.php* of the SendGrid library. On line 3, a new instance of the *mail* object is created and placed into the local variable titled *email*. The *from* address is set on line 4. This address must be an e-mail address that was used during sign-up to the service, as a verification e-mail will be sent by SendGrid. On line 5, the *subject* for the e-mail is sent. On line 6, the *to* is set indicating who we are sending the e-mail to.

On lines 7 and 8, the *addContent()* function is called to append content to the e-mail. This function takes two parameters, the first that describes the type of content that is being sent and the second containing the content to send. On line 11, the API key is appended in string format. This key is unique to your user account and must be included. The process of sending the e-mail is performed on lines 12–19. A *try-catch* surrounds the e-mail sending process to first attempt to send the e-mail, and if it fails, to capture the error. The status code, headers and body of the response can be accessed to identify if there was any issues when sending the e-mail. Typically, if errors occur with the API key or the address the e-mail was being sent from, they can be seen here.

```php
1   <?php
2   require 'vendor/autoload.php'; // If you're using Composer
    ↪ (recommended)
3   $email = new \SendGrid\Mail\Mail();
4   $email->setFrom("johnsmith@gmail.com", "Example User");
5   $email->setSubject("Sending with SendGrid is Fun");
6   $email->addTo("johnsmith@gmail.com", "Example User");
7   $email->addContent("text/plain", "and easy to do anywhere, even
    ↪ with PHP");
8   $email->addContent(
9       "text/html", "<strong>and easy to do anywhere, even with
        ↪ PHP</strong>"
10  );
11  $sendgrid = new \SendGrid('YOUR_API_KEY');
12  try {
13      $response = $sendgrid->send($email);
14      print $response->statusCode() . "\n";
15      print_r($response->headers());
16      print $response->body() . "\n";
17  } catch (Exception $e) {
18      echo 'Caught exception: '. $e->getMessage() ."\n";
19  }
```

SAMPLE CODE 11: sendmail.php — Sending an e-mail using SendGrid.

Example 5: SendGrid mail with attachment

A simple modification can be made to the original e-mail sending process to include an attachment, such as a PDF file. A new file is created titled *sendmail_attach.php* that contains the original e-mail code, along with a small modification for sending attachments.

Example code: sendmail_attach.php
In Sample Code 12, on line 11, the PHP function *file_get_contents()* is called to retrieve the contents of a file titled *samplefile.pdf* that is in the same folder as the PHP file. This is encoded in base 64 format using the *base64_encode()* function to convert the file into a format that can be sent by e-mail. On line 12, the *addAttachment()* function is called that takes a reference to the encoded file, the format of the file, the name of the file and finally identifying it as an attachment.

```php
1  <?php
2  require 'vendor/autoload.php'; // If you're using Composer
   ↪  (recommended)
3  $email = new \SendGrid\Mail\Mail();
4  $email->setFrom("kylegoslin@gmail.com", "Example User");
5  $email->setSubject("Sending with SendGrid is Fun");
6  $email->addTo("kylegoslin@gmail.com", "Example User");
7  $email->addContent("text/plain", "and easy to do anywhere, even
   ↪  with PHP");
8  $email->addContent(
9      "text/html", "<strong>and easy to do anywhere, even with
       ↪  PHP</strong>"
10 );
11 $file_encoded =
   ↪  base64_encode(file_get_contents('samplefile.pdf'));
12 $email->addAttachment(
13     $file_encoded,
14     "application/pdf",
15     "samplefile.pdf",
16     "attachment"
17 );
18 $sendgrid = new \SendGrid('YOUR_API_KEY');
19 try {
20     $response = $sendgrid->send($email);
21     print $response->statusCode() . "\n";
22     print_r($response->headers());
23     print $response->body() . "\n";
```

```
24  } catch (Exception $e) {
25      echo 'Caught exception: '. $e->getMessage() ."\n";
26  }
```

SAMPLE CODE 12: sendmail_attach.php — Sending an e-mail with an attachment.

9.5   HOSTING A PHP/JAVASCRIPT APPLICATION

Over the last number of years, the landscape of web application hosting has changed from restricted shared hosting environments to cloud-based hosting that requires little commitment to resources. A further advance on cloud hosting was the implementation of lightweight cloud hosting solutions that removed the need to configure a complete operating system and server. One of these solutions is the Amazon AWS Lightsail.[4]

In this section, the process of taking the solutions developed in this book and hosting them on the Amazon Lightsail is described. The main advantages of using the Lightsail include the speed in which the server can be deployed, the ease of management, and the overall cost of running the service per month, which is $3.50 at the time of writing. Before beginning, an Amazon AWS account is needed that can be created on the AWS homepage.[5] After a new account has been created, we can head to the Lightsail section of AWS. [6]

Example 6: Creating a Lightsail instance

On the Lightsail dashboard, we can first see any instances that are running. An *instance* is a single hosting solution that has been created. In Figure 9.6, one existing instance can be seen. On the right-hand side of this dashboard, click *Create Instance* to get started.

In Figure 9.7, an option then exists to choose the type of instance we wish to launch. The typical options dividing line is choosing a Linux based image or a Microsoft Windows-based image. As Linux images are cheaper to run, this will be chosen. Next, The *blueprint* for the image is selected. This is the name given to the software that is preloaded onto the image when it is created. As we are working with PHP and MySQL, the *LAMP (PHP 7)* is selected.

---

[4]https://aws.amazon.com/lightsail
[5]https://aws.amazon.com
[6]https://lightsail.aws.amazon.com/ls/webapp/home/instances

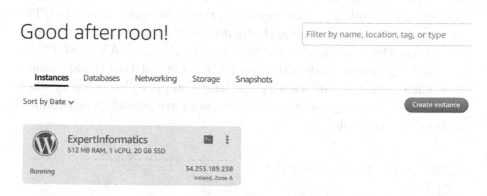

FIGURE 9.6: Amazon Lightsail dashboard.

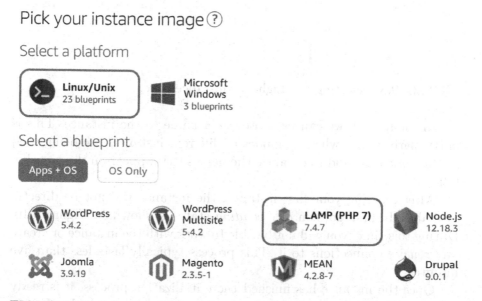

FIGURE 9.7: Selecting Lightsail image type and blueprint.

The next choice is focused on the overall RAM, CPU size, and hard-drive space that we wish to add. To keep costs minimal during the initial testing of the application, in Figure 9.8, the $3.50 option is selected. This can be changed at any time in the future if the application requires extra resources. This basic instance comes with 512MB of RAM, 1 vCPU, 20 gigabytes of a solid-state drive, and 1 terabyte of traditional storage. The choices that we are viewing are based on price. In scenarios where memory, processing, storage, or data transfer are important, customized options are available.

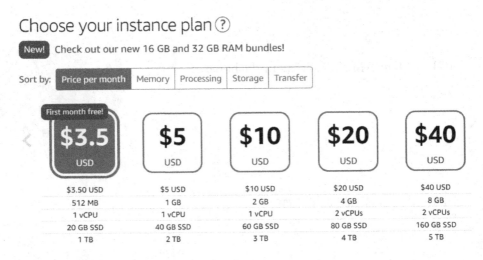

FIGURE 9.8: Selecting the Lightsail instance type.

In Figure 9.9, we can next provide a name to the instance. This is particularly useful when a number of different instances are being used at the same time and to organize the names that appear on the monthly bill.

After creating your first instance, the instance will not be directly available. It first goes into a *pending* state as shown in Figure 9.10. During this time, you will not be able to work with the instance or create any remote connections to it. This process typically lasts less than five minutes.

Once the instance has finished the initialization process, it is ready to access. To connect to the instance, a console can be opened by clicking on the console icon, as shown in Figure 9.11. This is a complete console replicating what would be seen on a traditional local operating system. Just below the console, the unique IP address for your instance can be

Identify your instance

Your Lightsail resources must have unique names.

TAGGING OPTIONS

Use tags to filter and organize your resources in the Lightsail console. Key-value tags can also be used to organize your billing, and to control access to your resources. Learn more about tagging. ☑

FIGURE 9.9: Providing a name to a Lightsail instance.

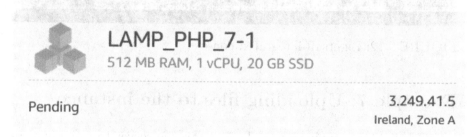

FIGURE 9.10: Lightsail instance in a pending state.

FIGURE 9.11: Running Lightsail instance.

seen. When this is typed directly into a web browser, a simple default HTML page will be shown.

In Figure 9.12 the console for the instance can be seen. To see what folder we are currently in the *ls* command can be used. After this command is issued, we can see that there is a *htdocs* folder that serves as the root folder for your web application. This is similar to the *htdocs* on a local Apache web server.

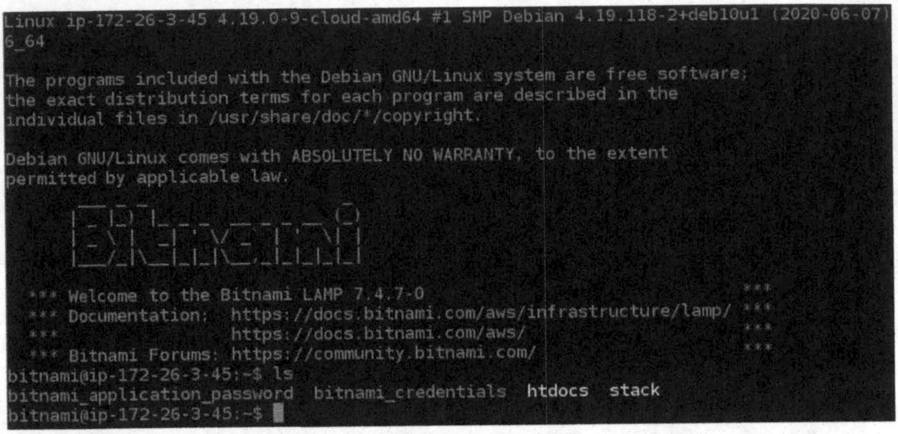

FIGURE 9.12: Lightsail-integrated console.

Example 7: Uploading files to the instance

Although we now have console access to the server to run any commands we wish, the main desire at this time is to upload the sample PHP/JavaScript examples that have been described in this book. To do this we first need to get the access key that will be used to authenticate with the server when external connections are made. To do this, the account section of the dashboard offers a keys management section.[7] In Figure 9.13, we can see that no custom keys have been added. Rather than creating a custom key, we can use the default key. This is done by simply clicking *Download* beside the regional area where your instance is hosted. This private key will contain a *.pem* extension and should be stored in a safe place.

To connect to the server and transfer files, we will use secure file transfer protocol (SFTP). The most common tool used is the FileZilla client.[8] FileZilla is a free and open-source tool that supports many formats for transferring files. To get FileZilla, simply click the *Download client* option as shown in Figure 9.14. Once the download had completed, it should be installed on your system.

---

[7]https://lightsail.aws.amazon.com/ls/webapp/account/keys
[8]https://filezilla-project.org

Manage your SSH keys ⑦

Choose a default key, create a key, or upload an existing public key to the AWS Region where you have resources.

You can store up to 100 keys per AWS Region.

Create New ➕   Upload New ⬆

▮▮ Ireland (eu-west-1)

◉ **Default** ⑦   Download ⬇

FIGURE 9.13: Options to create or download existing keys.

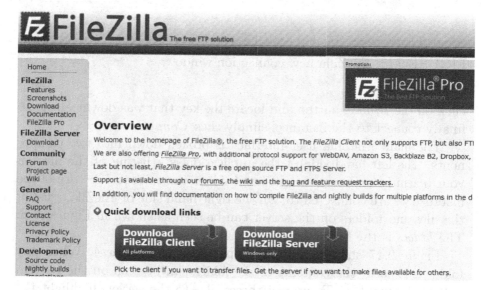

FIGURE 9.14: FileZilla homepage.

In Figure 9.15, after the installation of FileZilla, we can now begin the process of creating the connection. The option for a *New site* is first selected. Under the protocol section, *SFTP* should be chosen. The *host* is the IP address of your unique instance that can be found on the Lightsail dashboard under the console button. The *Logon type* is set to *Key file* as it will utilize the .pem file that was downloaded earlier. The default user name for this instance type is *bitnami*. Beside the *Key file* option,

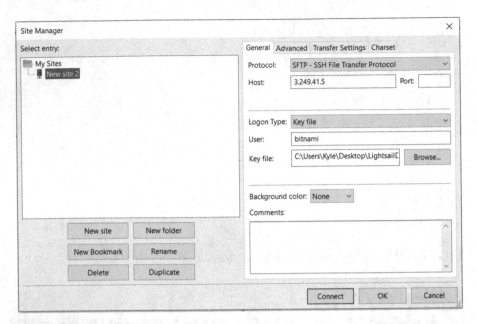

FIGURE 9.15: FileZilla new connection window.

click on the *Browse* button and locate the key that was downloaded. To finally connect to the instance, simply click *Connect*.

The main FileZilla user interface is broken down into two components. The left-hand side of the application is a listing of the files on your machine, and on the right-hand side is the current directory of the instance we are connected to. On the right-hand side of FileZila, a list of the files and folders on the server can be seen as shown in Figure 9.16. The *htdocs* is the target for our upload.

Figure 9.17 shows a list of samples files in chapter 4. When any folder is clicked, the contents of the folder can be seen on the bottom half of the window. To upload theses files to the server, highlight the files, right-click on the selected files and click *Upload*.

In this example, *dashboard4.php* has been uploaded to the server as shown in Figure 9.18. To access this page, the unique IP address of the instance is entered into the browser, followed by the name of the PHP file.

Remote site:	/home/bitnami					

```
⊟ ? /
   ⊟ ? home
      ⊞ bitnami
```

Filename	Filesize	Filetype	Last modifi...	Permissi...	Owner/G...
..					
.ssh		File folder	15/08/2020...	drwx------	bitnami ...
htdocs		File folder	24/06/2020...	lrwxrwxr...	bitnami ...
stack		File folder	24/06/2020...	lrwxrwxr...	bitnami ...
.bash_logout	220	BASH_L...	18/04/2019...	-rw-r--r--	bitnami ...
.bashrc	4,117	BASHRC...	15/08/2020...	-rw-r--r--	bitnami ...
.profile	1,398	PROFILE ...	15/08/2020...	-rw-r--r--	bitnami ...
bitnami_application_pass...	13	File	15/08/2020...	-rw-------	bitnami ...
bitnami_credentials	395	File	15/08/2020...	-r--------	bitnami ...

FIGURE 9.16: List of files and folders on the Amazon Lightsail instance.

Filename	Filesize	Filetype	Last modified
..			
samplefiles		File folder	30/06/2020 19:...
ajax.php	1,363	PHP File	30/06/2020 19:...
barchart.php	1,640	PHP File	30/06/2020 19:...
bootstrap.css	197,170	Cascading ...	22/01/2020 12:...
bootstrap.m		Cascading ...	28/12/2017 15:...
bootstrap.m		JavaScript F...	28/12/2017 15:...
Chart.bundl		JavaScript F...	28/10/2017 15:...
dashboard.c		Cascading ...	23/12/2017 17:...
dashboard4		PHP File	30/06/2020 19:...
jquery-3.1.0		JavaScript F...	28/12/2017 15:...
line.php		PHP File	30/06/2020 18:...
listFiles.php		PHP File	30/06/2020 19:...
popper.min.		JavaScript F...	28/12/2017 15:...
utils.js		JavaScript F...	28/10/2017 15:...

Context menu:
- Upload
- Add files to queue
- Open
- Edit
- Create directory
- Create directory and enter it
- Refresh
- Delete
- Rename

FIGURE 9.17: Selecting files in FileZilla to upload to the instance.

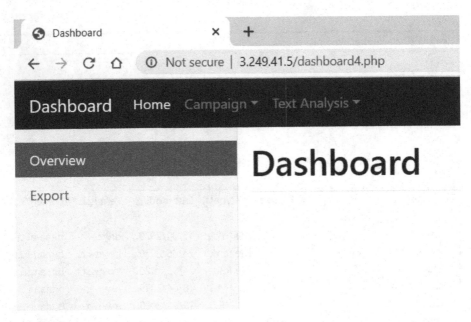

FIGURE 9.18: Sample application viewed in a web browser.

9.6 SUMMARY

This chapter closes the data analysis process by describing the fundamental components of any web application. Report generation was described, which is a quick and easy method of generating PDF reports using PHP. To provide a synchronous approach to reporting, cron and task scheduling were described for both local and external cron sources. As managing e-mail delivery has become a full-time job, the basics of cloud-based e-mail services were described as an alternative solution to in-house e-mail hosting.

Finally, to take the solutions that have been described in this book and provide a tangible application, a lightweight cloud web application hosting solution using Amazon Lightsail was described.

Index

Note: Locators in *italics* represent figures and **bold** indicate tables in the text.

Printed in the United States
by Baker & Taylor Publisher Services